True to Our Feelings

TRUE TO OUR FEELINGS

What Our Emotions Are Really Telling Us

Robert C. Solomon

OXFORD
UNIVERSITY PRESS
2007

OXFORD
UNIVERSITY PRESS

Oxford University Press, Inc., publishes works that further
Oxford University's objective of excellence
in research, scholarship, and education.

Oxford New York
Auckland   Cape Town   Dar es Salaam   Hong Kong   Karachi
Kuala Lumpur   Madrid   Melbourne   Mexico City   Nairobi
New Delhi   Shanghai   Taipei   Toronto

With Offices in
Argentina   Austria   Brazil   Chile   Czech Republic   France   Greece
Guatemala   Hungary   Italy   Japan   Poland   Portugal   Singapore
South Korea   Switzerland   Thailand   Turkey   Ukraine   Vietnam

Copyright © 2007 by Oxford University Press, Inc.

First published by Oxford University Press, Inc., 2007
198 Madison Avenue, New York, N.Y. 10016

www.oup.com

First issued as an Oxford University Press paperback, 2008

Oxford is a registered trademark of Oxford University Press

Library of Congress Cataloging-in-Publication Data
Solomon, Robert C.
True to our feelings: what our emotions
are really telling us / Robert C. Solomon.
p. cm. Includes index.
ISBN 978-0-19-536853-6 (pbk.)
1. Emotions (Philosophy)
I. Title
B105.E46S675 2006
128′. 37—dc22
2006045300

Printed in the United States of America

For Kathleen,
my love,
my spiritual mastermind,
my gentle but passionate companion,
my model of emotional integrity

Contents

Part III The Ethics of Emotion: A Quest for Emotional Integrity

Preface

I have always been fascinated by emotions: watching and dealing with them in other people, coping with and often joy-riding with my own. To be perfectly honest, I've also been terrified of them. As a child, I had a vile (though rarely violent) temper. As a young man, I fell in love often, and hard. As I matured, I learned to actually love, though perhaps more slowly and awkwardly than I would like to admit. And all along, I found myself brooding on, speculating about, luxuriating in, and terrified by my own emotional dispositions, responses, and preferences. I was already (although I did not know it at the time) a philosopher.

When I actually came into philosophy (from biology and medical school, where I had developed an interest in psychoanalysis), I brought with me that very personal fascination with the nature of the emotions, now as a scientific question, to be sure, but much more as a practical philosophical matter. What were my emotions, my passions, or—more vaguely—my "feelings"? Did they, as it sometimes seemed, just happen to me—"sweep me away"—or even possess me, "take over my personality"? Or were they, as they also seemed to be, what was *most* me, most mine, what best (or worst) defined me? Were my emotions good and good for me, or were they bad and bad for me (as my less emotional friends would continually caution me)? What did it mean—that sixties' expression—to be "in touch with one's feelings"? What was it to be an "authentic" person? (I had started reading and being captivated by Jean-Paul Sartre and the existentialists.) What was it, in other words, to be *true to one's feelings?*

Over the next thirty years, I explored those questions by way of philosophy, psychology, anthropology, and biology. (I remained fascinated by animals and animal behavior as well as by the behavior of my fellow humans). I had long been indignant that emotions were so neglected in philosophy, the self-appointed discipline of "rationality." But I started to argue (as Pascal and Nietzsche had years before me) that the emotions have their own rationality, their own reasons, their own *intelligence*. Back in the seventies, that was an argument that attracted little sympathy among my peers. Now, the philosophy of emotions, and the idea that reason and emotions are in cahoots rather than antagonists, is a major research area in psychology and the fast-advancing neurosciences. I have taken aboard these welcome scientific investigations, and I have accordingly changed my own views about what an emotion is over the years. (Although, my friends and critics will no doubt chime in, not that much.) But I hold onto the concern that got me interested in emotions in the first place: their intriguing and often troublesome role in our lives. That means that our emotions are first of all, for me at least, a personal concern, that is, an *ethical* matter (in the old classical meaning, having to do with living the good life rather than a moral question of right and wrong). The question, again, is how we can be true to our feelings. How can we get what I now call emotional integrity? How can we enjoy and thrive with rather than be plagued or haunted by our passions? That is what I have written about here.

Acknowledgments

I would like to thank and acknowledge two outstanding companies, each of which I am proud to say I have been working with for decades. The first is the Teaching Company of Chantilly, VA, which initiated this project with a series of lectures in a course entitled *The Passions*, released in March of this year (2006). Working on that course, and on a number of courses over the years with them, has been among the most rewarding activities of my long career teaching philosophy. The other is Oxford University Press of New York, which encouraged me to develop the same theme very differently presented, in book form. I want to thank Oxford University Press not only for their support on this project but for their support of my work over many years. This book is the product of the unusual collaboration and support between these two companies.

True to Our Feelings

Introduction

We are not only "rational" creatures, as Aristotle famously defined us. We also have emotions. We live our lives through our emotions, and it is our emotions that give our lives meaning. What interests or fascinates us, who we love, what angers us, what moves us, what bores us—all of this defines us, gives us character, constitutes who we are. But this obvious truth runs afoul of an old prejudice, and it needs to confront a new source of enthusiasm. The old prejudice is that our emotions are irrational and interrupt or disturb our lives. The new enthusiasm is that emotions will soon be thoroughly understood by science (especially neuroscience), which will render archaic our ordinary humanistic ways of thinking about them (derisively referred to as "folk psychology"). I will spend a good portion of this book attacking the old prejudice, but in doing so I will also be taking advantage of some of the new scientific research. But in isolation, experimental psychology, neurology, and the new methods of "cognitive science" tend to deprive our thinking of what I consider the most important dimension of our emotional life: its connection to ethics, to values, to living happily, healthily, and well. In this sense, but this sense only, I will be critical of the new zeal for hard-headed ("hard-wired") research perspectives. It is as living human beings, not just as scientists, that we want to understand and appreciate our emotional lives.

I want to defend a distinctively *ethical* view of our emotions, in contrast, many people would say (though I would not), to a strictly scientific analysis of their nature. But let me spend just a moment saying what this does *not* mean. It does not mean understanding our emotions in what some people would call moral or moralistic terms, that is, condemning some emotions as evil or sinful and praising a few others. This is, of course, what we find in a good deal of medieval philosophy, culminating in Pope Gregory's famous list of seven sinful emotions (including pride, anger, lust, and envy) and the Christian trio of virtues, faith, hope, and charity. But looking at the emotions through the lens of ethics does not mean damning and praising so much as it involves appreciating the insights, values, and subtle nuances of emotion and their many roles in making our lives worthwhile and meaningful. Emotions, to use the all-too-common image of popular ethics, are not either black or white but display all sorts of complex color patterns (I hate the dull image of "shades of gray"). Our emotional lives are not unlike the abstract expressionist representations of emotions in mid-twentieth-century American painting: rich, complex, and colorful. And that is how I would like to portray them here.

Pascal famously wrote "the heart has its reason which reason does not know." In this book, I want to explore this wisdom of the heart and pursue a new way of thinking about emotions and our passionate life in general. I will draw from such diverse classical sources as the wisdom of the ancients and the insights of the existentialists, as well as some of the latest theories in emotions research. But mainly, I want to appeal to our own collective if often unnoticed and unappreciated experience, or what is called "phenomenology," to get a grasp of the opulence of our emotional lives. Our emotions are anything but "just feelings."

Anger, for example, is not just a burst of venom, and it is not as such sinful, nor is it necessarily a "negative" emotion. It can be "righteous," and it can sometimes be right. Love is not always good and virtuous, and it is not always "better to have loved." Love can be foolish and destructive as well as wonderful. Shame and embarrassment involve harsh and humbling self-images, yet they are essential to our social consciousness and well-being. Such emotions can be more or less appropriate and ethically proper, depending on the person and his or her circumstances, and they are complex in a way that would not be possible if we were to understand them simply as "feelings." The emotions, according to many recent theorists, and summarized in a popular book by Daniel Goleman, are imbued with *intelligence*, that is, more or less insightful and knowledgeable ways of grappling with our world. In the chapters that follow, I would like to explore what this means. I want to show how the emotions provide insight and meaning to our lives, not just in special cases (falling in love, feeling awe in the presence of God) but across the emotional spectrum and in virtually every moment of our waking (and at least some of our sleeping) lives. With this in mind, I want to defend a concept of *emotional integrity*, or what one might call, "being true to one's feelings." But what sort of "feelings" are these to which we can or should be "true," and why should this be so important for the meaning of our lives?

I also want to contend that we are not merely passive victims of our emotions but quite active in cultivating and constituting them. In other words, we cannot just use our emotions as excuses for our bad behavior. ("I couldn't help it, I was angry." "I'm sorry, I was just jealous when I said that.") We *are* our emotions, as much as we are our thoughts and actions. Furthermore, I want to argue that emotions are not only intelligent but also purposive in a surprisingly robust sense. They are sometimes, perhaps even often, *strategies* for getting along in the world. They are a means of motivating, guiding, influencing, and sometimes manipulating our own actions and attitudes as well as influencing and manipulating the actions and attitudes of others. Accordingly, we are to a significant extent *responsible* for our emotions, something that we often deny for the most self-serving of reasons, to make excuses for ourselves. Thus I want to spend a good part of the book examining and to a certain extent rejecting the various theoretical excuses with which we try to get ourselves "off the hook," suggesting, for example, that our emotions are "psychic forces within us" or that "emotions are essentially irrational." Truly understanding the nature of our emotions and how they express and embody our deepest values is the beginning of emotional integrity.

For much of history, however, both common opinion and scientific orthodoxy treated human emotions as essentially irrational, if not by definition then because of their distorting effects on judgment and their often disastrous consequences. Our emotions supposedly make us misperceive the way things really are, make us do things that, with just a moment's clear thinking, we certainly would not do. But some recent research and thinking about emotions has dramatically turned this picture around. To talk about the "intelligence" of emotions is to say that there are good arguments that without our emotions, we would not be capable of rational decision making at all. Furthermore, there is a serious question whether our emotions distort our judgments about the world or rather make them meaningful. (A lover finds the beloved beautiful, but he or she is beautiful because loved, not simply loved because he or she is beautiful.) Moreover, the very idea that our emotions "make us" do such and such is rightly under scrutiny. To a much greater extent than we realize, we should take responsibility for our emotions. Our emotions orient us to the world and give us insights, even knowledge about our place in the world. But much of that knowledge is our own contribution. Our lives do not just happen to us.

These are the overarching themes of the book: the intelligence, purposiveness, strategic functionality, and integrity of our emotions. But just writing in such a focused way about the emotions and trying to theorize about them is also a significant part of a research boom in philosophy and science, including not only psychology and the social sciences but biology and brain science. For until just a few decades ago, the emotions were the prodigal child of psychology, the nemesis of rationalist philosophy, the supposed weakness of the "fairer sex," and an embarrassment if not a career-ender for their supposedly more rational male counterparts. Tears have ended presidential and other political campaigns. Bursts of righteous anger have ended relationships of all kinds. Even where such positive emotions as love were at stake, "better not to talk about it" was the usual word of wisdom. But of course, people always have talked about their emotions. They just did not see much point in doing so, except perhaps by way of "venting" or simply "expressing" their emotions or as a vehicle for gossip. For, after all, talking about an emotion was thought to be a lot like talking about the weather. You couldn't really do anything about it. And in the social sciences, silence reigned. Under the dark cloud of that pseudoscientific fashion of so-called "behaviorism," emotions were not to be mentioned at all. And philosophy continued to think of itself as the discipline of reason, logic, and argumentation—as a "science," in which emotion was not only irrelevant but the source of much unwanted disruption and fallacies.

But serious and proper talk of the emotions has finally come of age. Emotions are now a legitimate research enterprise. This is wonderful. But I want to be very careful that in our enthusiasm for science, we do not jettison the humanistic tradition within which the emotions have always been evaluated and understood. Interest in the emotions has a much older history in our age-old concern with ethics and the good life, dating back to Plato and Aristotle in Western philosophy and back to the Upanishads, the Buddhists, Confucius, and the Taoists in Asia. It was already clear to Aristotle, for example, that emotions (or what he called *pathé*, passions) had an essential role in the good life and were the key to the virtues. It was equally clear to the Stoics, who followed Aristotle, that the passions were significant but quite dangerous. According to the Stoics, emotions distort our reason, corrupt our virtue, and make us unhappy. (Nevertheless I will defend some of their brilliant insights into the nature of emotion in chapter 14.) The emotions also play an enormous role in the Judeo-Christian-Islamic tradition, and not just in terms of that supposedly singular passion called "faith" and Pope Gregory's "seven deadly sins." In the eighteenth century, ethics was dominated by the "moral sentiment theorists" David Hume, Adam Smith, and Jean-Jacques Rousseau, and morals once again became a matter of having the right kinds of emotions.

It was only toward the end of the nineteenth century that the study of emotions became a serious and widely discussed scientific subject, with the work of William James and Sigmund Freud in particular. This new attention to the emotions in science has proved to be both a blessing and a problem. On the blessing side of it, the new research, especially in the neurological and cognitive sciences, has been nothing less than fascinating, and it is progressing by leaps and bounds every day. The potential contributions to psychiatry and medical therapies are nothing less than miraculous. But on the problem side, it has encouraged our excuse making by way of an unfortunate reductionism, a tendency to "primitivize" the emotions, to rip them out of the humanistic contexts in which they have played such an enormous and important role and clinically examine them through a microscope, so to speak, with tweezers and rubber gloves or, more up-to-date, to view them as colored blips on the screen of an fMRI machine. What is sacrificed in humanistic understanding, I will argue, is not compensated for by the gains in technical knowledge. But neither, I want to make clear from the start, does that mean that we can or should ignore the insights that this new research can provide to our understanding.

In this book, accordingly, I will be focusing mainly on the emotions in the context of ethics and living well. I will also put considerable emphasis on those misunderstandings of our emotions that lend themselves to excuses that we use to duck responsibility. Finally, I will finish up with what I call *emotional integrity*. This has a lot to do with overcoming those excuses and taking responsibility. I will try to say something modestly informative about the new findings in neurology and something about the role of emotions in the larger world of evolutionary biology, but there are a great many new books on emotion that take on these tasks (see the Annotated Bibliography). So, too, I will not be saying very much at all about psychopathology and the medical complications surrounding the many ways in which emotions can go seriously wrong, as this, too, is covered in great detail by my colleagues in psychiatry and related fields. Those readers who are looking for psychiatric solace should probably turn elsewhere. I am here only concerned with the more "normal" vicissitudes of emotions, how and why they can make us unhappy, how and why they are sometimes irrational, but also how and why they are essential to happiness and central to rationality—to which they are too often thought to be generically opposed. Indeed, paradoxically, I would suggest that the emotions are more central to rationality than even reason and reasoning, for without them (as David Hume argued a few centuries ago in his *Treatise of Human Nature*), reason has no point or focus. Current psychiatric and neurological research tends to confirm this.

This humanistic or ethical perspective also dictates a way of carving up the proper domain of emotions. In current scientific research, with its emphasis on more or less automatic expressions, neurology, and brain processes, an emotion is typically defined as a very short-term physiological episode "triggered" by some event. Given the measures of emotion now in vogue, from a focus on snapshots and recognition of momentary facial expressions to the very expensive and therefore necessarily constrained use of fMRI and PET scan machines, this makes a lot of sense. Technology often determines the scope of investigation. (The history of microbiology, for example, is defined by the history of the discovery of various ways of making tiny organelles and tissues visible as much as by the discovery of new microbes.) But the emotions that count in our lives endure in ways that are hard to measure by such techniques. Our passions can go on a very long time. Love, for instance, can last a lifetime. So can anger and hatred. This is sometimes explained away by saying that such emotions are dispositions, that is, propensities to have emotions but not emotions themselves. But I don't think that this is right. Two people in love for twenty years do not just have an ongoing disposition to love. They will accurately say that they love one another every minute of every day, awake or asleep, in romantic moods and even during fights. A man who has hated his father since he was abused as a young boy does not just have the disposition to hate his father. He truly hates his father, all the time. The emotions that will occupy me in this book, therefore, will not be the sudden "bursts" of emotion that so fascinate neuroscientists and some psychologists but those long-term emotions and obsessions that have fascinated us throughout history, in literature as well as in life: the love of Abelard for Heloise, the conniving envy of Shakespeare's Iago, the murderous jealousy of his Othello, the subterranean resentment of O'Neill's Hickey in *The Iceman Cometh*, the explosive but life-long passions of Edward Albee's now-classic academic marriage in *Who's Afraid of Virginia Woolf?*

Love and hate and many other emotions remain active whether or not we are conscious of acting on them at any particular time. Thus I will insist that emotions are *processes*, which by their very nature take time and may indeed go on and on. They are not necessarily conscious. They also transform themselves, in all sorts of ways, into desires and courses of action (marriage and vengeance, for instance) and into other emotions as well. For example, love gives way to jealousy and grief, and the process of grieving typically includes denial and anger as well as the depressed feeling we specifically identify as grief. Hatred may well give way to guilt and even self-loathing. A big problem is our tending to think of an emotion as a discrete psychological event, since, after all, we do have singular names for our emotions ("anger," "love," "jealousy," "shame," etc.). An emotion is a complex process that incorporates many different aspects of a person's life, including his or her interactions and relationships with other people as well as his or her physical well-being, actions, gestures, expressions, feelings, thoughts, and kindred experiences.

What is an emotion? For reasons that will become clear in the book this is itself a highly controversial issue. Many scientific researchers would vehemently disagree with what I have just said above and no doubt as I go on their opposition will become intensified. But the stipulative definitions that begin most discussions of emotions tend to close off discussion instead of getting it going, and most of them are tendentious as well. Thus I want to say from the outset that this will be, in several different senses, a *political* discussion. That is, it is part of a much larger discussion about how people relate and respond to each other, how they understand themselves, how they manipulate both themselves and others, in part by the very language they use in ascribing and describing the emotions. (Think of the difference between calling a feeling of fondness "love" as opposed to "infatuation," or between calling a feeling of hostility "hatred" as opposed to "resentment.")

Indeed, the very term "emotion" is relatively new and still in flux, and the essential nature of emotion, if there is such a thing, is still very controversial. Calling someone "emotional" can be an insult, or a way of dismissing them. Saying that someone is "passionate," by contrast, suggests a kind of praise, even a recommendation. But the flux in the use of such terms indicates something profound about the way we research emotions, too. Emotions can be studied from many different perspectives, philosophical, ethical, psychological, physiological, biological, just to name the usual disciplinary categories. And the discipline of the person who attempts to define the emotions is bound to circumscribe the perspective, and his or her research tools will necessarily determine the sorts of things that will be observed, noted, and measured. And the aim of the study, too—clinical, professional, interpersonal, romantic, pharmaceutical—will make an enormous difference to the outcome. This, too, is "political," in the all-too-familiar sense that these disciplines are often at odds with one another, chasing after competitive university research funds and grants as well as public attention. But there is no one road to the understanding of emotion, and I want to keep reminding myself of that throughout this book. I am a philosopher, so my interest in ethics and living well will govern my use of psychology, biology, history, and literature.

What's more, and particularly important for my argument here, is the idea that in philosophy, the definition of a controversial term comes at the *end* of the discussion, not at the beginning. The "dialectic" of opposing views, even if presented by a champion of one of those views, produces a much more considered and inclusive definition than the usual stipulative definition. When the author of a recent edition of the prestigious *Encyclopaedia Britannica* begins his entry with the definition, "An emotion is a 'brief subjective, behavioral, and physiological response that occurs rapidly when a person is confronted with a situation of great personal significance,' " he has already narrowed the focus, slammed shut many doors, and restricted the analysis severely. A great deal depends on whether an emotion is thought of as a quick involuntary reaction or as a constructive process that progresses through time. It also depends on which emotions one chooses as paradigm cases, short bursts of anger or simmering resentment, flashes of affection or long-term love and commitment, simple sadness or the complexities of guilt and shame. So I would like to begin with the position—half-hearted and tongue-in-cheek though it may be—that we do not know what an emotion is, and that it really is a subject to be explored with curiosity and wonder.

This is not just an idle Socratic posture, however. The philosopher Nietzsche warned us that we are often most clueless about what is closest to us, and nothing, I would suggest, is closer to us than our own emotions. Nevertheless, we do not understand them. We are surprisingly often wrong about them, and we can be self-deceptively wrong about what they are. We all know from our own experience as well as from great works of literature that anger and love, for example, can drive our behavior and define our feelings for weeks or months or years without our recognizing what it is that moves us. People often deny that they are angry or hateful or jealous when their behavior shows quite clearly that they are so. More subtly, a change in atmospheric pressure or soft, barely noticeable background music can have profound effects on our moods and our behavior. More theoretically, most of us assume that we know what an emotion is, but a little discussion may be enough to convince us that we do not know, that we have accepted unthinking clichés and metaphors in place of careful observation and analysis, and that much of what we say about emotion is not only misleading but deceitful, falsifying both our own view of ourselves and the views that other people have of us. We have to learn how to recognize our emotions, how to deal with them, how to use them, and this is a set of skills that most of us have picked up only casually, unthinkingly, and inadequately.

Nevertheless, I do not want to suggest more confusion than there really is. For now, let me finesse the question as Aristotle did in his introduction to the subject and just say that we all know more or less what we are talking about when we talk about emotions, namely anger, fear, sadness, love, "getting upset," joy, and the like. There are serious ongoing debates about whether emotions form a unified class and whether all emotions are "really" physiological, as some would argue, or more like evaluative judgments or behavioral tendencies. Nevertheless, it's not as if we have no idea what we are exploring here. But understanding is much more than merely being able to agree on a subject matter.

In a recent influential book on the emotions, Paul Griffiths has suggested that our models of emotion are as antiquated as Aristotle's astronomy, now twenty-five hundred years out of date. But because I am primarily interested in emotions and ethics, I will take special interest in the wisdom of the ancients, Aristotle in particular, and other thinkers both in early Greece and Rome and in Asia. It is true that they had very little knowledge about the brain, but they were keen and wise on the role of the emotions in the Good Life and said many good things in defense of the wisdom of emotions. Aristotle was reacting against some of the warnings issued by his teachers, Socrates and Plato, but they, too, had wise things to say about the emotions, especially about the emotion of *eros* or erotic love. In Asia, wisdom about the emotions developed much earlier. While the Greeks were butchering one another in Troy, the early Hindus distinguished between the rather crude *bhavas* and *klesas*, on the one hand, and the more refined and aesthetic *rasas*, on the other. They developed whole schemes for the transformation of the former into the latter through art, theater, and music. Further to the east, Confucius conceived of a culture of virtue (not unlike Plato and Aristotle in the West), in which right feeling played a central part. Compassion, in one form or another, also played a central role in Asian thought, centuries before it became one of the defining sentiments in Christian ethics.

But closest to my own heart is modern European philosophy, especially existentialism and the movement called "phenomenology," which produced such outstanding existential phenomenologists as Martin Heidegger and Jean-Paul Sartre. I will also refer to Albert Camus's famous and popular novel *The Stranger*, which has a great deal to say about the emotions (and the striking absence of them in the titular character). Phenomenology is a movement founded by a mathematician named Edmund Husserl that reaches fruition in the works of Heidegger and Sartre. They took moods and emotions to be the key to phenomenology, as our ways of "being tuned" into the world. Sartre further suggests what I will take to be one of the most radical claims of this book, the idea that emotions are purposive. From him I will argue that our emotions are strategies through which we make ourselves happy or unhappy and give our lives meaning. By cultivating our emotions we determine the virtues and vices that make us good or not so good people.

More recently, there has grown a rich literature in personality theory and social psychology as well as the newer fields of neurobiology and psychiatry. But the modern interest in emotions, as I suggested, began at the beginning of the last century with William James and Sigmund Freud—two names that will often appear in this book—and it has been renewed in the past three decades or so with a resurgence of interest in emotion that is nothing less than remarkable. When I began writing about "the passions" thirty years ago, my complaint was that the emotions had been utterly ignored both by philosophers and psychologists. Today, that is anything but the case. The energetic research efforts of people like Paul Ekman, Carroll Izard, Nico Frijda, Richard Lazarus, and many others have opened up new dimensions of interest and established the emotions as a legitimate and prestigious dimension of psychology. Their painstaking research on emotion and "appraisal" have redefined a field that was a topic of marginal scientific interest in the centuries before.

But to conclude this introduction with a point I will make many times in what is to follow, *we live in and through our emotions*. Our lives do not just *include* episodes of anger, fear, love, grief, gratitude, happiness, humor, shame, guilt, embarrassment, envy, resentment, and vengeance. Our lives are *defined* by such emotions. Some readers may want to protest that so many of the emotions I will talk about are "negative." I will later challenge this notion—as it seems to me that one of the problems troubling our understanding of emotions is that we think of so many of them as "negative" when they are not. But for now let me point out, without making a big deal out of it, that most of our emotions, or at least most of our familiar emotions, *are* negative in an obvious sense. They have to do with our vulnerabilities, our mortality, our losses, our nasty surprises and disappointments in life. By contrast, our contentment and satisfaction tends to be much less dramatically emotional, usually manifesting itself in cheerfulness or peaceful calm. Moments of true joy are for most people exceptional, and happiness is more like the continuing hum of a life well lived than a momentous feeling at any given time. If one cares about anything —and it is virtually impossible to imagine someone not caring at all—one will have emotions. There is always the possibility—and for most of us the likelihood—that the world will let us down or offend us in some way. As Camus famously wrote, the world is "benignly indifferent" to our concerns, and this infuriates us. With that in mind, I would like to turn to one of the most human but often abused emotions, that red-eyed monster, anger.

PART ONE

Emotional Strategies

An Existentialist Perspective

❊

1

Anger as a Way of Engaging the World

Anger is an often clever, sometimes devious, frequently destructive emotion. It is the emotion that most often leaps to mind when the topic of emotion—and especially the topic of emotional irrationality—gets raised. Anger has a well-deserved reputation as the most explosive and most dangerous emotion. Thus it is usually a prime example of a "negative" emotion. It is one of the seven deadly sins. It is demonized by the ancient Stoics, rejected by the Buddhists as among the worst "agitations," and has an awkward place at best in the Christian tradition. ("Be angry but do not sin; do not let the sun go down on your anger, and do not make room for the devil" (Eph 4:26–27).) It is also an emotion that seems most obviously beyond our control, and such expressions as "losing one's temper" and "going ballistic" make this amply clear. Thus it is against anger that the entire army of historical wisdom, from the Buddha and the Stoics to the latest book on "emotional intelligence," is arrayed.

And yet Aristotle, who is often a wise and mollifying voice in such matters, is not so sure. In his *Ethics*, he insists that a man who does not get angry at the right time (in the right way, at the right person, in an appropriate situation) is a *fool*. The inability to get angry is a vice just as getting angry too easily is (though Aristotle allows that it is much easier to live with the former than the latter). Christians do not wholly dismiss anger, whatever its status as a "sin," but rather relegate it to God, who has much better judgment on such matters than we do. However, while New Testament passages on divine vengeance have often been systematically ignored or denied, the Hebrew God of the Old Testament is full of "wrath."

Even Buddhism endorses colorful stories about righteous indignation, and there is a central role for divine vengeance in both Hinduism and Islam. It is easy enough for us to appreciate the important role anger plays in life when other people do not always play by the rules, where one's territory and one's dignity are often trespassed against, in which our needs and desires are often frustrated. Indeed, given man's notorious "free will," we can even appreciate why a loving god would get angry. Not to get angry may be saintly, but anger is also sometimes *righteous*, meaning not just that the other person deserved it but that it may be good for one's soul to get angry. Piety may make saints of a few of us, but in the face of insult and offense, timidity can make us frustrated fools.

To support the argument that to be human is to be liable to anger, current scientific research on the physiological and biological basis of emotions suggests that anger, together with fear, are "basic" emotions. That is to say, it is not just a vice or a weakness of particular people but something common to all humanity (and many animals as well). As current theorists use the term, a basic emotion is one that is essentially neurological (or rather, neuro-hormonal-muscular). It consists of a complex more-or-less fixed response, a syndrome involving certain parts of the brain, the endocrine system, and characteristic "hard-wired" behavioral expressions, especially facial expressions. This all gets "triggered" by some provocative event. Because all of this is physiology, it is "naturally" trans-cultural and universal. It is a product of evolution rather than of learning or culture. Thus anger, as a basic emotion, displays a distinctive facial expression (including scowling and the gnashing of one's teeth) as well as characteristic autonomic nervous system responses (heart beating harder and faster, sweating, getting red in the face, more sensitive skin responses, the body getting tense and energized, etc.) All of this is spontaneous and not a product of thinking or deliberation. And, of course, one sees similar responses in animals, with appropriate anatomical differences. (Think of the peculiar tail movement of an angry cat, or the snarling posture of a dog whose territory has just been invaded.)

If anger is a basic emotion in that its manifestations and expressions are more or less automatic, is this what anger is, its essence? This is a question that I will raise throughout this book, but my answer, flatly for now, is *no!* No emotion, and especially anger, is just an evolved neurological response. There is no doubt that anger (and some other emotions) are part of our evolutionary heritage and include physiological responses that we share with other animals. But this is surely just a piece of the story.

To begin with, what place do *feelings* have in anger? Most people would say, as a matter of common sense, that anger *is* a feeling. (Even the grammar of "feeling angry" would suggest this.) But are feelings essential (as traditional theorists and most of us ordinarily think)? Or are they "epiphenomenal" embellishments, something like the red bulb on a Butterball turkey that pops up when the cooking is done but has nothing to do with the cooking or the turkey as such? I will have much to say about the relationship between emotions and feelings in what follows, so let me begin by insisting that, in one sense, it is perfectly plausible to insist that emotions are feelings, in the sense that they are typically *experienced*. (Leaving aside the difficult question of unconscious emotions for at least a little while.) But there is another sense, easily conflated with the first, that feelings are essentially unintelligent sensations, or much like sensations, even if these are not physically localized (like a pain, for example), or indicative of the physical appetites (like hunger, for instance). Among such sensations one might include a sense of "burning," perhaps—in anger or in passionate love—or "deflating," as in sudden humiliation or disappointment. I will have much more to say about the place of such sensation-like feelings in emotional experience as we go, but let me begin by roughly marking this very important distinction, according to which an emotion is (at least in large part) an experience (a "feeling") but is not at all to be identified with anything like a sensation ("feeling" in this other sense).

Moreover, what place do thoughts, plans, and full-blooded courses of action—for example, retaliatory or vengeful schemes and behavior—have in a proper conception of anger? Are these part of the anger or just common consequences of anger? Is anger a distinctive inner *experience*, or is it a full-bodied engagement with the world? In other words, is anger just a "basic" emotion, a merely bodily syndrome, or is it something much, much, more?

A major debate with many faces now rages about the "true" nature of emotions. On the practical side, much debated in the media as well as among doctors and public health officials, the debate is between interpersonal, psychological, and behavioral therapy, on the one hand, and pharmaceutical, biochemical treatment on the other (whether the drugs in question are organic and "natural" herbs and vitamins or highly restricted prescribables is entirely a secondary matter). Should hyperactive children just be give more playtime and reoriented toward more dynamic activities? Or should they be given Ritalin or other powerful (and possibly dangerous) drugs? Should mildly depressed people be put immediately on Prozac or some other antidepressive or should they be encouraged to talk more with their friends about what's bothering them? But the popular debate is mirrored by a much deeper theoretical debate about the nature of emotion. As the problems become less obviously pathological, room for debate becomes much more personal. Should angry people eat less red meat, or should they learn to control their tempers? is one rather frivolous way to put the question.

Many distinguished researchers, neuroscientists, psychiatrists, psychologists, and even some philosophers now insist that the essence of anger is just its neurological-hormonal-muscular core. Some philosophers would deny this but nevertheless distinguish between those aspects of emotion that are immediately part of the emotion and those that consequent, such as acts of retaliation and schemes of revenge (see Goldie, 2000). By contrast, I do not think that anger is just its neurological-hormonal-muscular core and I would include both lingering thoughts and far-reaching actions as part of anger. And, of course, there is the wealth of experience that is the emotion. I accept the neurological and clinical evidence, such as it is: Anger is, in part, a physiological phenomenon. But I would not even say that this is the "core" of anger, which is then shaped by culture and experience and subject to culturally derived constraints on emotional expression, what Paul Ekman calls "display rules." (Peter Goldie dismissively refers to this as the "avocado-pear model" of emotion, a hard neurological core surrounded by a soft fruit of culture, experience, and individual personality.) I, too, think this model is insupportable, neglecting both the pliability of the brain and the pervasiveness of culture in human development.

Anger (like all emotions) is a cognitively and value-rich phenomenon, not just a momentary state or event but a complex process that proceeds through time and can last a very long time. It necessarily involves feeling and judgment as well as physiology, and sometimes, especially after a short amount of time, there may be little distinctive physiological response at all. Nevertheless, the person might continue to be very angry. Indeed, I at least want to raise the question whether even basic emotions (notably anger and fear) always require such neurological machinery. What about long-term clearly noninstinctual fears (for example, of global warming) and long-term anger (for example, about ongoing government corruption and cronyism)? To be sure, *something* is going on in the nervous system, but is it sufficiently dramatic or distinctive to hold a place center stage and define what the emotion is? Or is it just one or another process in the neurological substratum that underlies all of our mental activity but certainly does not define it?

If there are basic emotions, mere physiology would dictate that they cannot last for a very long time. Thus I noted in the introduction that one of the basic disagreements surrounding the emotions in general and anger in particular is, How long does an emotion last? A burst of rage or panic may last only a second or two, and because of the temporal limitations and short-term measurements available in the laboratory setting, there is a decided prejudice in favor of treating anger and other basic emotions as just such phenomena of brief duration. Psychologists following Ekman who study the facial expressions of emotion look for the immediate reaction, before cultural and interpersonal influences and self-conscious display concerns come into play. But the very nature of basic emotions suggests that such spontaneous and quick responses do not easily endure. One can be truly surprised, say at a surprise party, only for a second. What follows is not part of the surprise as such. (Surprise, not surprisingly, is often identified as a basic emotion too, but whether this is a mere reflex, as in being startled, or more extended surprise, curiosity, or wonder, which is what old philosophers like Descartes were curious about, is a matter of considerable contention.) It is sometimes suggested, but with predictable hesitation, that only such emotions, basic emotions, are *real* emotions. The others, more drawn out in time, less spontaneous, more culturally shaped and highly self-conscious and "intelligent," are not real emotions but something else (vaguely summarized in such phrases as "higher cognitive functions").

I think that all of this is very wrong. First of all, as I already insisted, most emotions are not measured in fractions of a second but in hours, days, and weeks. Some emotions last years. Anger is one of these. (Love is another, but more on that later.) To be sure, there are short bursts of anger. We have all experienced them. Someone gives us a shove while we are standing politely in line, but we turn angrily only to see that some poor soul has just tripped. (Paul Griffiths [1997] imagines that it is a lovely young woman who is delighted to attract our attention, and our anger abruptly ends.) But anger is not just this. Anger often goes on for days or weeks or years. One can be angry with an offensive neighbor for as long as he or she remains a neighbor, and long after that, too. And this does not just refer to a disposition to be angry, that is, whenever one is reminded of the neighbor one *then* gets angry. The anger rather becomes a continuous structure of one's life, always in the background but easily brought to the center of one's attention. But the structure here is not just a neurological pathway (although that may well be happening too. That is how the brain gets "addicted" to certain emotions). It is a structure that includes one's thinking and behavior, what one pays attention to, what one remembers, what one imagines, even what one dreams, the metaphors one uses, and the way one engages in the neighborhood. Anger may be "basic" in that it is a common, powerful, dramatic, and near universal emotion, but it is not nearly so primitive as some theorists are suggesting. In this sense, not even anger is a basic emotion.

One would not go wrong in simply dismissing those bursts of anger that fit the basic emotion model as insignificant so far as ethics and the good life is concerned. No one worries about a brief spurt of anger (except, perhaps, in homicidal maniacs). It has little meaning and indicates very little about the person who "spurts" or how he or she sees that world. Tourette's syndrome, for instance, is characterized by such brief bursts of apparent anger, typically expressed in obscenities and impolite epithets, but indicates nothing about the personality, attitudes, or outlook of the patient. What worries us is protracted anger tending toward hatred and manifested in schemes of retaliation and vengeance. And even short of retaliation and vengeance, anger has a hostile judgmental nature, and these judgments are rarely simple or singular.

I will argue that anger is basically a judgment that one has been wronged or offended. Typically (but certainly not always) it is directed at another person, most often for a specific offense or, perhaps, a sequence of offenses. Often, too, it is directed at a situation or a task thwarted, as frustration, for instance, when I try unsuccessfully to thread a needle or when my flight is inexcusably delayed. But even in a relatively brief and impersonal bout of anger, for instance during my unsuccessful attempts to thread the needle, there will almost always be a series of thoughts and judgments (as well as shifting feelings), from one-word epithets to questions (probably just to myself) such as "why do they make this so difficult?" or "why am I so clumsy?" In other words, again, anger is a process, and when it further involves another person, these thoughts and judgments (and even the one-word epithets) become much more complicated. When such anger is expressed, moreover, the reactions of the recipient (whether a stony silence, fear, or anger in return) provoke a further process (including other emotions).

Why does anger inspire such reactions? Why should anyone worry about another person's anger? This seems like a simple-minded question, until we consider by contrast the basic emotion model or its more common-sense, simple feeling version. If anger were simply a neurological syndrome or something like a simple sensation, why would we think of it as anything other than a slight medical problem, like an itch or a headache? Of course, one might point out that such syndromes or sensations sometimes lead to violent behavior, but, first of all, this is usually not true. Most of the behavior directly caused by anger is not only nonviolent, it is not even hostile. (Anger leads far more often to apologies, letters written, and stony looks than to even modest acts of violence.) Second, even where anger does lead to violence (and much more likely a curse or a slap than a punch), it is not as if the behavior is just "triggered" by the neurology or the sensation. (Nico Frijda, as we will see, insists that all emotions—and not just basic emotions—are distinguished by characteristic "action tendencies," which may be much less than full-blown actions but "point in the direction" of certain sorts of behavior.) But it is the content of the emotion that explains both the behavior and our subsequent reactions to it (again, whether silence, fear, anger, or whatever). But that content is neither neurological or anything like a sensation. It is the way that those thoughts and judgments engage us in the world.

If anger is typically aimed at a person who has been offensive, the content of those angry thoughts and judgments will most likely concern the nature of the offense and the character of the offender. And that in turn gives us a clear picture of why we respond to anger—or even the threat of anger—as we do. When a person gets angry at us, we become quickly aware that we have offended (or at the very least frustrated) someone. For most of us, most of the time, this alone is sufficient to make us feel upset, even if we know that it is a misunderstanding or a mistake and that we did not do anything wrong. But the accusation hurts. The threat of retaliation or revenge, even if it is just by way of a cutting comment or a "dirty look," makes us anxious or defensive. On the other hand, a wrongful accusation, even if it is not fully articulated, might well provoke anger in return. In any case, anger is much more than a basic emotion or a set of feelings. It is a way of interacting with another person (or with a situation or a task) and a way of situating oneself in the world. And an offense is not just a particular piece of behavior. It is typically defined and circumscribed by one's culture and by one's language. (Most offenses in the civilized world are verbal.) If one person calls another a "mean S.O.B.," it makes an enormous difference whether the alleged S.O.B. has a self-image as "tough" and "uncompromising" or as "sensitive" and "congenial" as well as what sort of relationship it is (client or boss, friend or rival). In other words, an emotion is a self-aware engagement in the world, and to understand anger, we have to understand just what kind of engagement this is.

Many philosophers and psychologists now say that what is most often missing from the basic emotions model of anger are its "cognitive" aspects. While the more sophisticated basic emotions theorists acknowledge this and try to work it into their models, many of them rightly complain that what is missing in turn from cognitive models of emotion is precisely what the basic emotions model and common sense theory emphasize (I would say "overemphasize"), and that is *feeling*. While it is not built into the neurology as such, most basic emotions theorists are perfectly happy to acknowledge that some sort of feeling or sensation either accompanies or follows the short autonomic burst. (A few insist that such feelings are not necessary at all, for example, Joseph Le Doux at New York University.) Sensation theorists (for example, I will often cite William James) clearly emphasize the feeling aspect of emotions, but ignore (in my view) the cognitive aspects. The problem, simply put, is that both physiological and sensation views of anger fail to capture the essential fact that anger is always *about* something. Anger is not just a physiological disturbance. It is not just a feeling. And it is not just in a person's mind but rather in and about the world.

Philosophers (since the late medieval period) have referred to this "aboutness" of emotions (and other mental states and processes too) as *intentionality*. In other words, emotions are about the world. I will not go into this concept yet nor will I suggest its considerable scope and its limitations. For now, let me just leave it at this: Anger is always and necessarily an engagement in a situation or a relationship. It involves the perception and judgment of a setback or an offense. Typically it also involves an accusation of blame (although this tends to be irrational when it is directed at some thing or event, such as when one gets angry at the weather for interfering with one's vacation). Or as Aristotle defined it (in his *Rhetoric*) several millennia ago, "anger is a distressed desire for conspicuous vengeance in return for a conspicuous and unjustifiable 'slight' of one's person or friends." He adds that "anger is always directed towards someone in particular, e.g. Cleon, and not towards all of humanity," and he mentions only in passing the physical distress that virtually always accompanies such emotion. The key to Aristotle's analysis, however, is the notion of a "slight" as the cause of anger, a complex judgment regarding one's relationship to another person, and thus he gives a central place to the desire for revenge, introducing a behavioral component too at the very heart of the emotion.

I would add that anger not only involves judgment but is a distinctively and famously judgmental emotion. For this reason, a common retort to anger is "Don't be so judgmental!" Later, I will say much more about the contrast between anger and some of its kindred emotions, such as irritation and annoyance, moral indignation, and rage. But even before we get into the details, these contrasts are instructive regarding the nature of the judgments that are involved in anger. The difference between anger and "mere" irritation or annoyance is that the latter pair rarely involve blame, or, if they do, it is blame that won't stand up to even the slightest reflection or scrutiny. ("Oh, don't mind what I say. I'm just really irritated [or annoyed] this morning.") Anger differs from moral indignation, by contrast, in that the latter, not the former, necessarily involves a *moral* judgment, that is, much more than a personal sense of frustration or offense. Rage, by contrast again, involves minimal cognition (although it is still necessarily about something): It tends to treat with extreme hostility whatever crosses its path. Anger is rarely so indiscriminate, and when it is, we do not describe it as just an emotion but rather as a mood, as an emotional disposition, or, if prolonged, as a severe personality disorder.

In the introduction, I suggested that emotions are or at least can be *strategies*. To anticipate one of my central themes, this would suggest that our emotions do not just *happen* to us by way of disrupting our lives and distorting our rationality. Instead, I want to embrace an existentialist perspective and talk about what we *do* with our emotions and not simply about what causes them. Let me offer you a teasing example. I once worked

with a rather overbearing fellow—as have most of us—who had a notoriously "bad temper." When he was on the losing end of an argument, which
was often, he would rear himself up to his full height (well over six feet),
lean across the conference table in a menacing posture, and threaten to get
very angry. By raising his voice and sufficiently scowling, he got most people
to believe that he already was angry. And most people being as they are,
that is, anxious to keep the peace and unwilling to get into a needless fight,
my colleagues would almost always back down, at least for the moment.
(In the vote that would follow, they would quietly reassert themselves.)
But, for the moment, this fellow would get his way. He used his anger, and
the threat of his anger, to intimidate and manipulate those around him.

Now how did he learn how to do this? After all, an emotion is not something you can turn on and off at your convenience. The circumstances have
to be appropriate. And you can't just "fake it," for we all know how difficult
it is, even for an experienced actor, to convincingly feign an emotion. So to
make it convincing, my colleague had to really get angry. But emotions are
often habits, to some extent learned but also the product of practice and
repetition. It is very rare for a person to get angry *just once* (like Camus's
character in *The Stranger*). Anger tends to be recurring and habitual.
And here is one of the many places where we can really learn something
from the neurologists. Emotional habits are the product of pathways well
worn and chemical dependencies well established. To put the point a bit
dramatically, we become addicted to our emotions. We come to need the
biochemical "hit." Anger is an exemplary case. People such as my colleague
learn to energize themselves by getting angry. They actually *enjoy* it
(whereas most of us are sufficiently affected by shame or embarrassment
or fear of consequences to not much enjoy it at all). So, too, some people
can get quite literally "addicted to love," as a popular song puts it, and so
too sadness and jealousy and many emotions. (Clinical depression is an
extreme and special case, which lies beyond the scope of this book.)

We can do many things by practice and habit that we cannot simply
"do," say, by following the instructions in a booklet or even by watching
someone else. The American pragmatists William James and John Dewey
fully appreciated the importance of habit, whether it is a matter of learning
a language, learning to play a musical instrument, or even just watching
and appreciating someone else's performance. But habits are not clearly
voluntary or involuntary. (That is why it is so difficult to break a habit,
even a simple one.) Emotional habits occupy the middle ground between
just willfully getting angry and falling victim to one's own "bad temper."
One learns the habit, and one learns how and when to get angry. Here is
an imagined scenario, which I derive from many current examples of
child rearing. I imagine my colleague as a two-year-old child—a rather

formidable two-year-old, I would imagine—doing what two-year-olds do so well—throwing a temper tantrum. The response of his parents, I imagine, was terror, and to stop this impossible behavior they offered up any number of treats and entreaties. And inside that two-year-old brain a notion took form, something like, "Wow! I've got to try this again." The habit may have at some point become more or less "automatic," but nevertheless it was learned for a purpose and continues to be so motivated.

Now fast-forward quite a few decades and we can understand the adult behavior not as "a bad temper" but as a very well-rehearsed successful strategy, bolstered by years of practice and settled habits. Now I admit that this merely imagined model of another person's childhood may not in fact be correct; there are other plausible scenarios. But it does provide us with a way of understanding a good deal of emotional behavior that can be spontaneous, sincere, and, most importantly here, strategically successful. Not all emotions are like this, to be sure, but many are. And even when the notion of strategy seems quite out of place—as with grief, for example—it may be a valuable existential exercise to raise such questions as "Why am I doing this? What am I getting out of it?" And even with an emotion such as grief, the answer is not always what we would like it to be, namely, that it just "hits us." Grief is a reaction to an unwanted tragedy, to be sure, but how long grief goes on, how it is expressed, and how debilitating it is are not simply reactions to a loss.

We are used to thinking about emotions as first-person experiences, personal, private, uniquely individual. Thus the appeal of such expressions as "I feel angry." Or, by contrast, an emotion gets discussed from a "third-person" scientific or observational perspective, whether the impersonal study of brains in the laboratory or the casual voyeurism we enjoy sitting in a café at the airport, watching the behavior of those bustling around us. That leaves open the skeptical question of *how* we know or see that other people have emotions or have the particular emotions they do. But the idea that emotions are strategies suggests that the perspective in which we learn the most about emotions is in the *second* person, in personal interaction and exchange. Thus anger (and other emotions) are not so much "in" the mind (nor just in the body or brain) so much as they are out there in social and interpersonal space. Anger, and most of our emotions, usually arises with and in reaction to other people. Ronald de Sousa (1987) has captured this social learning aspect of emotions in a provocative and fertile phrase, "paradigm scenarios." We *learn* to be angry, whatever the underlying neurological and hormonal machinery, in social interaction. And what we learn has a lot to do with the seeming appropriateness of the circumstances.

Without the social context, anger really would be little more than pointless frustration and rage. There would certainly be no such thing as *righteous* anger. As Aristotle insisted, we have to learn when and where to get angry, how angry to get and with whom, and under what circumstances. We occasionally find that we come to understand our emotions by noticing ourselves in action and becoming aware of our emotions' effects on other people. Thus we learn what we feel not just by *feeling* it but sometimes by way of interpersonal feedback, including criticism and bad reactions from others. We get angry not only in order to intimidate others but in order to get their respect. So, too, one gets embarrassed, in some cases, to invite leniency (see Leary et al., 1996). We might promote our own sadness to invite others' sympathy. Emotions, even the most "personal" emotions, are often a mode of social action. They are therefore highly sensitive to and encouraged by specific cultures and societies. Anger, in particular, is an exceptionally encouraged emotion, and in American society today, it has become the main vehicle of emotional expression. (If you doubt this, listen to any random half hour of "talk radio," whether right or left, to hear how popular and wholly acceptable the provocation of anger and outrage has become.)

But the question "Why do we get angry?" has an even more fascinating answer, and it points to yet another sense in which anger (and emotions in general) may be manipulative. I anticipated this, in a rather general way, when I suggested that some people actually enjoy their anger, they find that it energizes them and so provides a rather positive experience. This may not seem to be true of the simplest cause of anger, frustration, when one finds one's goals or projects blocked or more difficult than expected. But even frustration may be considered in this light. It is "human nature," perhaps, that we seek out challenges. We start difficult crossword puzzles knowing that it is likely that we will be stymied and perhaps not finish. My friends undertake difficult rock climbing routes, bypassing the obvious and easier ways up (not to mention avoiding the climb altogether, or simply driving around to the top). Their aim, of course, is not to fail or be frustrated but to achieve something that might at first seem arduous or impossible. What I want to open up is the question whether part of the explanation for such typical human behavior (and some animal play as well) is the psychological pay-off of the attempt itself, even in the absence of success and in the face of failure. That would explain a great deal about our emotions.

Once we move beyond frustration to the more common sort of human anger where the object of the emotion is someone else's offense, someone who is *to blame* for the blockage or interference, the strategic value of the emotion is greatly increased. It is not just a way of manipulating the other person but an excellent way of manipulating *oneself*. Thus people might not only enjoy their anger because it energizes them but because it transforms the very nature of their way of seeing the world. I would agree with Jean-Paul Sartre that all emotions ("magically") transform the way we see the world, but the way that anger transforms the world is both illuminating and exceptional. To start with, consider how anger typically begins, in some sort of personal failure or humiliation, because of some offense or insult or slight. So one might say that in anger, we begin in a "one down" position. (I take the term from a really old Alasdair Sims, Terry Thomas movie, *School for Scoundrels*.) But then the exceptionally *judgmental* nature of anger becomes particularly important. Anger is judgmental in two somewhat different senses. First, like all emotions, it is constituted or structured by judgments, ways of perceiving, conceiving of, and evaluating ("appraising") the world. But, second, anger is distinctive among emotions in setting up a scenario that involves a particularly judgmental (magisterial) stance toward the world. This judgmental or magisterial stance, in turn, functions to strategically lift one out of the "one down" position and elevate oneself to something of a "one up" role in the situation.

Lewis Carroll, in *Alice in Wonderland*, makes a wonderful tongue-in-cheek observation. In a section called "The Mouse's Tail" he quips, "I'll be judge, I'll be jury, Said cunning old fury." This is, it turns out, a brilliant analysis of anger. Anger, in addition to being structured by judgments, is a literally judgmental or magisterial emotion. The offended subject turns the tables on the offender, thus saving face (at least as far as the subject is concerned). In anger, the subject casts him- or herself in the superior role of judge and jury. Thus the phenomenology of anger involves a sort of courtroom scenario, a "kangaroo court," to be sure, in which judgments are peremptory, there is no defense, and few people ever get a fair trial. But that is the point; in anger, the other is *put on trial*. Even more powerful, and more judgmental still, is moral indignation, an emotion in which one accuses the other not just on one's own behalf but on the behalf of some moral principle. Thus the kangaroo court expands its scope to become something of a supreme or world court, judging not just on the injury or offense sustained by the victim but on the judicial merits of such behavior on a global scale of justice. The strategic advantage of this set-up should be obvious. Emerging from a situation in which one has been hurt, offended, or humiliated, one repositions oneself as superior, even as righteous. It is a powerful psychological position. It is also quite presumptuous, which is why Christian tradition rightly warns against it.

Anger is typically contrasted with reason and being reasonable. In our ordinary way of talking, "don't get emotional" typically means, "don't be angry" or "be reasonable." But, to ask a basic question, aren't there times when it is perfectly right to get angry, to get emotional? Aren't there occasions when anger is perfectly reasonable? A friend of mine was brutally cut off from tenure at his university, despite a remarkable collection of published writings, excellent teaching, and devoted service to the institution. The problem, naturally, was politics. He had just rubbed someone in power the wrong way. But I was appalled when my friend failed to get angry, accepting his humiliation and forced change of life as "just one of those things," a good Stoic response. So, I got angry on his behalf, but I also got angry (though mixed with sympathy) *at him*. It seemed to me that not only did he have a perfect right to be angry but that he *ought* to have been angry. The emotion was both rational and, in my view, somewhat obligatory. You just don't let administrators get away with institutional murder.

Many people will reject this. They will say, "No. Anger is *never* the best strategy." And I will admit that this answer has much to recommend it. There is considerable virtue in my friend's response. But first, I want to argue the contrary and suggest that anger can often be a reasonable and rational response to adversity. But I also want to see just what the negative answer has to offer our understanding of anger. The idea that anger is always wrong is codified, most straightforwardly, in Pope Gregory's hepta-log of "deadly" or "mortal" sins. It is an idea that pervades a good deal of Christian and other religious thought (for example, Buddhism), and it can rightly be juxtaposed against earlier religious traditions that tended to sanctify or celebrate anger, for example, in the wrathful God of the Hebrew Bible and the destructive Shiva of ancient Hinduism. So, too, Socrates and Plato turned from the warrior wrath and the vengeful justice of the Homeric heroes to a more "civilized" conception of justice in which vengeance played no role. So the idea that anger is best avoided is an age-old idea with impressive philosophical credentials. Nevertheless, let's take a look at why this long-reviled emotion has such a hold on us, and why it is so often appealing and even reasonable.

Let me start by repeating what the detractors of anger and its would-be defenders must agree upon, the idea that anger is a way of engaging the world. We get angry *at* someone, *about* something. The important question, accordingly, is whether the anger is rightly aimed, whether has it picked out the right object (the offender), and whether the anger is warranted by the situation. (The person targeted may in fact be the offender but the offense is so minor that it does not warrant the anger.) If both the object is right and the seriousness of the accusation is warranted, then the anger is rational and reasonable. Of course, it is possible that future evidence and considerations might throw the original judgment into question, but then we would say that "given what he knew at the time" or "given what then seemed to be the case," his anger was rational and reasonable. But if anger can also be a *strategy*, there is an additional consideration, beyond accuracy and fairness, that governs the rationality of anger. Namely, does getting angry serve one's ultimate ends?

Getting angry at one's boss may be right and even righteous, but it is only rarely rational. Getting angry at one's professor before she has graded your exam may be right and righteous, but it is usually not a rational strategy. Thus anger is rational depending on whether or not it fits into a person's longer-term interests. What follows is that some modes of engagement, some strategies, are better than others. Some are foolish. Some are stupid and unwarranted. John's frustration because he cannot prove a mathematical conjecture that has long evaded the best mathematicians is foolish. John's anger at Sally for "slighting him" at a testimonial dinner because she failed to mention that he was the best lover in the world is stupid and inappropriate. (But perhaps one can think of odd circumstances in which this wouldn't be so.) Getting angry at a merely imagined slight is almost always a bad strategy and, when expressed, may be a moral injustice. But sometimes, it seems foolish *not* to get angry. After being humiliated in public, getting turned down for a promotion that one clearly deserved, or being repeatedly punched or pushed by a stranger while simply standing in line, one has a right to get angry, whether or not there are alternative avenues of expression or recourse. (The *Animal House* wisdom, "Don't get mad, get even," presumes that getting mad is the first step as well as the ongoing motivation to getting even.) Thus Aristotle insisted, in line with the Homeric heroes, that there are times when one would be a fool *not* to get angry, not only because the situation calls for it but because otherwise one degrades oneself as less than a fully functioning human being.

It is easy to appreciate the survival value of anger, even if it is just a means of energizing us for the fight that is soon to come. But anger seems to have a more complex evolutionary explanation, which might also count as a kind of strategy on a species-wide scale. In the evolution of cooperation, according to a now classic model by Robert Axelrod (1985), cooperation requires not only the willingness to make sacrifices for the group and work together (and all of those other "nice" things that we praise in our fellow human beings), but the inclination to be outraged and to punish. Otherwise, the cheaters will take advantage of the cooperators and the whole group will be at a disadvantage. (And things will get worse, as more cooperators note the advantages of cheating and become cheaters instead.) Thus anger, in addition to serving individual strategies, also serves larger strategic interests. Thus one might be warranted in suggesting that our readiness to get angry with offenders and cheaters is built right into our genes. One should add the Aristotelian proviso that we need to get angry at the right person, at the right time, and to the appropriate degree.

But the point is that anger turns out to be very valuable for a successful human social life.

Thus it is time to say something more general about the simple-minded Manichean distinction between negative and positive—good versus sinful?—emotions. This is, like many of the things both serious researchers and ordinary people say and think about emotions, a gross oversimplification of their complexity, their sophistication, and their intelligence. Anger is a perfect case in point. If the idea is that there are better ways to deal with the world than getting angry, that's fine. But that only makes anger a less good strategy, not a "negative emotion." It may well be that getting angry (or getting angry without adequate means of expressing it) is bad for your health, and in that sense it is on a par with overworking, overworrying, or overindulging. But that does not make the anger itself a "negative emotion" (any more than working, worrying, and indulging are negative in themselves). It may be that getting angry makes one feel bad, in part due, no doubt, to centuries of moral conditioning according to which getting angry is sinful. But anger at least sometimes feels good and right, and this is not necessarily due to any fatal flaw in character or misunderstanding of the nature of the cosmos. Anger transforms a situation in which we have been humbled or humiliated into one in which we are the righteous accuser, so it is easy to appreciate how it might feel good even in the absence of external expression. It is also true that anger expressed often invites anger in retaliation, and the results of this (if by your boss or your professor) may be disastrous. But it does not follow that anger is a "negative emotion," only that anger is not always the best strategy.

Instead of dismissing anger wholesale, across the board, here is a better way of thinking about anger as a strategy. Let us distinguish between anger in its cruder or more vulgar forms, including its more crude and vulgar forms of expression, and refined anger and more refined forms of expression. Picasso's *Guernica* is such a refined expression, and the ferocious anger that inspired it thereby becomes more refined as well. No one can say either that Picasso should not have been angry at the fascists' bombing of a small, neutral town, or that he should not have so expressed it. Some of Baudelaire's angry poetry could, with little imagination, be alternatively expressed in crude barnyard language, betraying emotions equally crude. But instead, Baudelaire expresses his fury with the world elegantly, movingly. Instead of talking about the "irrationality" of emotion (which as most people use the term means an absence of rationality rather than a poor strategy or a strategy gone awry), we would do much better to explore such aesthetic as well as moral evaluations, crude versus refined, appropriate versus inappropriate, vulgar and uneducated as opposed to insightful, exquisite, sensitive, and intelligent. Our emotions are as complex or as crude as our engagements with the world and other people. Our anger can be as elegant or as ugly as we allow it to be.

So what have we learned? That anger is not just a self-enclosed feeling but an engagement with other people and the world, an engagement that may be more or less warranted, more or less crude or refined, that may be more or less satisfying and more or less morally appropriate. As a strategy, it is not just something that happens to us but something we put into play, whether thoughtfully or not. This raises one final issue that I want to let dangle throughout these early chapters. Sometimes, perhaps often, what we do is not immediately obvious to us. Much of our emotional life is, as Freud insisted, *unconscious*. Since I am a philosopher, and philosophers love paradoxes to disentangle, let me put this by way of a paradox: Nothing is more immediate to us than our own emotions, but nothing about us is more prone to self-deception, suppression, lack of recognition, and even straightforward denial than our emotions. I take the unconscious to be not just a deep psychoanalytic discovery so much as a fundamental datum. People don't always know when they are angry, and they don't always know what they feel.

2

Why It Is Good to Be Afraid

Fear is perhaps the most important emotion, as unpleasant and as embarrassing as it may sometimes be. Without fear, we would allow ourselves to be vulnerable to all sorts of dangers, and we would recklessly face lethal situations without hesitation and without a thought of the possibly disastrous consequences—except perhaps an abstracted prediction ("Gee, I guess I could get killed doing this"). Hollywood protection professional Gavin de Becker writes in his book *The Gift of Fear* that the ability to be afraid is our greatest resource. We may occasionally think that we would like to be fearless, but that is a fantasy that will not survive scrutiny. Neurologist Antonio Damasio (who will appear several times in this book) describes the case of a young woman under his care who suffered a brain lesion and lost all fear of strangers. For those of us who are perpetually shy, this might sound like a boon. But her history suggests otherwise. Deprived of the "radar" that most of us take for granted, she trusted everyone and utterly failed to see how others were deceiving or manipulating her. Moreover she did not learn from her repeated bad experiences, and she suffered a predictable series of betrayals and cheats. Fear provides us with essential information about the world, namely, that it is, at least sometimes, *dangerous*.

Fear, like anger, is listed by virtually every theorist interested in these matters as a basic emotion. It is one that is universal in virtually all creatures that have any emotions at all. And for good reason. To be alive is to be vulnerable. Fear, like anger, is an engagement with the world. It is not just a self-contained "feeling." It is *about* something that endangers us,

something *scary*. Of course, fears can be mistaken, exaggerated, and sometimes just plain foolish. But many of our fears are perfectly reasonable and
necessary for survival, and they provide us with important information.
Our sensing of danger is often not something that we figure out. We *feel*
it before we are fully cognizant of what that danger is or even whether
there is a danger there. The world is dangerous, and while the nature of the
dangers vary—a walk in the jungle or down an alley on the wild side of
one of our rougher cities is not exactly like facing the boss in the midst of
a "downsizing"—some essential structures of fear seem more or less constant. Some of those structures are undeniably neurological and hard-
wired. The tingling sensations and the nervous attention to details of
shadows and sounds as we walk down a dark alley in a bad neighborhood
is not something we plan but something built right into our brains.
Surrounded by friends and acquaintances being laid off, we are sleepless
and nervous as we anticipate tomorrow morning's meeting in the boss's
office and we pay rapt attention to details (the looks from the secretary
as you approach the office, the demeanor of your boss in those first few
seconds of the meeting, the company's finances). These are not just matters
of curiosity but something far more primal and personal, not wholly
unlike the walk in the jungle or down a dark alley.

Fear, because it is so primal, is easily elicited in the laboratory. In rats
and dogs this is easily though not humanely accomplished using electric
shocks. Martin Seligman, who now leads the field of "positive psychology,"
made his initial reputation shocking dogs into a neurotic state of "learned
helplessness." Babies can be made to show fear if forced to crawl across
a transparent platform (something like a glass coffee table). When doing
research on undergraduates, given increasingly strict ethical guidelines,
researchers more often employ grade sheets and various devices manipulating peer expectations. But it does not take much to elevate the level
of fear in the average student. And fear's neurological manifestations are
easily measured, often using just the standard medical measures of quick-
ened pulse and breathing rates, of skin conductance and sensitivity. But
now that we also have an impressive arsenal of the latest in neurological
scanning and testing equipment that noninvasively gives us a remarkable
picture of the brain at work, the brain centers involved in fear turn out
to be particularly well identified, and this makes fear a favorite topic
of exploration. In fact fear has been much better explored, in terms of its
neurology, than virtually any other emotion. There is a danger here,
of course, that we will generalize too quickly from what we learn in the
carefully controlled conditions of the laboratory to the nature of all fears or
fear as such, and also that we will generalize too casually from what we
learn about fear to all other emotions. But what researchers have learned

about fear, just in the past decade, has challenged our established views about emotions and their nature considerably.

A little over one hundred years ago, William James published his now-classic account of emotions, in which fear played a central role. His example was coming across a black bear in the woods and the violent physiological reactions that immediately followed. In his account, he put a great deal of emphasis on the autonomic nervous system and related endocrine (hormonal) changes. It is because of these "peripheral" reactions that we find ourselves shivering in fear. (In anger, by contrast, our face reddens and we feel hot.) In both fear and anger, we feel our heart beating faster in that general pattern of excitement that psychologists call "arousal." But James's peripheral account of emotions soon came under fire, and recent theories have focused much more on the central nervous system and the brain in particular.

Neurologist Joseph Le Doux, for example, has argued that fear can be specifically located in a curious walnut-shaped central area of the "lower" (subcortical) brain called the amygdala. Other neuroscientists disagree about the exclusive importance of the amygdala, but it is generally agreed that it plays an important role in fear, in particular. According to Le Doux (1996), fear and other emotions are "biological functions of the nervous system." This is borne out by the fact that fear—for example, our reaction to suddenly seeing a bear—happens so fast that one does not have time to think or even process the idea "ohmygosh it's a bear." The time it takes for a nerve impulse to travel from the senses to the brain centers responsible for fear responses is a small fraction of a second. By contrast, the time it takes for a nerve impulse to travel from the senses to the "higher" or "cognitive" parts of the brain, the cerebral hemispheres, is much longer. One might compare this to an executive decision in an emergency that must be made quickly and without impediment as opposed to sending a set of alternative proposals through a democratically elected committee. Sometimes, it is important to be fast. (Philosophers don't last long in foxholes. They are too slow figuring out that they ought to duck.)

Moreover, our understanding and knowledge may be mistaken. Thus Le Doux polemically argues that fear does not even have to be conscious, that the feeling of fear is something like "icing on the cake." This seems to me to confuse feelings with consciousness, but the important finding here is that fear may have an in-born trigger, a certain "cell assembly," governed by certain fundamental "themes" (such as a dark shadow crossing our path) that may then be embellished by any number of learned variations. The risk is that the fascination with the speed and spontaneity of the neurology may suggest a reductionist account of emotion in which even matters seemingly so basic as feeling and emotional experience are treated as secondary issues. To be sure, emotions may be unconscious (as I noted at the end of the last chapter), and they may not at first involve the cerebral cortex. But to say that an emotion may be unconscious and even "noncognitive" is not to say that it is not felt. It may not be noticed or recognized or acknowledged, and the feeling may even emerge late in the game (in neurological milliseconds), but, whatever it is, the feeling of fear is not just "icing on the cake."

This fascinating research holds out many promises for further understanding and ways of dealing with and possibly curing dysfunctional emotions, from easing or ending anxiety and panic attacks to treating various phobias and other irrational fears. It also tells us a great deal about what goes wrong in those tragic patients with tumors, brain lesions, and head injuries who suffer from emotional deficiencies rather than emotional excesses. But what goes on in the brain is, at most, only part of the story. The other part has to do with fear as an engagement with the world.

I began by insisting that fear, like anger, is an engagement with the world, not just a self-contained "feeling." It is *about* something that threatens, something that endangers. Thus I would say, no matter what happens in the brain (and we knew very little about that until just a few years ago), fear is not fear unless it is about some perceived danger in the world. The relevant neurological syndromes, no matter how pronounced, do not manifest themselves as an emotion unless they have this external focus. (The neurological syndromes can be artificially stimulated, but without an external focus, they do not signify any emotion.) Typically, the threat or danger is outside of us, in the world. Sometimes, the threat may be merely imagined, or one might be mistaken, but what one is mistaken about is something in the world (namely whether there is a real threat there or not). It is thus confused, although we all understand what it means to say, "the danger is all in your head." The danger is necessarily perceived as *out there*, in the world, even if it is only our own imagination or projection or paranoia that puts it there. Sometimes the threat or danger may be "in us" in a different sense, in our bodies, or even in our minds, although this is a much more complex business than it may at first appear to be. I may be extremely anxious about my heart condition, or about what seems to be my progressive loss of memory. But my heart and my mind, in the relevant senses, are also part of the world. They are what I am anxious about. Fear is never just self-enclosed.

The idea that fear is directed outwardly even when the source is our own bodies finds a striking form of confirmation. When we find ourselves feeling the physical symptoms of fear we immediately look outward to detect the source of the fear, its cause, what it must be about. Two psychologists, Stanley Schachter and Jerome Singer (1962), did a famous experiment back in the early 1960s in which they gave subjects a stimulating drug such as epinephrine and placed them in a variety of circumstances. Consequently, those subjects who did not understand the cause of their arousal (they were told the drug was a supervitamin) identified their emotion according to the context in which they found themselves (infuriating, humorous, or fearful). The experiment suggested that people ascribe emotions to themselves based not only on their arousal but also on their perceptions of the situations. (The control group, which was warned of the effects of the drug, tended not to read their reaction as any emotion at all.) The idea is that even when the arousal is stimulated artificially, we look outward for an object, a threat or danger.

So, too, a dog suffering a sharp, sudden pain instinctively strikes out, trying to ward off what it takes to be an attacker. It does not comprehend, as we can, the idea that the pain has no external cause. A paranoid who suffers from outrageous delusions all too readily experiences the delusions as facts about the world (and may take great pains to confirm them). A paranoid who hears voices hears those voices as coming from outside. But even in these cases, fear is about some sense of threatening danger, whether literally outside in the world or in our bodies or minds, and whether real or imagined. The most horrendous fears, I would guess, are those that are most intimate, effecting our most basic abilities to cope, for instance, no longer being able to trust one's own mind, one's own judgment, or, in incipient senility, one's memory. Thus in horror movies and in some religions, I believe, the worst fears are generated by the threat of *possession*, that is, one's mind being taken over by an alien being. But this does not cast any doubt on the idea that the emotion of fear is necessarily *about* something and an engagement in the world. It only goes to show that, as sophisticated as we are about the notions of self and "my mind," our fears can be about a great many troubling possibilities that would be unimaginable to simpler creatures.

But if fear is always about the world, then it is a matter of considerable interest and concern that fear is sometimes immune to the relevant information about the world, namely, that the object of fear is really not dangerous. Accordingly, irrational fears can be notoriously difficult to eradicate, even in the presence of the relevant knowledge. We say (unsympathetically) to a friend, "how can you still have a fear of flying when you know that it is statistically much safer than driving to the airport?" or "how can you be afraid of that itsy-bitsy spider, when you know that it will not bite and wants nothing more than to get away from you?" How does the fear, which is about the world, get disengaged from the very information that it is supposedly about? It becomes increasingly evident that fear is not just about the world but involves something else as well. And the most obvious candidate for what that might be is located in the findings of the neuroscientists who have shown so persuasively that fear involves certain more or less automatic ("hard-wired") brain responses that may take place independently of *any* information about the world.

Irrational fears, phobias, and other intractable cases of fear might thus be explained: Sometimes the automatic ("hard-wired") brain responses take place regardless of what one knows about the world. Because of a brain chemistry imbalance, or because of some prior trauma, a person's brain gets locked into a certain kind of response, given even the most minimal stimulus. Thus the person who fears flying may have been traumatized by hearing about or seeing an image of a crashing plane, and the fear response takes over at the mere thought of getting on a plane. The person who is afraid of spiders may well have been bitten by a spider once and had a bad reaction. Subsequently he or she has a fear response at the very sight of a spider. William James (and many others) have suggested that there are certain primal experiences that we all react to instinctually and independently of our thought processes. (James cites seeing a snake or a bucket of blood, for example.) But whether the irrational reaction is learned or instinctual there are two different levels of processing going on, which we typically but misleadingly call the intellectual and the emotional ("Well, intellectually I know that but emotionally I nevertheless feel . . .") There is indeed an important distinction to be made here, but we need to be very careful how and where we make it.

The "two levels" here are not the two levels of the intellect and the emotions. Rather, we are talking about two levels of *belief* (or, better, "appraisal"). Given what we learn about the world, we come to have more or less well-founded beliefs or appraisals about the safety and dangers of such activities as flying and driving and such animals as snakes and spiders (and more generally crawling and creeping creatures). We form these beliefs on the basis of evidence in our own experience and from the testimony of others. But we also have beliefs that are not based on evidence or testimony, or are very loosely based on these. When these beliefs are fairly sophisticated, we call them "intuitions." When they are much more primitive, as in the cases here, we refer to them (misleadingly) as "gut feelings." Intuitions and gut feelings may or may not be easily articulated. (Often they are not articulated.) Nevertheless, they are still beliefs or appraisals of or about the world. How much these are emotionally charged is a further question, not necessarily decided by the nature of the belief. Very sophisticated, highly articulate, well-founded and well-argued beliefs or appraisals may be highly emotionally charged. Consider how people feel about abortion or any other "hot button" topic about which they have fought and argued often in current politics. By contrast, the most basic beliefs or appraisals that we have about the nature of the world, for instance, that the ground is solid, stationary, and will support us (assuming we have not recently been a victim of an earthquake or that we haven't just left a lecture on geology), may involve virtually no discernible emotions whatever, until, that is, these beliefs are thrust into view by being violated.

The case of irrational fear seems to make even more plausible the analysis of fear as a "hard-wired" and unintelligent (even if appropriate) response. Why else would we remain afraid, even though we know that the object of our fear is not dangerous at all? If what Le Doux (1996) calls the "low road" process to fear gets stuck, if the very sight of a spider triggers off this automatic response, we can understand how it is that no amount of information would alter that fear response. This is not to say that there is nothing to be done about it. Our fear just cannot be altered by way of the accumulation of further information and knowledge. But if the problem with many such cases of irrational emotions and phobias is, as I suggested above, a conflict of beliefs or appraisals rather than a conflict between fear and belief, then we can understand these cases in a much more humane and less problematic way. Some beliefs or appraisals are indeed "cognitively impenetrable," difficult to change by just adding further information. But this does not mean that they cannot be changed through further experience, for instance by repeated exposure to the disturbing stimulus in question. What's more, and more important for our general analysis, these are deviant cases of fear rather than prototypical cases.

Most cases of fear, I would argue, do not involve such conflicts of multiple layers of belief or appraisals (which is not to deny that they involve multiple layers of belief or appraisal). Rather, our primitive intuitions and gut feelings tend to be confirmed and reinforced on more focused, articulate, and rational examination by our articulate and justified beliefs and appraisals. So we first feel uneasy finding ourselves alone in a dark alley and hearing the odd creak ahead of us, but then reflecting on the fact that we are in a dark alley in a dangerous part of town where there have recently been several back alley muggings convinces us that we are *right* to be afraid and it is reasonable to be apprehensive and attentive. It is the odd case of fear, not the normal one, that involves a conflict of beliefs or appraisals. And it is the odd case of fear, not the normal one, that is irrational, that precludes further investigation and refuses to accept further evidence or testimony from others.

Many fears, it is plain to see, are straightforwardly rational. Being afraid of a grizzly bear when you have foolishly walked off alone in the Montana woods is not at all irrational (although walking off alone in the Montana woods may well be irrational). Being afraid of the taxman when you have under-declared your income by eighty percent is not at all irrational (although under-declaring your income by 80 percent is very irrational). Even when our fears are not so obviously rational, they may nevertheless be reasonable. There is or may well be something to be afraid of, although there may be much discussion about how real and how serious the danger is and how one should respond and behave toward it. We would not expect a Davy Crockett–type character to respond or behave in the same way that most of us would in the bear case—or for that matter, in the tax case, if his own Tennessee history is any indication.

The problem is that the irrational cases of fear have been taken not as deviant or exceptional cases but as the paradigm cases. Thus the "lower" symptoms of fear have been taken to be the essence of fear while the accompanying feelings and thoughts, not yet to even mention further reasoning, inquiry, and investigation, have been relegated to mere after-effects, inessential concomitants or consequences of fear. But no brain process whatever can be an emotion if it involves no feeling and no engagement with the "outside" world. This is not to deny that *all* fears are neurologically based. (And all emotions, too.) But it is to deny that, even in the most deviant cases, this is not all that there is to say about them. We should not too quickly generalize from the fact that some instances of fear, for instance phobias, are irrational to the claim that fear in general is irrational, much less to the much larger generalization that all emotions are irrational.

We are so used to thinking of emotions and rationality as opposites that we jump much too quickly to the unthinking idea that fear as such is irrational. I hope that it is by now quite obvious that this is not always or even usually so, and that fear is, more often than not, quite fitting, functional, and rational. But it is not just this. Emotions are necessary to rationality. The distinguished neuroscientist Antonio Damasio writes about some of his patients with damage to the amygdala who have lost not only the capacity to feel fear but the capacity to make rational decisions as well. They have no sense of *salience*, what is important and what is not, what is a risk and what is not. This is important neurological evidence for the thesis that I will be arguing throughout the book, that emotions and rationality are not opposed but complementary and intertwined. They are both necessary for a well-lived life.

There are many different varieties of fear. Some fears are largely "blind" neurological reactions, but others involve considerable sophistication and learning. An experience of fear may be sudden and utterly involuntary, as when one comes across a rattlesnake on a walk in the garden. But other fears grow over time and last a long time, even years, such as fear of government authorities or fear of hereditary illness. I am discussing both sorts of fear in this chapter. But when I say that fear (and other emotions) can last a long time, I am not just referring to *dispositions* to feel fear, as in the usual cases of fear of flying and arachnophobia. A person who is afraid of flying will probably experience fear only when he or she has to directly confront the need to get on an airplane. An arachnophobe will probably experience fear only when he or she sees (or seems to see) a spider. I am thinking much more of the unfortunate employee who is continuously afraid of his supervisor, or an abused woman who lives in terror of her husband. These are not just tendencies to have fear that occasionally get triggered by a specific circumstance. They are ongoing structures of a person's experience and personality that one might literally claim to be operative every waking moment of their day.

Normal fear can also be rational and reasonable, or it can be irrational and unreasonable. Normal fear requires an object feared, something threatening, something dangerous. Whatever else may be going on in the brain or the body, if it is not about something, some perceived or sensed danger, it does not count as fear. But we can be wrong about such fears. What passes for knowledge may in fact be based on ignorance, misinformation, or foolishness. The object may in fact not be so dangerous (it is a king snake, not a rattler), or it may only seem dangerous (it is indeed a rattlesnake, but it has had its fangs and its venom removed), or the situation may involve a prank rather than an unreasonable fear (it is a dead, stuffed rattlesnake, animated by a primitive electrical device). But ignorant or misinformed fear may nevertheless be reasonable, if one had good reason to believe in the danger at the time. Foolish anger, by contrast, implies that the belief or appraisal was not warranted and lacked any adequate reason to believe the object in question was dangerous.

Normal fear can also be subconscious, under the radar, so to speak. Often, when one faces a danger, one is so engaged in the process of extricating or otherwise saving oneself that one pays no attention to the symptoms of fear. After a close call in a near-miss auto accident, it might seem that the fear begins only after the danger has passed. It is probably true that we notice the physical symptoms—heart racing, sweating, breathlessness—only later, when we have safely stopped. But we should not mistake the physical symptoms for the fear, any more than we should equate the fear with our awareness that we are afraid. The fear was the recognition of the danger. This example reminds us of the fact that even intense fear can be unconscious, notably when overwhelmed by some other engagement, in this case controlling the car, or in a different kind of case, when eclipsed by another emotion, such as anger. The fact that fear is unconscious, however, is quite independent of the question of whether it is rational or not. An emotion may be unconscious, but it can still be rational if it can be explained with good reasons. When an emotion is conscious, however, the burden of rationality moves to the subject, who should be able to supply those reasons.

We can say of fear as we did of anger that it is only with some gross over-simplification said to be a "negative emotion." The truth is: Fear is invaluable. We would not survive without it. Security consultants insist that it is our first line of defense. ("Trust your fear.") Thus fear is not an emotion to be avoided. "The only thing to fear is fear itself" is a brilliant political line in the midst of an economic depression but poor advice as a general psychological caveat. To be sure, too much fear, generating paralysis, is a bad strategy. But fear itself is one of our most essential ways of engaging the world. Here, there is a trap that awaits us, and we should make a seemingly innocent but in fact quite important distinction. There is the negativity of the danger, the object of the emotion as something to be avoided, but it does not follow that the emotion itself is negative. A quick and obvious example is the fact that people often go out of their way to feel and enjoy feeling fear, whether by going to a horror movie or, more courageously, by going bungee-jumping. On the one hand, there is the danger to be avoided, but on the other there is the emotion that may be sought out for its own sake.

Aristotle worried at some length about the paradox that people enjoyed going to see tragedies because they evoked fear and pity, two decidedly unpleasant emotions. Today, more people may prefer to avoid tragedies but they do put themselves in circumstances where the danger is real but minimized. By bungee-jumping they get to experience the sheer thrill of finding themselves falling rapidly through space but with the confidence (only occasionally misplaced) that the apparatus will slow down and stop the fall and leave them ready to try it again, or to sign up for the white-water rafting excursion just down the river. Their own descriptions of the experience (and the ways in which those experiences are promoted) emphasize the fun, the *desirability* of feeling fear, the more the better. How do we explain this? It would seem that fear, like anger, is not a "negative" emotion at all, despite the fact that the situations that normally cause us fear—namely, real dangers, are not at all to be desired or sought after. Thus Aristotle suggested that make-believe fear allowed us to "discharge" the fears that we experienced in life ("catharsis") and Freud followed him not just in his vocabulary but in his model of fear released, though through therapy, not in the public theater. Nevertheless, this raises some tantalizing questions. How can we get pleasure from such a "negative" emotion, and if we do, doesn't that suggest that the emotion is not so negative after all? How can fear and pleasure, or horror and entertainment, be made compatible? Or is the emotion not really fear, or not really horror (or not really pleasurable) at all? Such questions suggest that we have not yet tapped into the intricacies of fear.

3

Varieties of Fear and Anger:
Emotions and Moods

There are, as I said, many varieties of fear and anger. The range of fear reactions alone is breathtaking. There is fear of snakes, fear of heights, fear of authority, fear of success, hypochondria, fear of public speaking, fear of being alone, fear of crowds, fear of being embarrassed or humiliated, fear of being mugged on the same street that one was robbed on before, fear of the gruff-looking stranger who eyes you suspiciously on the subway, fear of the tornado that seems to be bearing down on you no matter how fast you drive, fear as you suddenly jam on your brakes when the traffic stops ahead of you on the freeway, fear of an oppressive regime, fear of being arrested for participating in an unpopular political protest, and that unfortunate fear that at times seems to be fear of everything. Then of course, there is always the fear of death, which seems to afflict mainly us humans. (Animals certainly fear being harmed or caught by a predator, but that they fear *death* is a very different proposition.) But in addition to these many types and objects of fear, we noted in the last chapter that fear admits of some other tantalizing variants, whether these are deviant instances of fear or rather more basic and paradigmatic examples of that emotion. There are utterly irrational fears and phobias. There is fear that takes place so quickly that it does not even enter consciousness. There is panic, which is decidedly different than fear. And then there is what we might call for the moment "mock fear," the experience of fear sought out precisely because one knows that there is no reason for fear (because the movie monster isn't real, because the bungee cord is guaranteed to be secure). And in addition to fear, there is also anxiety and dread, which seem to have no objects at all, and terror and horror, which are interestingly different from fear, the former more like panic, the latter something quite different entirely (and more, perhaps, like disgust, another supposedly basic emotion).

Moreover, I mentioned in passing that for some unfortunate souls, fear is not just an occasional emotion. It is what Heidegger would call "a way of being." In such cases, fear seems to lack any particular object. Or rather, it seems to take *everything* as its object. In such cases, we might say that fear is more like a mood, where moods, like some mysterious emotions, seem to be without an object, or in any case, without a specific object. Thus Heidegger says that through the mood of *angst* (or anxiety), we tune in to the reality of our lives in the world. This might be triggered by the recognition of impending death, the realization that we are mortal, but it suggests a more pervasive nothingness in our lives, a lack of substantial "authentic" being.

Anger, too, admits of many varieties. We briefly discussed annoyance and irritation as trivial or minimally accusatory versions of anger, and I suggested that moral indignation is sort of a supreme court version of anger, anger with suprapersonal moral clout. I also suggested that anger, too, can be or can turn into a mood, for instance when someone "wakes up on the wrong side of bed" and gets angry at everyone, indiscriminately, or when anger at a single, specific offense morphs its way into anger at the whole world. In such cases, the anger seems to be about everything, or about nothing in particular. It, too, is a way of "being tuned" to the world, a way of being-in the world, in a particularly unpleasant and manipulative way. And so we need to look a bit further at this distinction between emotions and moods. It is a distinction that is often and inconsistently misunderstood. Sometimes, and by some serious theorists, emotions are taken to be short-term and abrupt outbursts while moods are taken to be more enduring. In popular culture, by contrast, emotions are more often taken more seriously (and more readily feared) while moods are taken to be like passing mental weather in a fast-changing climate. ("The angry mood is now passing, with a bit of sunshine on the horizon.") Paul Ekman thus suggests that moods (as opposed to emotions) may be unnecessary for human survival and confesses that he would be quite happy to give up his good moods in exchange for being freed from the bad ones as well.

I doubt that the distinction is so neat or clear as either view suggests. Emotions tend to have specific and more or less discrete objects. Moods tend to have underdetermined or less specific objects. Thus I think that it is correct to say that the angry man is angry about everything or, perhaps, "angry at the world." Camus's mythological character Sisyphus expresses his anger at the cosmos "with scorn and defiance," though putatively his ire is directed at the gods who ordered his punishment. So, too, the fearful person may fixate on the fragility of his own health or the likelihood of imminent unemployment but he is afraid of everything and anything, even of "his own shadow." There are emotions, such as anxiety (angst) and dread, which are said to have no objects but in fact have very peculiar objects. It has been said, for example by the existentialist Søren Kierkegaard, that their object is the Unknown, or, more straightforwardly for many religious thinkers, God. It has also been said, notably by Heidegger, that their object is Nothingness. But without trying to pin down these evasive metaphysical entities, we should take careful note of both the variations of fear that are without distinct objects and those with peculiar objects such as the Unknown, God, the Cosmos, or Nothingness.

The person who is afraid of death, however, seems not to be afraid of everything but of something, but its object is not just death as such. The medieval image of the "grim reaper" allows us to focus on something particular: in its usual characterization, the scary but cartoon image of a skeleton in a monk's habit carrying a nasty-looking scythe. But what scares us about the image of the reaper is not death. Death itself cannot be depicted. Philosophers and preachers have long waxed eloquent on how evasive that concept can be. Thus it makes good sense to say that a person is afraid of the Unknown, or of Nothingness. Kierkegaard tells us that dread or anxiety (Danish *angest*) opens the door to faith, if only we would follow it through, and Heidegger tells us that *angst* is not just a mood but a profound ontological insight, if only we would grasp it. It reminds us of our mortality, our "Being-unto-Death," and consequently of our possibilities for leading an authentic life. It is often said that the ultimate fear, not just the last but the foundation of all fears, is the fear of death, but this would suggest that even the fear of death might really be the fear of something else.

The shift from emotions to moods and vice versa is as common as shifts in focus from the specific to the general. Often when we are in the midst of an emotion, perhaps fear of crashing in a turbulent aircraft, perhaps angry at being interrupted in the middle of our presentation, we shift our focus to a larger issue, the issue of mortality as such or the increasing rudeness and hostility of one's colleagues and the culture in general. Just as often, the shift goes the other way, from the general to the specific, so as we are raging against the universe some poor unfortunate undergraduate pops his head into the lecture hall and the whole weight of the rage gets focused on him (during the brief moment before he manages to escape from view). Fear of one's mortality easily finds a focus in any odd passing faintness or discomfort, which can then become a very narrowly focused obsession.

Depression and joy are especially instructive when this distinction between moods and emotions comes into focus. Depression (and I am not here referring to the very serious clinical variety that involves imbalances in brain chemistry or other neuropathology) involves a global attitude to the world. Ludwig Wittgenstein, who often suffered from depression, rightly said that "a depressed man lives in a depressed world." But depression can be "triggered" by a particular setback. So a person might get depressed *about* his rejection from law school, an emotion about a specific event. But the depression gains in scope, spreads over other aspects of his experience, and so starts affecting all the things he does, which now seem no longer worthwhile, and his relationships, which come to seem inadequate to make up for the disappointment, and before long he is depressed, not just about something but about everything. A cure for depression (again, not the clinical kind) may be to come to grips with the incident that initiated the depression and come to understand that it is not so serious or life-damaging. This in turn, however, may involve some serious self-examination and a reevaluation of one's life goals and abilities.

So, too, on a happier note, the emotion of joy—joy about some particular event or the enjoyment of some particular activity—may well expand its scope to include other things and people associated with that event or activity and may even become global, about everything. Then joy becomes a mood—a really good mood—and with some luck and training it can come to define one's life. This expansive mood is often referred to as happiness, but as a philosopher I must politely demur. Happiness is not just joy, nor even joy expanded. Happiness is not a mood or an emotion but a way of living, involving a life well-lived as well as, of course, a substantial component of joy and a feeling of subjective well-being. But happiness is not just a sense of subjective well-being and a "positive" feeling. It is possible to drug or delude oneself into believing that one is doing fine when it is or will soon become evident that this is not the case, and it is easy to induce good feelings, if only very temporarily. But the idea of thinking about happiness in relation to moods is a good one to the following extent, as we shall see later. Happiness is not just a specific good feeling or emotion but an all-embracing evaluation of one's life that takes into account not just every aspect but the *gestalt* of an entire life, not at a moment in time but through time, a lifetime. (I will discuss this further both in chapters 6 and 23.) But one would not be on the wrong track—although it would not apply to everyone—if one insisted that joy can be a key ingredient in happiness. The trick that many of us need to learn is to be as efficient at expanding our joyful and enjoyable moments into an all-embracing sense of the world as we are in expanding our disappointments into global complaints about our lives.

What is particularly interesting is how anxiety, especially, gets focused on something particular and becomes mere fear—or vanishes altogether, a topic that Freud made the cornerstone of his psychoanalysis and his theory of the Unconscious. According to Freud, emotions as such cannot be unconscious because feelings (or "affects," as he called them) are necessarily in consciousness. But emotions are conjunctions of feelings and ideas, he insisted, and while feelings cannot be unconscious, ideas can be, or, alternatively, the connections between an idea and a feeling can be unconscious. So the various defense mechanisms, as they came to be called, tended to displace or disassociate a feeling from its idea, that is, its proper object, and the result was anxiety, a feeling (an emotion) without an object. But through the process of analysis, one could learn the proper connection between the current feeling and its original cause (for instance, a recurrent memory, disguised in symbolism, of an upsetting incident from the past). Thus we might say that anxiety, à la Freud, does have a particular object but the link between feeling and object has been hidden or disguised or, as Freud would say, repressed.

On the other hand, Sartre, who is in many ways opposed to Freud (in particular to his notion of the Unconscious, but also to his general sense of "psychic determinism"), interprets the difference between fear and anxiety in a very different way. Here he borrows heavily from Heidegger and his analysis of angst. Fear, he says, is the recognition of a very specific danger, for example, the fear of falling off a high ledge as one tries to walk along it. Anxiety, by contrast, is the fear of one's own freedom, that is, the fear of what one might *do*, say, gratuitously leap off the ledge of one's own free will. There is a dramatic difference here, but it is not the difference between mood and emotion. It is the difference between fear directed at the dangers in the world (including one's own poor sense of balance or the insecurity of the trail) and anxiety directed at one's own choices. It is a distinction that plays a weighty role in Sartre's existentialism, that puts great emphasis on the importance and pervasiveness of human choice. But it is also a novel understanding of anxiety as significantly different from fear.

We saw that both fear and anger can be either rational or irrational. It depends on whether the object of the emotion is right or reasonable and whether the intensity of the emotion is appropriate to the situation. I also noted, especially with regard to anger, that its rationality in part depended on its being conducive to one's long-term goals and well-being. So, too, fear can be irrational even if it is correct and appropriate to the situation but destructive of one's long-term interests. During wartime, for instance, there is always good reason to be afraid. But as the war goes on, it becomes antithetical to life to remain in a constant state of fear. One needs to take chances. One needs to show courage. And so even with good reason it can become irrational to remain in a state of fear. In anger as in fear, there is the real possibility that neurology may overtake good sense and provoke overwhelming irrationality. In the case of fear, this irrationality manifests itself as panic. In anger, it manifests itself as rage.

Here we get back to the neurological dimension we briefly discussed in the last two chapters (when we were talking about basic emotions), but we are no longer talking about emotions that are usually listed as basic. Indeed, it is curious to me that panic and rage, although they are extremely primitive and essentially programmed emotions, are not usually included as basic emotions. Too often, it is simply assumed that fear and panic are the same, and anger and rage as well, as if all cases of fear were variations on panic and all cases of anger were variations on rage. Paul Ekman, for instance, speaks noncommittally of "emotion families," of which fear and anger would be two primary examples. But panic and rage are extreme reactions, and it is with good reason that some neuroscientists, for example, Jaak Panksepp (1982), have distinguished fear and panic, for instance, as quite distinct emotional responses. In our brief discussion of irrational fears and phobias, I suggested, following many contemporary scientists and clinicians, that a neurological disorder gets "stuck" in such a way that fear becomes unresponsive to new knowledge and information. So, too, irrational anger may also involve such a "getting stuck." But what is not sufficiently appreciated is how odd an occurrence this is. So I might suggest, as a hint at least, that panic and rage are something like "stuck" variations on fear and anger.

Many years ago, I was discussing the nature of emotions with Patricia Churchland, an excellent philosopher and the founder of "neurophilosophy" who was then just developing her views. She argued against my own emerging views about anger as a kind of judgment, stating that she could induce rage in a cat just by stimulating a particular network in its brain. Thus rage needed no provoking object at all, much less anything as intelligent as a judgment. I took her argument very seriously and I still do, but I now think that she was only talking about rage, not anger. Rage, to put the point a bit oversimply, is largely a neuromuscular reaction with minimal intelligence, minimal attention to its object (if there is one), and minimal prudence in its lashing-out behavior (in a cat, claws bared and swinging, a hissing, biting frenzy). A notoriously extreme version of rage in humans is the phenomenon known in South Asia as "running amok." (This is the only Malay word I can think of to make its way into standard English.) When someone (usually a young man) runs amok, he goes homicidally insane, apparently for no reason. Like the cat whose rage has been induced, this person acts in a physiological frenzy, not for any ostensible reason, his behavior only minimally but violently directed at one or another passing victim for no reason whatsoever.

Panic, to pursue the parallel, is also a primarily neuromuscular reaction that involves minimal intelligence, minimal attention to its object (insofar as there is one), and minimal prudence in its flight behavior. Thus in a panic one runs wildly and aimlessly, sometimes even (disastrously) in the direction of the danger. After striking a utility pole in an automobile, people have been electrocuted when they panicked and jumped out of the car. (The safety manuals all emphasize, "Stay in the car!") Panic and rage are irrational, in other words, in a multiple sense. They tend to have minimal intelligence and thus are often off target, unreasonable (without reason), and imprudent. But when it turns out well, the flight in panic makes fast escape possible and the rage allows one to attack and over-whelm a formidable offender. Even so, we are rightly loath to call the behavior "rational." Sometimes, not surprisingly, evolution has equipped us for survival quite independently of our much-celebrated rationality and intelligence. Thus both panic and rage can serve us well, but that does not mean that we should endorse either of them. Indeed, we tend to treat both of them (in ourselves and in others) with some horror and disdain. The efficiency of emotions is not the only or the primary argument to be made on their behalf.

Panic and rage are both unreasonable, in fact, without any reason at all. After the fact, one may be able to supply reasons—or in any case an explanation—why he or she acted so. But at the time of the panic or rage, physiology takes over and medical not psychological intervention may be required. It would again be a huge mistake, however, if we were to general-ize from these extreme cases to the nature of fear or anger or all emotions. What characterizes fear and anger and most emotions is their intelligence, their insight, their attunement to the world. Through them, we often get to see and sense what our merely rational minds might ignore, blunder over, or merely rationalize. It is through our fears, our ordinary, normal, reasonable fears, that we rightly recognize that the world is a dangerous place. It is through our anger, our ordinary, normal, reasonable anger, that we rightly recognize that the world is sometimes an infuriating and offensive place. But even in the absence of such reasonable fear and anger, our bodies and brains are built in such a way that fear and anger, or panic and rage, come quite naturally even when reason has not had a chance to intervene.

Finally, let me briefly talk about terror and horror, two other seemingly extreme members of the fear family. Terror lies midway between fear and panic, insofar as one can discuss any two emotions along a single dimension. That is, terror might be thought of as extreme fear, but it has considerably more intelligence and more prudence than panic. Terror, happily, is relatively rare for most of us, but we know it vicariously all too well as we follow the news bulletins from Israel and Palestine, from Iraq and Kashmir, from eastern Africa and other troubled, literally explosive parts of the globe. Fear is aimed at a more or less specific object, but it usually does not occupy the whole of our consciousness. One can have serious stage fright but nevertheless perform brilliantly. A student can have test anxiety and nevertheless do very well. One dimension of rationality regarding fear and anger, suggested in Aristotle's advice regarding the right object and right amount of an emotion, is the *scope* of an emotion, that is, the range of its field or objects. One may be rightly afraid or angry, but when that fear or anger becomes obsessive and obliterates any larger or more perspicacious view, that is another way in which it can go wrong. (The same is true of love, which I will talk about in the next chapter.)

Fear is usually more or less circumscribed in our experience. We can overcome it, or work around it, or even ignore it. Terror, by contrast, is not so circumscribed. But normally, fear is not terror. It does not take up the whole of consciousness. Thus terror, like extreme irrational fear, is marked by its obsessional quality. The person who suffers from fear of flying is not just a nervous flier. He or she is a terrified flier, aware of nothing else but the airplane, its vibrations, and the likelihood of its crashing. The arachnophobe is not just uncomfortable around spiders. That itsy-bitsy spider comes to occupy the whole of his or her consciousness. Nevertheless, although terror differs from fear in its scope, it may sometimes be rational and justified, for instance in wartime situations. War is a terrible experience that no one would rationally choose to have just for the sake of having it. (I am not sure about "green-line" journalists, who seem to thrive on being on the front lines of the most dangerous trouble spots in the world.) But even so, as I suggested earlier, in times of war it may be necessary to modulate one's terror into fear and give it a more adaptive proper place in consciousness.

Horror, like terror, differs from fear in that it leaves us utterly helpless. There is nothing that we can do. Fear, in general, is a useful emotion with obvious evolutionary as well as personal advantages because of its built-in "action tendencies," that is, propensities for directed behavior, built into the nervous system and musculature, preparing the body for fight or flight or whatever else it may have to do. In some circumstances, however, and for some animals as a matter of instinct, *freezing* counts as an appropriate if not always successful evasive action. (My old dog Beefeater used to corner possums in the yard, but since he was in it for the chase and not for the meal, he would stare at the motionless critter for a minute or so and then walk away, totally frustrated, leaving the possum to scamper into the woods.) In horror, too, there is a tendency to freeze, but in this case it doesn't seem to be any kind of strategic action. We might say that horror is a "spectator" emotion, although this is not for a second to say that it is a detached or disinterested emotion. To the contrary, horror is usually an overwhelming emotional reaction. It is so obsessive that it blocks virtually any other response or emotion.

I would argue that the fact that horror is so overwhelming also means that it is not one of those emotions that can be "mixed," and, in particular, it does not mix with pleasure. Thus the "paradox of horror," that is, how horror can be pleasurable, which has worried philosophers since Aristotle, is, I would argue, impossible. Fear can be pleasurable, especially if one knows or believes that there is no real danger. (The adrenaline rush in bungee-jumping, for example, is enjoyable precisely because it is an instinctual response to falling from a great height combined with the confidence that one is in no danger at all.) Horror, by contrast, cannot be pleasurable. And yet, horror, even more than fear, fascinates us. Drivers slow down and gawk at the twisted bloody body on the highway after a terrible accident, willfully obsessed despite the knowledge that they will probably be greatly upset for days or weeks to come. Young people pay to see "horror movies," despite the high probability of nightmares to follow. But even if they do so to "entertain" themselves, I doubt that they get any pleasure out of it, that is, pleasure out of the horror. They may well take pleasure at the artifice of fright, or at their bravado in subjecting themselves to such a sight. But of course, rarely do horror movies provoke actual horror. They may provide suspense, which is pleasurable enough, especially when merely fictional and happily resolved in less than two hours. Often, they provoke laughter (at their silliness or at our silliness in reacting to them), and they can evoke appreciation for the acting (though this is rare, given the genre) or for the special effects (all too often the film's only virtue). We do take pleasure in vicarious fear, but we do not take pleasure in horror, which eclipses any possibility of pleasure. I'm not sure that there is such a thing as vicarious horror, although we can certainly react with sympathy or empathy to someone who is horrified. But if we are horrified too, it is no longer vicarious. It is now *our* horror.

The peculiar nature of horror helps to solve another, related philosophical paradox, how we allow ourselves to be moved by situations that we know to be unreal. (The highway accident, of course, is very real. It constitutes what I call "real horror," as opposed to the "art horror" in the theaters.) Samuel Coleridge summed up the paradox with the glorious phrase "the willing suspension of disbelief," but he does not tell us how we can or why we should do this. The distinction between fear and horror gives us a partial answer. Philosophers ask, how can we see the Tyrannosaurus Rex charging toward us and not run from the theater? If we were truly afraid, it would be hard to understand why we do not. An essential aspect of fear, some psychologists would argue, is the triggering of action tendencies. But it is the standard case in horror that there is nothing to do, no action to be taken, so no action tendency can be triggered. Thus philosophers' desperate attempts to define some unreal or "make believe" fear become unnecessary, for horror can be genuine in the absence of action. (I'm thinking, in particular, of Kendell Walton's ingenious book *Mimesis and Make-Believe,* which argues that both the situation [or work] and the resultant emotion are "make believe.") Horror is essentially the same emotion, whether its object is real or it is a response to a work of art. There need be no "willing suspension of disbelief," for unlike fear, horror does not admit of an easy distinction between responding as if there were some real danger and actually responding to such a danger. A painting of a merely imagined horrific, twisted, mutilated face is horrible in exactly the same sense that a real and present horrific, twisted, mutilated face is horrible, although the meaning and thus the consequences of the latter, needless to say, might be very different.

Since I have briefly introduced the subject of horror movies perhaps I should add that just as horror should not be confused with fear, it should not be confused with *disgust* either. Given the trashy quality of a great many so-called "horror" films (more accurately described as "slasher" or "splatter" films), it is important to make this point. What is horrible may also be disgusting, but the two emotions are not the same. I should similarly insist that shock and brutal surprise are not horror either, as popular as these cinematic devices may be with B- and C-level horror directors. In fact, one of the most often used dramatic devices is the cheapest, in terms of requiring no talent, no scripting except for a modicum of suspense, and no particular content. It is that physiological reaction to sudden surprise called the "startle reaction" (imagine a loud unexpected bang just behind your ear). But this is not an emotion at all. It has no conceptual content, no intelligence whatever. But the best horror films (I would nominate *Invasion of the Body Snatchers*) evoke horror without either being disgusting or startling. They appeal to our intelligence and sophistication as well as to our "gut reactions," which are typically rather crude.

Given the varieties of fear and anger and their deviant forms, perhaps this is the best time to introduce yet another provocative problem into the emotional stew that we are concocting. This one is a problem having to do with the familiar category of "emotion" as such. There are an amazing variety of emotions, and they are very different from one another. Not only is fear very different from anger and from love, it also seems to be very different from other members of the fear family. The fear you feel as the three-hundred-pound tackle comes running toward you is the not the same fear you experience when you get wind of the fact that your tax return may soon be audited. Some emotions do seem to be momentary episodes, then they are done with, but others tend to be enduring experiences with many phases, twists, and turns, the stuff drama is made of. Some involve minimal intelligence and information about the world (panic and rage, for example). Others involve a great deal of sophistication and refinement, aesthetic appreciation, for example, or exquisite mastery of the morals and customs of the local cultural scene. Some emotions expand into moods, and some moods turn into specific emotions. So the question presses itself upon us, is there any single phenomenon that is clearly designated by the term "emotion"? Is there any single feature or quality that all of these various phenomena share in common? In biology-talk, do emotions form a specifiable type, a "natural kind"? Or are we talking fruit salad here, apples and oranges and a few nuts and marshmallows thrown in for variety?

The philosopher and science historian Paul Griffiths, in his book *What Emotions Really Are,* challenged the idea that emotions are a *natural kind.* Using biology as his base and defending a very strong version of basic emotions, he claimed that there are at least two very different kinds of emotions, basic emotions (which he tended to treat as *real* emotions) and "higher cognitive states," which would include most of what most of us think of as real emotions. (As you have probably gathered, there tend to be a very small number of so-called basic emotions, five or six by most accounts, including fear and anger, and then perhaps sadness, surprise, and disgust, while there are arguably hundreds or even thousands of other emotions, depending on how finely we want to distinguish them.) But Griffiths's challenge is very real. Amelie Rorty made it much earlier, back in the early 1980s. (See her more recent essay in my book *Thinking about Feelings,* 2005.) I myself have pointed out that the category of emotions is rather like the broad category of "produce," fruits and vegetables and a few other things besides, but when push comes to shove, I find myself, as does Griffiths, tending to write without very much hesitation about emotions. As I said in my introduction, I do not think that anyone is confused about what we are talking about. I noted that I would follow the example of Aristotle, who, when asked what he meant by "*pathé*," commented that he included "anger, fear, pity, and the like, as well as the opposites of these." It has never been very clear to me what he might have meant by "the opposites of these," but I am confident that my readers, like Aristotle, take "emotions" to be a more or clear conception of a distinctive subject matter. But now we are no longer willing to settle for simple agreement. Griffiths suggests that emotions must be understood in terms of their evolutionary development, a notion that Aristotle could not possibly have comprehended. And on this basis he insists that emotions cannot be a natural kind but have to be understood in a very different way, in terms of their evolutionary history.

The classification of emotions, however, depends on a different kind of history, the history of a word and its meaning. That we have become used to the word "emotion" (and the range of examples that it covers) does not mean that it refers to a "natural kind," something supposedly as specific as a particular species of animal or plant (which is where Aristotle gets his notion). It is not even clear that any single emotion type or family (fear, for instance) is anything like a natural kind. An excellent account of the emergence of the word "emotion" and its current usage is Thomas Dixon's recent *From Passions to Emotions: The Creation of a Secular Psychological Category*. What we call emotions were called "passions" and "affects" for many centuries, but the study of these phenomena was so thoroughly caught up in Christian theology, ethics, and practical psychology that there remained little room for secular, scientific study. So in the nineteenth century, the category of "emotion" was more or less invented (by Thomas Brown) to include virtually all of those mental states that were neither simple sensations (like pain) nor intellectual states (such as thoughts and reasoning), with no theological ax to grind. The word had been used before, to be sure, notably by René Descartes and by David Hume to refer to particularly unruly passions, but the word "passion" (which was their focal subject) was already becoming a bit archaic. (The word "affect," or Latin *"affectus,"* used, for example, by Spinoza, also referred to more primitive and unruly feelings.)

The Christian psychologists, notably Aquinas, had elegantly distinguished a huge variety of passions and affects, mainly on the basis of their guiding us toward either salvation or damnation, but the new psychology forced those passions all into a singular category, more or less without distinction or hierarchy. Thus the chaos facing the student of emotions today. The category of emotions is indeed something very like a mixed salad, with no evident common characteristics other than the fact that they all signify something of significance, whether by virtue of the intimacy of physiological upheaval or the personal and social significance of the context. But in this egalitarian category, it is hard to know how to weigh the various emotions and the various dimensions of emotion. Today, the neurological underpinnings of emotion seem to be getting the most attention and respect. Five hundred years ago, it was the ethical and theological dimensions of emotion. But most emotions seem to involve a dramatic balance between mere arousal and meaning, and perhaps this is no more evident than in that most melodramatic of human emotions, *love.*

4

Lessons of Love (and Plato's *Symposium*)

It is with considerable relief that we move from anger and fear to love, perhaps the most overdiscussed emotion. (Picked up any celebrity magazines lately?) Although there are many kinds of love, I am here concerned mainly with the most exciting variety, erotic or romantic love. It is a bit embarrassing to admit that virtually everything I will have to say here has been anticipated by one or another country and Western song and in love poetry both great and awful, but such is the nature of love in our society. It is, in a word, *hypercognized.* In other words, we talk about it all the time. We talk about it when we're in love. We talk about it when we're looking for love. We talk about it when we're hurt in love. We talk about it when we've lost love. We talk about it for gossip, scandal, and titillation. Only a tiny part of all that talk is revealing and insightful, but all of it is grist for our mill. The truth is that love, romantic love at least, exists in part *because* we talk so much about it. "Would anyone ever fall in love," asks the French wit La Rochefoucault, "if they had never heard the word?"

The Greeks distinguished a number of different varieties of love. What I will be mainly concerned with here is *eros*, which is the word Plato uses. It is erotic or sexual or what we now (since the romantic period) call "romantic" love. Aristotle talked at length about *philia* (friendship), which also applies to family relations. Then there is *agapé* (Latin *caritas*), which I will discuss in the next chapter, which is generally characterized (by the early Christians) as asexual, unselfish, and altruistic. A great deal can be learned from the historical interaction between these terms. (This is true of all emotion terms, as indeed of the word "emotion" itself.) The fact that *eros* and *philia* were distinguished seems quite reasonable to us, for we, too, distinguish erotic love and friendship, and although most reasonable people hope that the two be found together we all know from experience (our own or others') that often the two are not. But the distinction between *eros* and *agapé* provides a profound lesson in the politics of emotion. Eros has always included sexual desire, but despite Plato's attempt to etherealize it the history of *eros* through the Christian millennia has been one of degradation and abuse. Through the ages, *eros* degenerated into selfishness and lust. *Agapé*, by contrast, became increasingly altruistic and giving, even divine, until Christian theology ultimately declared that it was an emotion only God could truly have. *Agapé* fit quite well with the Christian denunciation of all things flesh and sexual and the glorification of ideal if impossible passions. Nevertheless, *eros* has managed to hold its own, no doubt because we are flesh and we are animals and some primitive version of this variety of love evolved in us as biological creatures.

It is generally believed that love is a "positive" emotion, despite the fact that anyone who has ever been in love can attest to its nastier, negative, and anxiety-provoking aspects. But whereas anger and fear reveal the world to us as infuriating and dangerous, respectively, love at its best reveals the world to us as wonderful. Love is (among other things) about beauty, and so it is easily inferred that love is beautiful and wonderful, too. Indeed, it is not just that love reveals to us a single person who is beautiful and wonderful. As philosophers and dozens of popular songs have made amply clear, the world as a whole is illuminated thereby, from the "street where you live" to the far reaches of the cosmos. "Love makes the world go round" is a thesis at least as old as the ancient Greek philosopher Empedocles, and it is in the ancient Vedic *Upanishads* as well. But, of course, this "beautiful and wonderful" stuff is often a lot of romantic nonsense, thoughtless expressions of enthusiasm or desperate longing for what one so lacks in life. And yet, love is real, and it can, sometimes, be a beautiful, wonderful, and lifelong experience.

But it can also be irrational and foolish as well as rational and wise. What I want to avoid is an overly mawkish and nonsensically abstract discussion of love, and at the same time, overly utilitarian "advice to the lovelorn," in other words all of those love-pundits that I once dismissed as "foggers and facilitators" (2001). Love is, after all, just a "secondhand" emotion (as Tina Turner sings). True, one's love is rarely original (however we may fool ourselves into thinking it is). We follow love along a well-worn road. Speaking even less romantically, love has an intentional structure and displays several strategies, some of them self-interested, others not. (I have not yet talked about this, but not all emotional strategies are self-interested.) And love displays a more or less specific physiological substratum as well as an evolutionary past. In love, the heart may be our favorite metaphor, but love is also a physiological reality. That physiological reality, however, is not cardiac but sexual.

So, to get to the emotional basis of erotic love, before we talk about ethereal *eros*, perhaps we should first look at sex, sexual desire, and attractiveness. Sexual desire, I quickly add, is not the same as lust, which has condemnation built into the very word, though such a view is promulgated by moralists who (publicly) condemn almost all passionate sexual activity. But sexual desire is perfectly natural and perfectly normal. Furthermore, it is not a form of cheap reductionism to trace the origins of the emotion of love to our natural desires for sex and companionship, but of course I will insist that love is much more than this as well. Nevertheless, as in fear and anger, there is a physiological basis (or bases) for love that may or may not be evident at any particular time, especially since love, more than either fear or anger, often lasts for a very long time and goes through many permutations. Sexual arousal in love may be explicit or not, it may be sporadic or frequent, and sexual desire may be consummated, satisfied or not. But it is pretty clear that the *energy* of love, what Freud called the *libido*, has its origins in more primitive and clearly biological features of human psychology. What we call (romantic) love is built on, shaped, and molded on the natural desires for intimate contact and with it the reproduction of our kind.

Sexual desire may have many manifestations, from the urge to grab and caress to inspired poetry and high-minded resolutions. Courtship rituals, of course, are not unique to human beings. Our feathered friends display some remarkably complex and elegant mating dances, and even cats and dogs show signs of selectivity, fickleness, and some subtlety rather than simply jumping on one another. Sexual attractiveness, too, may have its hard-wired origins. It may well be, as some psychologists have very controversially argued, that there are certain proportions and traits that serve as innate triggers for both sexual attractiveness and an appreciation of beauty. (Some psychologists hypothesize that in women, somewhat child-like facial features combined with high cheekbones to show maturity, and a substantial hip-waist ratio, are found attractive because those traits seem to represent optimal fertility and health.) So, too, there may be "chemistry" between people that has (at least prior to reflection) little to do with real compatibility, backgrounds, beliefs, values, or shared interests. None of this is love, of course, and it is adolescent confusion (or worse) to think that it is. We rightly distinguish between love and infatuation, between the real thing and a teenage "crush," between finding someone attractive and falling in love. Love is not sex and it need not even involve sex. And love is not just attraction, although love certainly nurtures, cultivates, and promotes attractiveness and even beauty in the beloved. But I want to keep love grounded in its biological realities in order to guard against the fog of simplistic romanticism and the obscurantist idea that love is just a "mystery."

"If you're in love, you will know it," says the well-meaning friend, ignoring the testimony of hundreds of novels and thousands of experiences that suggest otherwise. "Love is so beautiful, you can't really describe it," gushes the newly beloved, oblivious to the millions if not billions of words that have done just that. Love is said to be "ineffable," indescribable, but love is an emotion. As such, it has what philosophers and cognitive scientists would call "an intentional structure," a certain way of putting the world we experience in order. The intentional structure of love, just to begin with, has to do with putting the person loved—the beloved—in a very special position. But perhaps more dramatically, the intentional structure of love, though often derided, allows the lover to see and appreciate all sorts of charms and virtues in the beloved that have gone unnoticed before. (They may still be missed by less infatuated friends and acquaintances.) Love is, in part, the continuous discovery or adding on of these charms and virtues, a process that the French novelist and essayist Stendhal poetically called "crystallization." But this means that love can be described. And like all emotions its description will focus first of all on its object, the beloved. Not the beloved as a physiological organism, to be sure (although there might be many charms there to be found too) but as a reciprocating conscious creature whose very existence becomes of tantamount importance. But the focus on the beloved is only the primary focus. The larger scope and focus of the emotion is on the effects of love and the beloved on the lover and the nature of the relationship. So it is probably wrong or misleading to say that love is about the beloved. It is more appropriate, if clumsier, to insist that love is about the joining of two people. It is not "a feeling deep inside" but an interpersonal emotional dance. Love is about a relationship.

But this cannot be quite right either. To say that love is an emotion that concerns the joining of two people in a relationship seems to deny the obvious, that people often fall in love before there is any hint of a relationship and there is unrequited love that never gets to the joining-together stage. Love, one might say, is not an objective relationship in the world but rather a subjective experience involving (along with much else) the other person. It might also include a possible or projected relationship, one that the lover imagines or hopes will come into being. I think that this is basically right, but the philosophical notion of "subjectivity" has to be carefully understood. There is a sense in which all experience, all emotions, are subjective, that is, they are specific to the subject (or subjects, if it is an emotion that is shared), and it is special to the peculiar perspective, tastes, and values of that particular subject. But this is often taken to mean that love as such is irrational, out of touch with reality, a *mere* projection and fantasy. I think that this is wrong, but it cannot be simply dismissed.

There are qualities in the world that we might call subject-dependent properties. These are *in the world*, not in the subject's head or mind or imagination. But they also depend on the subject in a way that the shape or color of a thing arguably does not. The best known of these is beauty. Beauty, according to the old platitude, is in the eye if the beholder. This is especially the case in which we are talking about the beauty of the beloved. It might also be true of great works of art, but then there is a further consideration, namely, the fact that many connoisseurs, art experts, and aesthetically sensitive people agree on the art object being beautiful. But in the case of someone's beloved, where it may be just one person (and possibly his or her parents) who perceives the beloved as beautiful, there seems to be no ground for objectivity or intersubjectivity. Objectively, the beloved might not be beautiful at all but he or she only seems to be beautiful, subjectively, to the lover. But it is a short step from this to the argument, frequent enough in the history of philosophy, that the lover is bedazzled, his or her perception is distorted, that he or she sees what is simply not really there. Indeed, we see the same argument repeated for emotions in general. The great German philosopher Leibniz called all emotions "confused perceptions." But subjectivity is not necessarily a matter of being mistaken or confused.

In love, it is for the most part a meaningless question whether the qualities we admire are subjective (that is, *only* the product of our individual perspective) or objective (wholly independent of our individual perspective). If I love you because you are beautiful and charming, it might be a matter of indifference whether my friends see you that way or not. But, fortunately or unfortunately (and depending on the situation), we all know that the opinion of one's friends can make a significant difference, and whether this is the desire for objectivity (intersubjectivity) that is sneaking in here or rather just the desire to keep the respect of one's friends is not at all clear. A good way to think of this is that in love, we *bestow* charms and virtues on the beloved. The language of bestowal is the terminology introduced into this discussion years ago by Irving Singer (1973), one of the best modern scholars of the nature and development of romantic love. To say that we bestow charms and virtues is to say that we do not just find or project these but we endow them to the beloved. This is not something we do voluntarily or deliberately. It may well seem that we simply *perceive* these charms and virtues as objective facts. But they are not objective facts.

They belong to "the eye of the beholder." But neither is our perception falsified or distorted. It is a cruel misunderstanding to say that love "distorts" our perception.

Love *enhances* our perception. But when love crosses the line into irrationality and self-destructiveness, as it sometimes does, then we depend on our friends, who are not just disinterested observers to check or "correct" our perception and judgment. This is easier said than done, of course. We usually expect our appraisals and bestowals to be confirmed or at least respected by others, especially those closest to us. (Many conflicted lovers drop their friends before taking their advice to ditch their beloved, even when they know full well that their friends' advice is right.) So our subjectivity in love, our ability to bestow charms and virtues, is not just a personal matter. It is always open, even when it is "blind," to intersubjective confirmation, which is not to say that love's perspective is necessarily intersubjective but only that the qualities of the beloved are not just the private domain of the lover.

Love is not, as such, irrational. Like any emotion, it can be on target or off, warranted or unwarranted, based on the facts or wrong about the facts, wise or foolish, life-enhancing or self-destructive. Thus falling love with a conman or a liar, if one can see the truth but refuses to, is irrational. It is in such cases that "love is blind." But this is not usually the case. Usually, love sees more clearly and deeply, with much more attention to and appreciation of details, than ordinary perception. Of course, bestowing charms and virtues has its limits. Usually it is not appropriate for others to challenge or correct us in our finding the beloved beautiful, but there are qualities we cannot bestow. One cannot make his or her beloved an accountant or physician, no matter how hopelessly in love one may be. One cannot bestow on his or her beloved intelligence he or she does not have, no matter how uncritical one makes oneself. And one cannot bestow on his or her beloved sensitivity or kindness. These are facts, not bestowals. They are not just subject-dependent properties but intersubjective and to a significant extent objectively determined properties. Thus we do (or should) depend on our friends and family to tell us when we are making a mistake, although their viewpoint will not always be graciously received nor is it necessarily correct. But it is not as if love is as such irrational. Many of the charms and virtues of the beloved are not in the realm of fact but properly in the province of one's own personal perspective, and they should be respected as such. Subjectivity is not irrationality.

The idea that love is irrational, however, has its apt applications. Love can be inappropriate, falling in love with your sister, for instance, and that is a matter of irrationality. Love is sometimes obsessive, and that is irrational too. Even if the person is right, the relationship is not. We sometimes fall in love with the wrong person, "wrong for us," as they say, and that is irrational, or we may fall in love with the right person but go about it in a disastrous way. Being obsessive is just one of a long list of potential bungles. There is also being too aggressive, too timid, too "cool," too fast, too slow, too arrogant, too humble, and so on. These can be irrational too. If love is a process, and falling in love is just the first step to *being* in love, then any flaw in the process might be a candidate for irrationality, from the first approach to the final scenes.

There is another argument that love is as such irrational, however, because love does not have *reasons*.

> It does not appear to me that my hand is unworthy of your acceptance, or that the establishment I can offer would be any other than highly desirable. My situation in life, my connections with the [appropriate] family, and my relationship to your own, are circumstances highly in my favor; and you should take it into further consideration, that in spite of manifold attractions, it is by no means certain that another offer of marriage may ever be made to you.

So said Mr. Collins, the pompous suitor, when he proposed to Elizabeth in Jane Austen's *Pride and Prejudice*. I think that I would not be radically misrepresenting the most common reaction (and the one intended by the author) as repulsion, or at the very least, the sense that such an alternatively pompous, threatening, and insulting proposal lacks any semblance of charm and romance.

Why? Many people would say, "because you don't love someone for reasons. You just love them, or you don't." Most philosophers are less thoughtlessly romantic, so they might say, "not for *those* reasons." But I think that we do love for reasons, just as we have any emotion for reasons, and love without reasons is unintelligible, suggesting psychotic obsession, blind, blithering, helpless attachment, or mere frivolousness. To be sure, love is often misdirected, with damage to the lover and consternation, concern, or amusement for the lover's friends and family. But even misdirected love and love gone wrong must have their reasons, even if, all things considered, these reasons may be unreasonable.

Perhaps Mr. Collins was giving reasons why Elizabeth should accept his proposal of marriage and not reasons for her to love him. But what nevertheless rubs our romantic fur in the wrong direction are the *kinds* of reasons advanced by Mr. Collins and others like him. Loving someone for his or her money, or connections, or status, or, for that matter, even for his or her looks seems like love for just the *wrong* reasons. Or, rather, it usually turns out that one doesn't love the other person at all; one just loves the money and puts up with the person, or covets the connections or status and is willing to be not only tolerant but even affectionate in order to share them.

One kind of reason that has been celebrated since Plato, however, is the beauty of the beloved. Loving someone for their looks is a difficult case insofar as one cannot readily separate a person from his or her looks as one can with some ease separate a romantic fool and his money. This is complicated again by the consideration that beauty is one of those bestowed, rather than objective or intersubjective, properties in love. But I think that it is a mistake to focus on just one kind of reason, *properties-of-the-beloved-*type reasons. Too often, these reasons turn out to be self-interested and so they seem not to be reasons *for love* at all. But here is another kind of reason, and I call them *Aristophanic* reasons for a reason that will soon become evident. Aristophanic reasons have to do with the special role of the beloved *in the relationship.* The common insistence on loving a person "for him or herself" is badly misconstrued as appealing to some sort of personal essence when it most often refers to something essential about the uniqueness of the relationship. So "because we have been together for twenty years" can be a pretty good reason for love, even if there are cases in which twenty years together is a good reason for *not* loving the person any more. "Because we fit so well together" is an excellent reason for love, and so is "because we share the same sense of humor." The best reasons for love are such Aristophanic reasons, and we shall see in a moment why I call them that.

There are also bad reasons for love. For example, it is not unknown for a young woman to fall in love, not once but in an unmistakable pattern, with married men who will not abandon their wives and families. So too, the idea that the beloved satisfies more neurotic needs—the need to be punished or martyred, the desire to take care of a truly pathetic human being, the need to play God with someone. These are bad reasons for love that might be quite effective without ever being acknowledged. Then there is love that arises out of jealousy. Such jealousy is, in the truly perverse cases, the sole reason for love's existence: A has no interest in B until C shows an interest in B. But I want to be cautious here. It is a staple of sitcom romances that a little bit of jealousy (usually based on an easily resolvable misunderstanding) is good for a relationship. It reminds one of the contingency of this (or any) relationship. There need be nothing irrational about this.

The fact that there are many ways in which love can go wrong and accordingly that there are many bad reasons for love too often leads to an unfortunate cynicism, a favorite form of rationalization of too many frustrated and disappointed teenagers and divorcees. (There are also a multitude of bad reasons for *not* falling in love.) Philosophers have picked up on this. Erotic love is said to be the passion that makes fools of us all. Love, we are told by Sigmund Freud (1966), is "lust plus the ordeal of civility." (What a phrase!) Millennia ago, Hesiod, Sophocles, and Euripides all denounced *eros*. Tragedies such as *Antigone*, *Medea*, and *Hippolytus* made love out to be disastrous. The great poetess Sappho, around the time of Plato, likened *eros* to illness, even to madness.

It was against such cynicism that one text, more than any other, set the stage for the glorification of love in the Western world. That is Plato's *Symposium*, written some twenty-five hundred years ago. We can ignore the fact that Plato was writing mainly about homoerotic love. What he says about love, through some half dozen or so characters whom he has placed in the symposium, would sound quite familiar in today's women's magazines. One speaker (Eryxymachus) praises love for its healthy effects. Another (Phaedrus) praises it for promoting virtue (as no lover would want to shame himself in front of his beloved). Still another (Agathon) gushes about the sheer beauty of love and its pleasing the gods. But I want to mention in a bit more detail three speeches from the *Symposium* because they are deeply insightful about the nature of love. The first is by Aristophanes, the famous playwright (and a contemporary rival of Socrates), who offers up a fanciful tale about prehistoric humans, double creatures (four arms, four legs, two heads) who are split apart by Zeus (for their *hubris*) and left to wander around the earth "looking for their other half." Thus love is more than a mere physical craving. It becomes a metaphysical need, the need to reunite oneself with one's other (better?) half.

The second and central speech of the *Symposium* is by Socrates, who is usually Plato's mouthpiece (although there is reason to doubt that Plato wholly agrees with him here). Socrates' speech is eloquent and revolutionary, for what he does, prefiguring the teachings of Christianity (and "Platonic love" in the late Middle Ages) is to urge the true lover to see beyond mere beautiful bodies and even beyond beautiful souls to the divine form of Beauty itself. One of the most important features of Socrates' argument is that it challenges the centrality of sexuality in erotic love *(eros)*. A less obvious feature of the argument is that it radically depersonalizes love, as the object becomes the abstract Good, the True, and the Beautiful rather than the concrete beloved. Thus Socrates prefigures the teachings of Christianity and "Platonic love" in the late Middle Ages in which love is ultimately the love of God. In "Platonic love," the Good—or God—is loved *through* the beloved, who thus becomes a means or a medium. Thus love becomes the love of the divine, and the true lover is the philosopher.

The last speech of the *Symposium* rounds out the evening's increasingly ethereal message by bringing it back down to earth with a thud. Alcibiades was in fact a student of Socrates, and he was also in fact one of the most treacherous (and most handsome) men in Athens. He enters into the symposium drunk and ranting, and he declares in quite crude terms that love is a hang-up, a trap, a fixation, and not at all ethereal, not aimed at the good or any god or any virtue. He begins to insult and abuse Socrates (his beloved) as if to show us what love is really like. It can be cruel. It can be jealous. It can be mean-spirited and most unhappy. That, sadly, is how love sometimes turns out for many of us, however promising it may have begun. But Plato does not end the dialogue on that sour note. Alcibiades passes out (as do most of the revelers) and Socrates, cold sober, walks home to a beautiful sunrise, as if he has won a contest. But what Plato has given us is a brilliant cubist portrait of love, from the most divine perspective to the most vulgar. Despite our delusions of simplicity, love is among the most complex emotions. That is why we need to talk so much about it.

So, what is love? There are very different views about this, as Plato makes clear. To put the scene in contemporary American life, we can think of love from a typical young person's view, love as all excitement and discovery, as sexuality and passion. Or we can view it from the point of view of an older happily married couple who view their love in terms of comfort and fidelity, trust and affection. It would be foolish to call one of these right or "true" and deny the other. We might think of them as different "phases" of love, so long as we don't insist that everyone has to go through both of them. Passionate love only sometimes lasts into long-term love, and lifelong love does not always begin with passion. Good friends from high school gradually get more intimate and eventually get married but never go through that passion-filled period of temporary insanity enjoyed by others. But I think that the critical clue as to what love is ultimately about can be found, of all places, in Aristophanes' odd tale.

What all forms of love share is a peculiar intentional structure, the conception of one's self as intertwined and fused with another. Animals that don't have a sense of self may feel affection, but they do not experience love. (We can love them, but they do not love us in return. Sorry, dog and cat lovers. You'll have to settle for affection and dependency.) In parenthood, one loves what is quite literally a part of one's own identity. In friendship—true friendship, that is—one comes to think of one's friend as inseparable from oneself. But it is in erotic love, which tends to be exclusive, that this "merging" of selves is most profound. (The difference between parenthood and friendship on the one hand and monogamous love on the other is that one can obviously love more than one child or friend. Whether it is possible to romantically love more than one beloved and what this might cost psychologically is way beyond our scope here. Let's just say, at the very least, it can be logistically labyrinthine.) But I want to make this idea of *merging* the centerpiece of the intentional structure of love. It is coming to see another person as sharing an identity with oneself.

Here is the often underappreciated genius in Aristophanes' odd story of love in the *Symposium*. His fanciful tale about prehistoric creatures split apart by Zeus and left to wander the earth "looking for their other half" provides us with an important picture of love as a "merging" or "fusion" of souls and the idea that love "completes us" as human beings. It is, looking back from the twenty-first century, a marvelous reminder that we are not—as our dominant ideology keeps telling us—first of all individuals who are for the most part alone in the world. We are social creatures who are born into a network of relationships, and each of us alone is incomplete. Love makes us whole.

But this is not just a series of edifying metaphors. It embodies an important literal truth. Love is all about the self. I thus interpret Aristophanes' allegory as an account of love as an emotion in which a person (and preferably both persons) come to understand his or her identity (or their mutual identities) with and through the other person. Note that this makes room for the sad fact of unrequited love, but as a degenerate case, not as the paradigm. But the usual paradigm, I would argue, is wrong. It is love as admiration or desire for the beloved, and it is a secondary matter whether the beloved responds in kind. This is true in Plato (one longs after the Beautiful), and it is also true of much of romanticism, in Stendhal, for example, and in Goethe, who famously said, no doubt as a joke, "Yes I love you, but what business is that of yours?" But understanding love as a "fitting together" leaves open the myriad ways in which two people come to fit together. Needless to say, it is rarely the case that two people, often from different backgrounds, simply fit together as two halves of an original whole. I often marvel at the many different ways in which couples work out their lives together, many of which are virtually unimaginable to me. But Aristophanes is right, I think. Love is a matter of two souls coming together, and, as Aristophanes speculates, if Hephaestus (the smithy of the gods) would weld them together forever, body and soul, they could not be more delighted.

What this also means is that love is not selfless, as we so often hear, but essentially involved with the self. But love isn't selfish either. (Nietzsche, despite his romanticism, thinks that it is.) The self in love is an enlarged or expanded self that includes or embraces the other. That is why I say that love is altering one's self-identity such that it becomes with and through the beloved. And when all goes well, the resulting emotion is something beautiful and enduring. It's not as if love as such is a "positive" emotion, but love at its best is one of those grand passions that we live for—even occasionally die for—and it is rightly said to be one of the most important ingredients of the good life.

5

We Are Not Alone:
Compassion and Sympathy

One of the several words for love in Greek, which became especially prominent in Christianity, was *agapé* (Latin *caritas*). Sometimes translated as brotherly love, sometimes as divine love, it involved neither the sexuality nor the exclusivity of *eros*, erotic love. In the last chapter, I mentioned that *agapé* in Christian theology became increasingly idealized, to the point where it became an emotion possible only for God. But in a more mundane and secular way, *agapé* is interpreted as the name of an ordinary emotion, or perhaps we should say "a moral sentiment," namely compassion. In this chapter, I do not want to talk much about Christian *agapé* because I do not want to tackle the theological issues that are involved. Instead, I would like to begin by going back to the eighteenth-century Enlightenment. Then, the reigning theory of human nature in many quarters was that people are essentially selfish. The philosophy of Thomas Hobbes was exemplary: Life (in the "state of nature") was "selfish, nasty, brutish, and short." Against this, a number of philosophers, including David Hume, Jean-Jacques Rousseau, and the great economist Adam Smith, defended what they called *sympathy* as a natural "moral sentiment." (Thus Smith was not the uncompromising defender of self-interest that he has since been made out to be.)

Sympathy is essentially the same as what we call compassion. It provides, these philosophers argue, the basis of ethics. Not reason, not custom, but emotion. The philosophical thesis is that we are not just selfish creatures—which is not, of course, to deny that we do pursue our own interests. We are also compassionate and sympathetic with others. We might note that sympathy and compassion all have essentially the same etymology, as "feeling with." Hume, Rousseau, and Smith, and later the German pessimist Arthur Schopenhauer, all rejected unemotional and purely rational approaches to ethics and insisted instead that ethics was all about compassion. I think that this is right. More than two thousand years ago, the Confucian Mencius wrote, "No man is devoid of a heart sensitive to the sufferings of others" (1970). Two millennia later, Adam Smith wrote, in his *Theory of the Moral Sentiments,* "How selfish so ever man may be supposed, there are evidently some principles in his nature, which interest him in the fortune of others, and render their happiness necessary to him, though he derives nothing from it except the pleasure of seeing it. Of this kind is pity or compassion, the emotion which we feel for the misery of others." Without compassion (sympathy), there would be no foundation and no motivation for ethics.

Compassion is a basic emotion, argues the English philosopher Peter Goldie. It characteristically involves a distinctive emotional experience as well as characteristic emotional expression, although this can usually be read as such only in context, and it tends to motivate action, namely helping or at least nurturing behavior. It is not yet clear what the neurological patterns might be, although Wisconsin psychologist Richard Davidson (et al., 2002) has done some fascinating work with the Dalai Lama on the curious relationship between meditation and compassion. It bears out the commonsense idea that relative selflessness and compassion may go hand in hand. It also points to evidence that compassion may in fact be basic in its intimate connection with physiology. But the idea that compassion is a basic emotion is an important contemporary claim that reinforces the eighteenth-century "natural moral sentiment" view of Hume, Rousseau, and Smith. It might also be worth noting that Goldie separates himself from Hume's views on sympathy because Hume (and Smith too) emphasizes "imaginative identification," which requires far more mental effort than simple compassion. So, too, there is the German concept of *verstehen* (which also emerged in the same century), which similarly involves a reflective attempt to "put oneself in the other's shoes." But the basic thesis about the natural moral sentiments is something more radical, that we naturally feel compassion for other people without thinking about it at all.

This is not to say that compassion does not have any intelligence, in the sense that I have been developing that idea here. The idea that there are natural moral sentiments makes a whole lot of evolutionary and biological sense. We are "by nature" social animals, and we need a quick way of reacting to a fellow creature in need. To be sure, compassion can and must also be cultivated. We must learn to understand what other people are feeling

and we must learn, with some effort and moral education, to "put ourselves in another's shoes." But prior to that, we have a "gut reaction" to
other people's perils. Without that, it is doubtful that we could learn
to "feel with" other people at all. Nor would we enjoy novels, autobio-
graphies, movies, and plays, as we could not "identify" with the characters
in them. We might have some merely academic theory about such works
and the people in them, but we would have a greatly impoverished social
life, if, indeed, we could have any social life at all.

But what is compassion? The way Adam Smith uses the term
"sympathy," it suffers from two serious ambiguities. First, and less prob-
lematically, Smith sometimes treats sympathy not only as a disposition
to have emotions, but sometimes as an emotion itself. I say that this is
unproblematic because many if not most emotions have this dual nature.
They are emotions (with more or less immediate manifestations in feelings
and behavior) and they are also dispositions, which can result in any number and variety of episodes including other emotions. (Love, for example,
can evoke jealousy and anger, depending on the circumstances.) But second, and much more confusingly, Smith's word sympathy encompasses
both what we call sympathy (or compassion) and the much more recent
concept of *empathy* (which seems to have been invented by the German
psychologist Edward Titchner in the nineteenth century). The two terms
are still often conflated, but I think a useful distinction is that sympathy
and compassion have as their basic structure "feeling sorry for" someone
(who is presumably in some sort of trouble or distress), while empathy
means more like "fellow feeling," that is, understanding what another person feels (whatever he or she feels). It is the latter that was mainly intended
by Smith, but his conception still exhibits a tension between being a natural or innate response to another person, feeling (more or less) what he is
feeling, and the more intellectually sophisticated act of imagining oneself
in the other's place. Compassion (sympathy), by contrast, can easily be
envisioned to be a "gut feeling" that need not involve any thought whatsoever. Hume, Rousseau, and Smith all seem to waver between the two.

Eighteenth-century moral sentiment theory was actually concerned with
a family of emotions, including benevolence, sympathy, compassion, and
pity, all of which were sometimes grouped together. Care and caring were
not much mentioned in the theory, but in much theorizing since, especially feminist theory, they have emerged as central. "Feeling sorry for" can
be a sign of caring, but a minimal one, as we can feel sorry for strangers
and even for our enemies. Benevolence has much in common with the
more activist concept of "caring for," but benevolence has much greater
scope than sympathy. We can feel benevolent in the abstract without any
particular object, and we can be benevolent to someone whose feelings are

utterly malicious, for instance, in being merciful to a condemned killer. Pity, finally, has a much more convoluted history. Although in German, pity is a translation of the same word as compassion (*mitleid*), it is employed by Schopenhauer as the basis of all of morality and then condemned by Nietzsche as the height of sniveling, self-deceptive weakness. I won't go into this fascinating story here, except to say that Nietzsche sees quite clearly that pity can easily be self-serving and hypocritical, an attitude of one-upsmanship rather than genuine selfless concern. He's right, but it is an enormous mistake to generalize this to all instances of the emotion.

Compassion, or what we also call sympathy, is defined by the psychologist Nancy Eisenberg (2002) as "an affective response that consists of feeling sorrow or concern for the distressed or needy other." It also involves distinctive action tendencies, namely, helping. It does not matter how much one talks about compassion or verbally expresses it if he or she makes no movement, even a futile one, to help out. Nietzsche is probably right when compassion is just self-indulgence, but his view makes less sense when compassion motivates helpful behavior. It is thus that sympathy lies at the heart of ethics, as Schopenhauer insisted, but not as an isolated feeling. It is sometimes supposed that in compassion one *suffers with* the other, but one need not actually feel his or her actual pain. I feel sympathy for an acquaintance who has broken his leg, and I may even have a "sympathetic" twinge in my leg, but I do not share the severity of his pain. Indeed, compassion suggests that one somehow stands safely "above" the misery of the other, affording one the luxury of commiseration. (This is one of Nietzsche's points.) A student who has just flunked his exams does not feel compassion toward a fellow student who has also flunked his exams. They just feel miserable together. It is the student who has passed her exams with flying colors who is in a position to feel compassion for the other two, though the giddiness of her own success may make it difficult to do so. It is compassion, this ability to feel for those less fortunate than oneself, that I would argue is the cornerstone passion of our sense of justice.

To feel sorry for someone already presumes that one in some sense understands what they are feeling, and therefore compassion or sympathy already presuppose empathy. This is why Smith and the others so easily ran them together, but what we now call empathy is philosophically a much more interesting emotion. Empathy, in contemporary psychology, is defined as "an affective response that stems from the apprehension or comprehension of another's emotional state or condition, and that is identical or very similar to what the other person is feeling or would be expected to feel" (Eisenberg, 2002). How is it possible to feel what another person is feeling? But empathy is not, like compassion or sympathy, a singular emotion. Indeed, one might even question whether it is an emotion at all rather than a capacity to have any number of emotions depending on the emotions of others. One can empathize with another's joy as well as his or her suffering. One can empathize with the winner's feeling of success as well as with her grief. Compassion, or sympathy, is thus a straightforward emotion in the sense that it is a distinctive emotion, an emotion dependent on the emotions of others, perhaps, but it is only a response to them, not in any sense an imitation or reproduction of them. It is, essentially, feeling bad because another feels bad, combined with a feeling of reaching out to them (which may or may not be inhibited by fear of getting involved or repulsion at the plight of the other). One might sympathize with another person and get his or her emotional situation completely wrong. Empathy, by contrast, seems to require in some sense replication of the emotions of the other person.

Empathy, however, can also be extremely primitive and unthinking. It may be as simple as what psychologists call "emotional contagion," the tendency of people to pick up the emotional vibrations of the people around them. So, at a funeral, even of a person one did not know at all, one may come to feel sad just because the people around are grieving. Walking into a comedy club, one will probably get mirthful even before he or she has heard a single joke, just because of the mood of the crowd. But empathy can also be thoughtful and imaginative. I try to empathize with illiterate villagers caught up in a complex civil war in Africa. It is by no means easy, but with some effort I can sketch the outline of how their world must feel to them. Indeed, with some intellectual and imaginative effort, I can always empathize with other people and even other creatures, no matter how different they are from me. Pain behavior, at the very minimum, usually expresses pain. Dogs *yip*, cats *yeow*. Wriggling and writhing are common pain behaviors throughout the animal kingdom. Even grimacing can be recognized in a surprising variety of mammalian species. Birds cannot grimace but most people (and many animals) easily recognize their stress and pain behavior.

Sometimes, empathy takes research. It is not always evident when a creature is suffering, and our ability to "empathize" with members of other species can be misleading or wrong-headed. Animal rights activists once complained loudly that chickens were being kept in cages with wire bottoms, presumably for the sake of the convenience of their keepers. We easily imagine how uncomfortable it would be for us, with our sensitive feet on thin wire netting. But it turned out, on investigation, that chickens actually prefer wire netting floors to wooden or linoleum or plush carpeted floors, and our well-intended concern turned out to be wrong (Dawkins, 1980). So, too, naive dog owners may think (or rationalize) that their animals are much happier without the discipline and conditioning of "training," assuming that a free dog is a happier dog. But such dog owners should be told that an untrained dog is usually a confused and unhappy dog, unsure of its owner's desires and expectations and unsure of what it is to do. Compassion with animals as with humans requires knowledge as well as feeling. The argument against "do-gooders" has to do not so much with their feeling of compassion as with their lack of knowledge.

It is important to distinguish empathy from just being upset or "personally distressed," and it minimally requires the "cognitive" separation of self and other. Infants, accordingly, cannot feel empathy although they can get very upset when their mothers are upset. By contrast, getting upset because someone else is suffering may be wholly self-involved and aversive (for instance getting uncomfortable as someone regales you with their tale of woe and you just want to leave the room). This is not empathy either. Both empathy and compassion/sympathy are affective responses and cognitive; that is, they involve concepts and ways of construing the world. But this does not mean that empathy (or sympathy) needs to involve thinking or imagining oneself "in the other person's shoes." Understanding may be minimal and merely tacit, not articulate, and it need not involve any projection at all.

There is a good distinction to be made following Nell Noddings in her book *Caring* between being *receptive* to the feelings of others as opposed to imaginative projection and contemplation of other peoples' feelings ("putting myself in the other's shoes"). Empathy is *not* needing to ask, "How would I feel in such a situation?" She gives the example of a mother whose baby's diaper is wet and asks: Does the mother really have to ask herself what it must feel like to be wearing a diaper soaked in urine? The answer is obvious. Her empathy is not thoughtless but neither need it be thoughtful or explicit.

What this example also shows is that empathy is not sympathy nor is it the literal sharing of emotion. One can feel sorry for someone without in any way sharing his pain, and one can, perhaps, share someone's pain without feeling in any way sorry for him. I feel terrible about you breaking your leg, but my feeling terrible is nothing compared to what you're feeling. I sit watching an early James Bond movie *(Goldfinger)* in a theater. The bad guy's bodyguard ("Oddjob") grasps Bond in a death grip, and Bond responds by (how to put this politely?) kicking him in the groin. There is a collective "ungh!" from the men in the audience. (There is no such response correlative to any of the other punching, gouging, slamming, etc.) I take it that this is a straightforward if crude example of imaginative empathy. To say the obvious, no one in the audience suffered at that moment from an actual pain in the groin, and yet the response (including the twist of a self-protective gesture) was quite specific.

This is a crude sort of empathy, to be sure, but moving up in gentility, as well as cognitive sophistication, I remember sitting through any number of romantic films in which I "felt for" the hero or the heroine. I found myself quite freely "identifying with" the character as I watch him or her on the screen. I also note the ease with which I empathize with characters in novels and nonfiction biographies. It is often said that part of the effort of reading is "filling in" the details, fleshing out the skeleton provided by the verbal descriptions with use of one's imagination, adding colors, smells, and tastes (whether or not they are described in the book). What is less-often noted is the extent to which one "identifies" with the characters in a novel or biography by way of adding one's own personal details, including one's emotional reactions (again, whether or not they are so described in the book). This can be thoroughly narcissistic and self-indulgent, perhaps, but a certain amount of this is necessary if we are to identify with a character at all. (I would say this is true even in films, but there is far less open space to insert oneself.)

Sometimes, empathy requires quite dramatic leaps of imagination. I try to imagine, for instance, Joan of Arc's feelings as she first approached Robert Baudricourt to offer her services to Charles VII. Let me point out that I am not a young woman—I am no longer even young, and I am not religious, much less devout, and have never to my knowledge been spoken to by God or any other ethereal spirit. I do not live in the Middle Ages (and know much less about that millennium than I do about other periods of Western history). And yet, with considerable effort, I can empathize with young Joan's feelings by comparing them, with considerable trepidation, to my own remembered experiences (of youthful enthusiasm, self-righteousness, intimidation by authorities, and aggressive ambition).

I think that it is a mistake to think that compassion (sympathy), too, is just one emotional phenomenon rather than several (or many). These emotions range in cognitive sophistication from the mere fellow feeling of "emotional contagion"—simply "picking up" another person's distress by virtue of mere proximity—to the "higher cognitive" sharing of emotion through imaginatively and quite self-consciously "putting oneself in the other's place." At the "low" end of the range, "emotional contagion" involves only minimal intentionality, some vague sense of shared discomfort or merriment, and it is by no means necessary or even likely that the subject of such an emotion would be able to say clearly what it is "about," much less what it portends or what it means. The question "why are you feeling this?" gets only a causal answer, for instance, "because I'm with her, and she's upset." Considerably more sophisticated is Nell Nodding's "receptivity." Intentionality may still be minimal, but whereas "emotional contagion" happens by virtue of mere proximity one must "open oneself up" to be receptive. One "lets it happen" (often hidden behind the observation that such emotional empathy is "spontaneous"). This involves a decision of sorts (although the crucial decision may have been made many years ago, for instance, to have a child or to foster this friendship.)

A final caveat: We sometimes use "sympathy" or the verb "to sympathize" to register agreement or approval, although this is not a literal use of the term. One need not agree with or approve of the feeling in question any more than one must always enjoy, like, or approve of one's own emotions. Sharing a feeling is one thing but accepting or approving of the feeling is something quite different. The feelings may agree but we need not. In grade-B movies we might well share the offended hero's rather fascist sense of revenge, as we might share the envy of someone who has been similarly deprived while berating ourselves for just that feeling.

But a final word of good cheer. Adam Smith is often misinterpreted as the apostle of selfishness, which I have suggested he certainly is not. But what is true of Smith might also be true of the economic system he championed, "capitalism" or, more accurately, "the market economy." Think of it this way: The primary forms of exchange throughout most of human history have not been very civilized: warfare, with all of the cruelty and dehumanization that goes along with it, and Christian and Muslim missionary zeal, which makes the claim that it intends to "civilize" the world but more often than not ends up killing thousands of innocent people and being indifferent or downright hostile to the local cultures and institutions it uproots and destroys. But then there was commerce and the market (which antedated both Christianity and Islam). The overwhelming virtue of the market was and always has been that it *of necessity paid attention to the needs and preferences of its customers.* Thus Smithian sympathy (empathy) played an essential role in this supposed arena of selfishness. It is necessary to understand what people want in order to provide it for them. This is not to deny the persistence of corruption, exploitation, monopoly, and profit-mongering in the market, nor is it to deny that most businesses want and need to be profitable, but it is to say that the market in its essence and at its best is not just the expression of unbridled self-interest but the opposite, a mutual concern for mutual satisfaction.

I take compassion and empathy to be of enormous importance in understanding our emotional lives; they are part of our natural ability to tune into the emotions of others without the intermediary of a rich empathetic imagination and to feel the urge to respond without the need for a great deal of thought. Thought, however, needs to come soon after, so our responses are in fact helpful rather than merely expressive. Thus sympathy, however "natural," is a combination of both inherent dispositions and acculturation and education. Our emotional lives are largely imitative, learned in what philosopher Ronnie de Sousa (1987) calls "paradigm scenarios," and it is in the presence of other people's suffering that we learn the appropriateness of compassion and the expectations surrounding it. We do not just have our own interests. We *share* interests with others. Empathy is neither altruistic nor self-interested. It rather exemplifies the implicit solidarity of human nature.

This, I think, is the lasting and contemporary importance of those eighteenth-century theories, and, we might mention, those similar religious messages emanating from Buddhism, Confucianism, and Christianity, just to name a few. Against the perennial cynicism that depicted human nature as essentially selfish they all argue for a much more humane and admirable portrait, one that greatly qualifies and limits the selfish aspects of humanity and renders human nature not a Hobbesian "war of all against all" but a sympathetic community defined by fellow feeling and an abhorrence of seeing one's fellow creatures in pain or suffering.

6

Extremes of Emotion:
Grief, Laughter, and Happiness

From love and compassion, let's move on to explore an odd trio of emotions: grief, laughter, and happiness. Grief and happiness might be thought of as extremes of emotion, perhaps, with laughter acting as something of a transformative medium between them. Or, you could think of this as a judicious mix of affects, something like balancing the sweet with the spicy and the bitter, like a good Mexican *molé* sauce. But together, grief, laughter, and happiness raise profound questions about the role of emotions in the good life. To start with, grief cannot be excluded from the good life even if it is one of the most painful and devastating emotions. If loving and caring are essential to life, then so is grief, which is nothing less than the realization of our extreme vulnerability to loss. Thus it is an essential part of life even if some lucky souls should never suffer it. Laughter, and happiness, by contrast, tend to be so overpromoted in our "pursuit of happiness" society that they are often assumed to be tantamount to the good life as such. But this is not the case, or at least that it is not so simply the case, because a rich human life is only sometimes a life of happiness and laughter, as ultimately desirable as these may be. Fools can spend a wasted life of laughter. Even happiness, perhaps, is not the be-all and end-all of life, Aristotle to the contrary. This chapter, in other words, is intended to put into perspective two extremes of our emotional life: devastation, on the one hand, and what we call happiness, on the other.

There is another thesis that I would like to toy with here, however, and that is that grief, laughter, and happiness are all emotions that are most meaningful when they are shared. This is not the prevalent view, at least in much of our own culture. Grief is often described as a very private, personal emotion, characterized by social withdrawal and shutting oneself off from the world. Happiness, especially in America, is too often characterized as a strictly individual emotion, a feeling that one might have and maintain even if all of those around him are suffering. Worse, happiness is often identified with mere cheerfulness and this is depicted as admirable and desirable in itself, again quite independent of context and without regard to the well-being of others. Laughter, too, is too often celebrated without regard to content or context, in other words, without reference to what it is *about*, as if it, too, is good in itself. But when happiness is depicted as an individual emotion, a buoyant sense of personal well-being, I think that we have made a profound philosophical mistake, and this is, ironically, the source of a great deal of *un*happiness. Or so I will suggest. Grief, laughter, and happiness are not always what they are said to be, and furthermore, the great virtue of all of these emotions, as opposed to many others, is that they are (or should be) noncompetitive. It is in this sense in particular that they are often and preferably shared, not just individual at all.

Grief and laughter tend to be ignored by philosophers, the former because it seems like such a gloomy emotion, the latter because philosophy itself tends to be a bit gloomy. ("I tried to be a philosopher," said Dr. Samuel Johnson, "but cheerfulness kept breaking out.") Happiness, of course, has been a topic of central philosophical concern since Aristotle. But what old Aristotle meant by happiness (Greek *eudemonia*) and what we usually mean by "happiness" are two quite different matters. For him, and for many philosophers since, happiness has little to do with our subjective states, with "feeling happy." So it is probably fair to say that philosophers tend to dismiss happiness *as an emotion*, even if it is central to their thinking as the more general aim of a good life. Nevertheless, I would certainly not deny that our emotions, in general, are essential to our happiness.

Grief

First, grief, which philosophers do not like to talk about. There is death, of course, about which many philosophers have chosen to wax eloquently (if obscurely). But philosophers, they will be quick to say, are not grief counselors and not therapists, and the bereaved should look elsewhere than to philosophy for solace. What we philosophers can tell them, unhelpful but in all good conscience, is that we all have to die—sometime, anyway. ("Gee, thanks.") Outside of philosophy, in the world of those who actually have to cope with death and grief, the more hopeful among us might add something about the deceased having "gone to a better place" while the rest of us offer our "condolences" and remain respectfully silent. But in most cultures, whether or not they believe in an afterlife, mourning—the process of public grieving—is one of the most important social rituals. By contrast, Americans have an attitude toward death and grief that can best be summarized as denial, and one reason is that they focus on grief as a personal loss and do not tend to see it in terms of solidarity.

Grief is said to be the most negative of "negative" emotions, but as I have already suggested in previous chapters (and will argue again), I find this opposition of positive and negative emotions to be simple-minded. This is once again true of grief. And again, we should carefully distinguish between what causes an emotion and its functional role in our psychological economy. Grief signifies a serious loss, that is true. (A note here: I will be talking about just one paradigm of grief, that which follows the more or less sudden loss of a loved one. There are others, the family who loses their ancestral house to a hurricane or tornado, the woman who mourns for her unborn children, the lost soul who grieves for the life he might have had, the abandoned lover who grieves for his or her beloved who is now happily married in Seattle, the lingering illness that not only allows but demands grieving-in-process over the final months or years of a loved one's life. But the loss of a loved one is sufficiently terrible and devastating and trauma enough to focus our attention).

But that trauma isn't the whole of grief. The other side of grief, its precondition, is love. Thus I want to argue that grief is not only bemoaning the loss. *Grief is also a way of keeping the love alive.* Think about how badly we think of a person who, having just lost his or her spouse or child, is up and active again, without a hint of grief or grieving. At best, we might be generous and suppose that he or she is in denial and repressing it, but less sympathetically we might just conclude that he or she is callous and incapable of love. Furthermore, we too readily tend to think about grief as being just about the past. But grief is also about the present and the future. Think about what I will call the *commemoration* factor in grief. People dedicate novels, name buildings, and create fellowships and foundations in order to maintain the memory of those they have loved and lost. We may think of grief as a "negative" and unwanted emotion, but would any of us like to live in a world without grief, where people die without an emotional trace? Think about your own funeral, and just imagine that no one bothered to come.

Grief is neglected not because it is unimportant but because it is so unavoidable in life. It forces itself upon us. It is easy enough to see why we should think of grief as a so-called "negative" and undesirable emotion. Its very presence means that we have suffered severely, which is not to be confused with the claim that we have suffered *from* grief. We talk of grief as a painful emotion but it is the loss that is painful, not the emotion. Furthermore grief is a *moral* emotion, in ways that I will try to spell out here. It is for this reason that grief is not only expected as the *appropriate* reaction to the loss of a loved one, but it is in a strong sense *obligatory*. We are not just surprised when a person shows no signs of grief after a very personal loss. We are morally outraged and condemn such a person.

Consider Camus's character Meursault, in *The Stranger*, who is condemned as "inhuman" because he fails to grieve for his dead mother at her funeral. If grief were simply a negative reaction to a loss, or even a physical condition that (it has often been pointed out) fits the definition of a mental disorder, a medical illness, this would be incomprehensible. Such a person would be considered fortunate, like an athlete who has a high threshold of pain, or a brave risk-taker who remains unafraid in circumstances that would scare the wits out of most normal people. But grief is not merely "normal" or "natural" nor is it only customary or "appropriate." It is morally obligatory because grief like love is woven deeply into the fabric of our moral lives. Meursault does not grieve because he does not (cannot) love, and this is what condemns him.

Another problem is that grief is looked down upon in Western culture as "unmanly." The classic line is from *Hamlet*, a play that can be read as being all about grief (rather than about revenge, as it usually is [see Faccio, 1999]).

> 'Tis sweet and commendable in your nature, Hamlet.
> To give these mourning duties to your father,
> But you must know that your father lost a father,
> That father lost, lost his, and the survivor bound
> In filial obligation for some term
> To do obsequious sorrow. But to persevere
> In obstinate condolement is a course
> Of impious stubbornness. 'Tis unmanly grief.
> It shows a will most incorrect to heaven,
> A heart unfortified, a mind impatient,
> An understanding simple and unschooled. (*Hamlet* 1.2.91–101)

"Unmanly grief." That says it all. Grief is a refusal to accept the inevitable, an "impious stubbornness." To be sure, Claudius acknowledges the propriety of a (very) brief grief, "for some term . . . obsequious sorrow" but he is quick to add that *real men* don't grieve (and in this age of gender equality perhaps *real women* don't, either). So how should we understand this "simple and unschooled" emotion, charged with being out of touch with reality? Does it show "a will most incorrect to heaven," or does it rather indicate something essentially human, namely, the capacity to love?

True grief can be profound. Like love, grief involves a shared self, but in this case that shared self has been seriously damaged. To turn once again to Aristophanes' myth, the completed self is once again sundered. Thus grief involves nothing less than the loss of one's self—or a substantial portion of one's self—and the withdrawal that expresses grief is neither the rejection of society nor the simple retreat of a wounded being but rather the necessary attempt to rebuild and reestablish one's sense of self. Contrary to the common view, grief is not just pain, and the "action tendencies" associated with grief are not, as is so often supposed, merely withdrawals or expressions of pain. Grief, like Heidegger's *angst*, prompts reflection, and this is the purpose of the withdrawal. The idea that grief has no action tendencies further ignores this obvious feature of grief, although to be sure withdrawal and reflection are not exactly "vigorous" actions on a par with punching an offender in the nose in anger or running for one's life in fear. (It was William James who insisted that "an urge to vigorous action" is what distinguishes emotions from cold rationality. But he was thinking of anger and fear, not grief.) Also significant are the action tendencies of other people, in a healthy community, which give support and help keep the memory of the deceased alive.

I once thought that grief might be viewed as a kind of degenerate emotion, a *breakdown* of emotion rather than an emotion itself. Many philosophers now argue (as I have) that most emotions are "rationally assessable" and involve complex motives, goals, intentions, and actions. But this poses a problem for grief, which seems to include a straightforwardly irrational desire—namely, wanting the deceased to come back to life—and therefore produces no intelligible goal or intention, and no action. Grief, unlike most emotions, seemed to entail no actions but rather withdrawal and an inability to do much of anything at all. Thus I believed that grief was a loss of intimacy and the rupture of an intense emotional dependency. That meant that the phenomenology of grief would be better understood not as an emotional outlook but as the sudden destruction of an emotional outlook, a breakdown. But I have come to see that this underestimates the value and significance of grief and provides an inadequate and unimaginative analysis of the emotion.

But grief is exemplary in another way. Grief is not a single emotion but a process. Elisabeth Kübler-Ross (1975) plotted out what has been many times confirmed as the "normal" process of grieving, which includes denial, anger, distraction, and guilt as well as sorrow, with which grief is often narrowly identified. So it would certainly be wrong to say that grief is a "basic emotion" in the sense we have been suggesting, but in another sense, it is hard to think of an emotion that is more basic to human life, its social nature and its mortality. Once again, it is essential that we think of an emotion as a dynamic engagement with the world and not just a self-enclosed feeling.

That engagement with the world is dominated by a peculiar kind of perception, the perception that someone, the beloved, is *not there*. Such perceptions of *absence* are important, if neglected, in philosophy, as Jean-Paul Sartre so persuasively insists in his "Pierre is not in the café" discussion of "nothingness" in his great book *Being and Nothingness*. The phenomenological and psychological fact is that an absence can be more poignant, more noticeable, more obsessive, than any presence. Thus the phenomenology of grief is almost inconceivable without a phenomenology of memory, because, to say the obvious, grief refers ineluctably to the past, or rather to the past as remembered. One remembers, perhaps obsessively, times together with the dearly departed. Indeed, one of the paradoxical pains associated with grief is the realization that one cannot remember as much as one would like to, that one's memory of the lost beloved is diminishing with time. This is both frustrating and, to some extent, itself a cause for further grief and guilt. Thus what is an essential part of the "recovery" from grief is thus also an aspect of the suffering of grief.

But I noted that grief is also aimed at the future. It is not just about the past. Most emotions include a characteristic desire (or set of desires), and this is what makes them so motivating. But what is the desire attached to grief? It has been suggested that grief involves only one desire, an impossible desire, and that is the desire that the loved one not be dead. But this ignores one of the most dramatic features of grief, its strong desire to commemorate and honor the deceased, to satisfy at least one of the departed's most basic (though not necessarily spoken) desires and wishes. Thus Janet McCracken, a dear former student of mine, writes of the "dedicatory" nature of grief. "The dedicatory quality of grief's relation to the dead is reflected in some of the things we commonly say about the deceased, such as "she would have wanted it this way," "let's win this game for her," "she's turning over in her grave about this." When someone we love has died, we desire to *do honor* to that life as a whole, above and beyond whatever honors or rewards he or she may have received for particular accomplishments during her life. It might seem perverse to some people that we dedicate our books to the dead or name stadiums and schools after them, for "after all, they aren't here to appreciate it." But someone who does not understand this "dedicatory" urge can be judged insensitive (at best).

Grief, however, can also adopt a strategy, one that may begin as an expression of love but soon leaves that behind. It is well expressed by Edina, the obnoxious protagonist of the television show *Absolutely*

Fabulous: "What's the point of grieving, if there's no one there to see you do it?!" Thus grief (like pity, according to Nietzsche) can be self-indulgent. But even when it is sincere, grief serves a strategic purpose, to attract sympathy and care through a difficult time and to remind oneself of one's continuing membership in a community. So far I have not paid sufficient attention to the public and social expression that I claimed was so important and neglected by American culture. The social expression of grief, of course, is the ritual of mourning.

In many cultures mourning goes on for years, sometimes for a lifetime. In some societies, for example, among the Maori in New Zealand, grief is not considered an interruption of life but rather the continuation of the rhythm of life. A Maori funeral lasts three or more days. In America it may take less than an hour. Maori grief is tightly communal and really shared, and not just as a matter of sympathy. The loss is everyone's loss, a loss to the community as well as to the next of kin. Accordingly, the logic of grief gets entangled with the social structure of mourning, as opposed to the common American attitude that grief is antisocial withdrawal. One of the most striking things about American culture (insofar as this can be distinguished from the many ethnic subcultures that make it up) is the comparative absence of established mourning rituals. Within a few days or even a few hours after a funeral it is perfectly appropriate for the mourners to go back to their ordinary lives, and within a few weeks or at most one or two months it is simply expected that they will "get over it." In other cultures, by contrast, the idea of "getting over it" is considered utterly offensive not only to the loved one lost but to the honor of the entire community.

Thus grief is vital to human community and our own larger well-being, but at the same time it seems to interfere with our ongoing lives and projects and thus be ineffective if not "unmanly." Thus mourning rituals not only have the purpose of helping the grieving parties to rejoin the larger community, but they also serve the function of reminding us all of our mortality, the fact that we are ultimately significant not just because we exist as individuals but because we together form a people that will outlive us and give our lives meaning. In this, too, grief has positive value in that it gives us good cause for reflection, a renewed sense of social solidarity, as well as a new sense of what needs to be done, not just for ourselves but for the memory of those we have lost and the community that we share together. The loss suffered in grief may be enormous and irredeemable, but the further loss suffered by ignoring or denying the importance of the grieving process and the significance of mourning rituals only amplifies, and does not ease, the suffering. The denial of grief, as the Stoics saw so clearly, first requires the denial of love, and that is a price that most of us are unwilling to pay.

Laughter

Having gone through grief, let's lighten up and go to what would seem to be the opposite pole of the painful-to-pleasant spectrum of emotion, laughter. Laughter, one might think, doesn't fit here at all, not just because it doesn't go together with grief (though it sometimes can, and very well) but because laughter isn't an emotion. It is an expression of emotion and, what's more, several different emotions. As children we laughed when we were tickled. We also laughed excitedly when we were just playing, running around and chasing one another. In some Asian cultures and for some sorority girls, laughter is a standard expression of nervousness or embarrassment. If we have been given nitrous oxide ("laughing gas"), we laugh for no reason at all. But mainly, one might think, we laugh because something is *funny*. But that itself is a huge question. What makes something funny? (Nothing is so unfunny, I should warn you in advance, as trying to understand what makes something funny. Do not expect what follows to be a laugh riot.)

What emotion is it that is being expressed in laughter? Paul Ekman and others have hypothesized that certain facial expressions characteristically express definite emotions. Is this true of laughter? In the United States, laughter often expresses cheerfulness, but this is not clearly laughter about anything. Tickling and embarrassment aside, I used to think that laughter was all about humor, an expression of one's "sense of humor." But what is it to have a sense of humor? It is not enough to laugh a lot, or even to find a lot of things funny. This may merely make you a moron. So what is laughter about? I spent several years trying to analyze what makes something funny, in other words, what makes us laugh. I did a delightful few years of serious research into the pathos-drenched humor of Charlie Chaplin, the shenanigans of Laurel and Hardy, the punsical wit of Shakespeare, the self-mocking satire of Seinfeld, the physical humor of Steve Martin, Robin Williams, and M. Hulot, the wry political humor of *The Daily Show*, and the Three Stooges. (I was a big fan.) But what is funny, I asked, about three adults acting like idiots, poking each other in the eye, and hitting one another with hard and heavy implements? What is so funny, in short, about bad things (apparently) happening to other people? From this perspective, it did not look as if either our laughter or our humor was conducive to virtue. On the contrary, laughter and humor, it seemed, was often at the malicious expense of others, the very opposite of the compassion that I earlier suggested was the basis of ethics and human fellow-feeling. (That is why the French philosopher Henri Bergson thought that humor was antithetical to sentiment and emotion.) But if humor and laughter are essential to the good life, the implications of this are pretty awful.

I started to see the error of my ways at a psychology workshop in which a young mother (on film) was shown playing peek-a-boo with her infant, and both were laughing hilariously. I was tempted—to save my theory—to insist that they both found this tremendously funny. But for the life of me I couldn't see what this had to do with the humor I had been analyzing. It was not even slapstick. In a sense it was play, but that seemed to be much too advanced an activity given the age of the infant. It became evident, as I distanced myself from the "what is funny?" question, that laughter is first of all a profound interpersonal mechanism. The emotion expressed isn't mirth or amusement (much less amused sadism) so much as it is mutual delight. This isn't to deny that some things are genuinely funny (at least in a certain context, for a certain audience), nor is it to deny that many things are just *not* funny (at least in some contexts, for certain audiences). But if laughter is first of all an expression and a vehicle for solidarity then we can understand how it is that humor is so contextual and variable. Laughter in the midst of grief not only can be a great relief but it can also be very much in the spirit of the deceased, who would, one expects, be laughing along as well. In such circumstances one should, however, choose one's humor cautiously. (After the death of someone lacking in humor, laughing behavior would be particularly disrespectful.)

The fact that laughter is interpersonal bonding does not in itself make it valuable or virtuous. Racist and sexist humor tends to enhance solidarity, but this hardly makes it worthwhile, much less virtuous. But is solidarity the essence of humor? There are quite a few distinguished thinkers who have argued that racist and sexist humor is not exceptional but the norm. (It is just that these two areas are, at the moment, "politically incorrect" and inappropriate.) It has been argued that humor is all about aggressive superiority and that laughter is essentially ridicule ("the roar of the victor," writes Thomas Hobbes). Aristotle, too, insisted that humor is an expression of superiority, especially the superiority of the "better" people (the aristocracy) over the "vulgar" (everybody else). Of course, sexism and racism often fit in here (as anyone who has seen the comedies of Aristophanes will appreciate), but more than anything else, laughter is directed at poor manners (thus the "comedy of manners" remained a staple of humor until modern times). On the plus side, laughter could be appreciated as having a certain therapeutic value, as ridicule is a powerful deterrent for small misbehaviors. But laughter, on this view, is nasty, even vicious (a point often made by distinguishing between laughing *with* as opposed to laughing *at* another person.) This would explain the humor of the Three Stooges, and perhaps the pathos of Chaplin's tramp. But is all humor like this? What about the mother and her infant playing peek-a-boo? Isn't there a more innocent way of understanding of humor and laughter, which we all take to be a great virtue and an essential part of human life?

The superiority theory is not the only theory of humor, although it obviously has its problematic domain. There are other conceptions of humor. John Morreall (1983) has distinguished three different philosophical theories of humor that construe laughter in very different ways. The first is the "Superiority Theory," but not all humor presumes any such combative stance. Thus Morreall distinguishes a second type of "Relief" theory that takes particular aim at sex jokes and their like. Its best-known promulgator was Sigmund Freud. Freud insisted that the function of humor was release of forbidden libidinal and scatological impulses, and in the repressed world of the Victorian middle class, this seemed to make a lot of sense. Perhaps this theory would also explain why, in some societies, laughter is an expression of embarrassment, a different kind of release. Its application to the Three Stooges is a bit more dubious, but the fact that those short films still appeal mainly to adolescent boys (and grown-up adolescent boys) suggests that humor might release a different kind of urge, neither sexual nor scatological but nevertheless naughty in its own way. But communal laughter isn't always an expression of noble sentiments, and the idea that something is "naughty" already puts it in a category of the social, "the forbidden," and that alone is capable of bringing inhibited people together. So humor, according to this interpretation, has to do with *violating* manners, not just poor or inferior manners, and breaking taboos, including taboos on violence. (Thus the popularity of such films as *Animal House* and *American Pie.*)

Such a theory, however, does not seem to make humor any more virtuous than the superiority theory, especially if it encourages violence. But we should not leap too quickly to outrage here. No one ever gets hurt in a Three Stooges comedy. They are cartoonish characters. Immediately following a bit of violence, they are back in good form, and the supposed hurt is of no consequence whatever. Like so many cartoon characters, they suffer no lasting pain. The unhappy coyote in the old Roadrunner cartoons may fall hundreds of yards into a canyon, but he is up and ready with a new plot two second later. Here we back into some rather deep philosophical issues about the status of fiction and fictitious persons, akin to our worries about vicarious fear and horror in chapter 3 and 4. But more troubling is the argument that if pretend violence is humorous, might not real violence be even more so? If breaking taboos is humorous, wouldn't really breaking them be more humorous than just pretending to break them?

There are, to be sure, pathological people for whom only real violence will do, and there are extreme situations in which such an argument may make some sense. But a precondition of humor for most of us is that the taboos in question not actually be violated. Freud was quite clear that sex jokes are jokes and not actual sex. So, too, the difference between violence and pretend violence is a critical difference. Imagine the following slapstick scenario in real life: A person slips on a banana peel, falls, is embarrassed, is obviously not hurt, and so we laugh (although this might seem as much like a case of superiority as relief). We would probably say that we are laughing at the other person's expense, or, more simply, we are laughing *at* the other person. The case becomes more complicated but also more congenial if the person laughs *with* us. Not only does this show that the person is not hurt. It also shows that he or she is not humiliated but, like us, amused. A more complex case still is where the person is not at all amused at the time but perfectly willing to share the humiliating experience with us after the fact. Friends often tell us embarrassing stories about themselves, obviously amused, but after the fact. A popular television example these days are those rather obnoxious "home video" programs that invite the audience to show humiliating examples of their own (or their family's) mishaps and slight misfortunes. There are also those cases in which the humiliation itself is staged by the supposed victim, who finds it amusing not only after the fact but beforehand as he or she plans it. But if the person who slips or trips doesn't move or is bleeding, whatever humor the situation might have evoked disappears immediately and the laughter ceases. So the relief theory is more subtle than it might originally appear to be. We are back into the "willing suspension of belief" mode, and it is much more the suggestion of violating a taboo than the actual violation of it, which is why innuendo is so often so much more funny than crassness. (Though our cultural standards here are visibly degenerating.)

Both aggression and relief make humor look pretty bad, but Morreall offers us a much more civil (but much less precise) theory of "incongruity" as the source and nature of humor. This comparatively polite view of humor explains a good deal of wit—puns, for example, and a great deal of stand-up comedy, which relies on jokes (often one-liners) whose point is sheer cleverness, not sexual provocation or an expression of superiority. Illustrious philosophical defenders of this incongruity theory include Immanuel Kant, Arthur Schopenhauer, and the existentialist Søren Kierkegaard. My objection to the theory is not its civility, which makes the welcome point about laughter's intrinsic sociality, but its vagueness. One can find some "incongruity" in almost any joke or comedy skit. But it is a good observation that humor often involves a breach in our expectations, a surprise, or some oddity that is itself amusing. But here, of course, is the problem. Explaining why an oddity is amusing seems to just repeat the question, what makes something funny? Indeed, not all incongruities are amusing. Life is filled with incongruities, and most are not amusing. So it starts to look as if the incongruity theory is not much of a theory at all.

But this does not just leave us with those antisocial superiority and relief theories. I want to go back to the insight that laughter expresses sociality, and hypothesize that what strikes us as funny (a more modest formulation than "what *is* funny") depends largely on context, not just the context of the joke or even the context in which the joke is told but the people with whom one is enjoying the joke. The joke, in sort, is an *excuse* to laugh and establish social solidarity, although some such excuses are obviously more widely appropriate than others. Jokes—that is the very form of jokes—set up an occasion for laughter and solidarity. We have all enjoyed the scenario of a young child who has mastered the form of a joke (say, "knock-knock" jokes) but has not yet grasped what makes such jokes funny (cleverness, rudeness). The child tells a "joke" in that form and more often than not breaks into peals of laughter, knowing that this is a cause of humor but evidently not knowing why. (To be sure, our enjoyment usually fades well before the child tires of the seemingly infinite variations.) But I suggest that all humor is like this, an excuse for laughter and solidarity rather than something funny as such. To be sure, there is a great deal of room for cleverness, wit, expressions of superiority, and the breaking of taboos in all of this, and it is in appreciation of this (or in appreciation of being part of the "in" group that is presumed in the humor) that the solidarity is realized. But the humor is in the laughing together, not in the joke itself.

This explains why, unless you are a somewhat unusual person, you will not laugh as loud or as much when you are alone. You may break out in a laugh or guffaw occasionally, but laughter is an interpersonal and social expression of emotion, and humor is an essentially social emotion. So one might laugh at the Charlie Chaplin movie alone but it is much better and funnier in a theater with a hundred other people also laughing. The humorousness of the movie might not change with the audience, but laughter, I have come to understand, is first of all an interpersonal and a social expression of solidarity. The humor is only secondarily what the emotion is about.

Laughter is, first of all, a bonding gesture, and the emotions it expresses may be any combination of love, affection, camaraderie, and solidarity, including the problematic solidarity of racism, sexism, and shared prejudice. Aristotle and Hobbes are right, that one familiar source of solidarity is a shared sense of superiority (which may well be, as Sartre argues with regard to anti-Semitism, no more than a pathetic mutual defensiveness). But they got it wrong insofar as they suggested that this sense of superiority was what all laughter is about, much less the source (rather than just the target) of the humor. Solidarity need not require either superiority or defensiveness. A family or fraternity can laugh in solidarity at films or videos of themselves in earlier adventures. We can sit laughing together with a couple hundred strangers in a theater showing witty repartee between two or more other strangers. The sense of humor here is itself dependent on the feeling of solidarity. This is not to say that what we are laughing at is not funny, but it is funny in part because of its shared social content.

The differences in humor between different cultures is, of course, well-known. (Just think about the Germans, Italians, and French, not to mention Japanese, Arabs, and South Sea Islanders.) It is not just that they find different things funny. That is the superficial data. The cultures themselves have different customs, expectations, taboos, etc. But if humor is only superficially what the emotion is about, then, again, what seems so simple, straightforward, and "natural" is on investigation immensely complex, sophisticated, and steeped in the particularities of a culture.

Happiness

And, at last, and all too briefly, happiness. But first the question: Is happiness even an emotion? I already suggested that it is not an emotion in the usual sense. I instead agree with Aristotle that happiness involves a quasi-objective judgment that covers one's whole (or a good part) of one's life. Happiness, or what Aristotle called *eudemonia*, is living a whole life and living it well. Nevertheless a well-lived life involves—necessarily—substantial moments of happiness as a subjective state, that is, as an emotion. So we are once again facing what promises to be a complex and controversial formula where we might have expected or hoped for a simple feeling. So, on the one hand, one could argue that happiness is not an emotion at all. On the other, happiness would seem to necessarily involve many emotions, one of which might be those light-hearted states that we characterize as "feeling happy," but there are many others.

At least as important are all of those feelings of satisfaction and contentment, which may sometimes not seem like feelings at all. They are more like a soothing hum than a raucous arousal. Then there is joy. Joy can be raucous, but it, too, is more like a sweet melody than a violent passion. More ethereal is the quasi-religious experience of bliss, which the philosopher Spinoza (and some Buddhists) listed as the highest of human feelings, a transcendent connection to something much more than human. On a more secular plane there is also what Mihaly Csikszentmihalyi (1991) calls "flow," the temporary "high" that is experienced by many athletes and other people at the peak of their performance. Granted, this is not a common experience, even among happy people, but it certainly contributes, in those who have it, to one's larger well-being. Perhaps, too, we should mention cheerfulness, which seems to be more of an expression or even a way of being rather than an emotion or even a mood. (Cheerfulness has become mandatory on television commercials and for many people in the work place, which should rightly lead us to be suspicious of it.) But all such states, as opposed to Aristotelian happiness, may be merely transient, even momentary. Happiness must be much more than that. Such states may also be no more than "subjective" in the sense that they could be wholly illusory. That is, we might be wholly mistaken or oblivious about the true state of our world. Our feeling might be grotesquely inappropriate, or a short-term "high," or it could be like the euphoria of a down-and-out drug user whose life is a shambles but whose momentary feeling is blissful and without concern. Some people (including the ancient Epicureans) have insisted that happiness is no more than freedom from life's problems, just as (for Epicurus) pleasure may be nothing but the absence of pain. But is a good life really nothing but a life without pain and worry? Doesn't it also require achievement, good times, self-fulfillment, and all of those other good things? All of this is much more than we can hope to deal with here, so let me offer you a promissory note. We will keep coming back to happiness and its emotional constituents throughout this book (but especially in the final chapter).

In holding out for happiness, I am not denying that joy is a delightful emotion. But it is too easily trivialized, as is the more modest mood or expression of cheerfulness. If joy has nothing to sustain it, it is not an indicator of the good life, no matter how intrinsically desirable it might be as an experience (and I would argue even against this). If cheerfulness is nothing but a facade, a way of congenially encountering situations and other people, that may well make it desirable but it might still express nothing about a person's well-being. And if it is so "superficial" that it remains exactly the same across a wide variety of situations, then it becomes even more an object of suspicion (as in, "what is she hiding?"). Cheerfulness is certainly not that grand form of happiness that Aristotle insists is the highest end of human life. Again, this is not to demean or condemn cheerfulness, an attitude that I could use a lot more of myself and has been similarly lauded by some of the grimmest philosophers (notably Nietzsche). But it is to say that we should not put too much weight on its significance. It is instructive to remind ourselves, for instance, that the American emphasis on being friendly and cheerful (encapsulated in the Boy Scout Oath and in all of those corporate reports) is considered both inappropriate and insincere in many of the more somber cultures in the world. It has too little to do with the hard realities of life.

But even if joy and cheerfulness are superficial or for the most part insignificant in themselves, few of us would choose to live without them.

The mistake is when we confuse these for happiness, or when we tend to think like an accountant as if happiness is some sort of proportion of good feelings to bad feelings in the accumulation of life. The pessimist Arthur Schopenhauer thought something like this, and his argument, hard to refute, was that the bad feelings eventually come out on top. When parents and older professors chasten their overly fun-loving offspring or students, they warn them, "Just you wait!" The good times may be frequent enough now, they say, but eventually disappointment, illness, and mortality—and perhaps karma too—will take their toll. (Schopenhauer's own ability to enjoy himself, we might note, was quite notorious among philosophers. Bertrand Russell enjoys reporting how the old pessimist used to enjoy good dinners and fine wines, not to mention other pleasures of the body not recommended in his philosophical works. But there is no evidence he ever displayed cheerfulness.)

Even for those of us who find our lives getting better and better (even as the creaks and aches get more frequent), the question of simple accounting as well as the simple-minded distinction between good feelings and bad feelings seems to be quite inappropriate. One could do such a calculation, perhaps, assuming that one could accurately remember how one felt in the past without appealing to the significance of the events prompting the feelings, but I do not much see the point of doing so. Living well is not just maximizing the good feelings and minimizing the bad.

And yet, happiness and well-being depend in part on having "positive" emotions. According to this view, positive emotions are conducive to happiness and well-being and negative emotions are not. I do not think that any of us would take issue with that on the face of it (although what counts as positive or negative emotion needs to be further scrutinized), and on hearing this we are all pretty clear what it means. I think that, contrary to the Stoics and the Epicureans, the good and happy life need not be a life of tranquility and peace of mind but can rather be a life of passion and engagement. Of course, a life of passion and engagement can be happy or unhappy, but this is just to repeat that a happy life is not necessarily filled with happy moments. An unhappy life, too, can be filled with happy moments. People might be cheerful and enjoy themselves throughout their youth and adulthood and yet deeply feel that they wasted their lives. But notice that we are now talking about a mix of subjective and quasi-objective evaluations. This does not get captured in the idea that happiness is a momentary and possibly transitory feeling. Nor is happiness just the fulfillment of publicly established standards of success. Powerful moguls and smiling celebrities often reveal that they are exemplary in their misery.

Current researchers refer to this complex feeling as a sense of "subjective well-being," and unlike those moments of unwarranted euphoria enjoyed even by the dope addict, "subjective well-being" requires concrete and more or less realistic engagement with the world. I say "more or less realistic" because our self-evaluations are, of course, subject to all of the biases and distortions of personal perspective and selective memory. But the object of such feelings of subjective well-being are the facts of one's life over (at least) a substantial amount of time. They can, accordingly, be evaluated and, if need be, corrected by sympathetic friends and sometimes by sympathetic biographers, who might note, for instance, that one has overemphasized one particular course of events or the significance of one shameful or embarrassing incident in a lifetime of noble feelings and deeds. Nevertheless, it is the subjective feeling and not just the facts that are at stake here.

Still, the relationship is intricate. Aristotle rejects the idea that pleasure is the goal (the "end") of life, in part on the grounds that pleasure itself is not an end but rather the accompaniment of well-done and enjoyable activities. He says, and I have always found this unintelligible, that pleasure is like "the bloom of youth." It is like a bonus that gets added to meaningful activities and "excellence." Thus happiness is tied to actually doing something. Of course, it is still possible to deceive oneself about what or how well one is doing: Inebriated people may enjoy what they are doing although they do it very badly, and they might well believe (wrongly) that they are doing it well. But the best pleasures, Aristotle is telling us, are not mere feelings but aspects of satisfying activity. We do not enjoy pleasure but rather enjoy doing what we do well, and pleasure comes along to "complete" the activity.

Perhaps, too, we can include in this Aristotelian analysis the phenomenon of "flow" studied by Csikszentmihalyi. When I introduced this above, I referred to activities such as endurance sports, the source of "runner's high." I can attest to the fact that it is also available to us more sedentary types. There is a "writer's high" that makes writing, on occasion, a genuine joy. I should admit that the product of such ecstatic activity is, on further inspection, not always up to the standard one briefly imagined, but the writing itself, like any activity that results in "flow," is an experience of effortless yet total concentration and engagement. But to come back to one of the persistent themes of this book, happiness, insofar as it is an emotion, necessarily involves engagement with the world. It is not just a feeling, no matter how pleasant or even thrilling. And it does not merely accompany the activity or engagement. It *is* that engagement with the world.

The feeling of subjective well-being is, as I argued, dependent on the facts of one's life. But perhaps to a certain extent it can also be independent of those facts. Ed Diener (2003) and others have argued that people tend to live at a certain level of satisfaction and have a "set point" for happiness. It is an observation we have all made, that some people just seem to be happy all or most of the time, whatever the circumstances, and other people seem to be somber or even unhappy, no matter what good fortunes befall them. What Diener reports is that both people who suffer terrible debilitating accidents and those who win lottery jackpots, after a relatively short adjustment time (a year or so), return to their old levels of subjective well-being and how they felt before. So it is not as if we can just "make ourselves happy," as self-help books are always promising. Each of us can and should do what we can do, but our "temperament" seems to set some sort of limit to what is possible. Nevertheless, it is worth noting that neuropsychologist Richard Davidson, working with the Dalai Lama, has suggested that meditation can shift this set point considerably.

Some great philosophers have argued that true happiness is possible only by eliminating virtually all of the emotions. The Stoics, notably, and many Buddhists have defended some such concept of happiness devoid of emotion, though compassion would be allowed (as a feeling for other people's suffering) and perhaps an objectless notion of bliss (at release from the suffering caused by emotions). Spinoza shared this emphasis on bliss (though he disagreed with the Stoics' general dismissal of emotions), and bliss properly understood, I think, is best conceived as a particularly enlightened but not necessarily religious conception of happiness. But bliss, like happiness, demands a connection with the facts of one's life. It is a form of engagement. But unlike happiness, in bliss the connection tends to transcend the facts, the accomplishments and failures in one's life, to focus on one's life in a larger, more philosophical or more spiritual sense. (In the last chapter of this book, I speculate on the nature of bliss and spirituality more fully.)

Thus Spinoza, who by all accounts had a miserable life (he was excommunicated from the Jewish community, in terrible health, and thoroughly impoverished) nevertheless had a sense of his life in union with God that allowed him a sense of bliss. So, too, many religious thinkers have taught of a "higher happiness" (as opposed to the pagan happiness of Aristotle) that does not require either success in life or many momentary good feelings. Of course, there may be serious obstacles to bliss if one has been wicked in life, and many religious thinkers have tried to finesse the case for bliss by insisting that it encompasses both happiness and transcendence. But I think that the idea that one can have a kind of happiness that does not consist of happy emotions is insightful.

My own concern is drawn more from Romanticism, and, to be dramatic, the myth of the suffering artist. My philosophical source on this is, more than anyone else, Friedrich Nietzsche, who insisted both that

(a) happiness is not the most important thing in life and (b) happiness is not incompatible with suffering and unhappiness. The first seems to presume that happiness is something specific, perhaps a feeling of well-being but not well-being as such. Such "happiness" is not as important as adventurous creativity, which Nietzsche thinks is the most important thing in life. The second is more of an Aristotelian conception of happiness as well-being, and a life of adventurous creativity might well be a happy one even if it is filled with pain, suffering, and failure. (That is, what might seem like failure to the subject during his or her lifetime.)

The test of a life well lived, however, may well involve some sort of success consideration, just not any sort of success that might be enjoyed by the subject. Nietzsche himself comes to mind, perhaps also his artistic doppelganger Vincent van Gogh. Thus we might distinguish between a superficial (bourgeois) happiness and a "deep" happiness, the first involving persistent good feelings, the latter largely consisting of high aspiration and not infrequent frustration. But even here, it is impossible to understand such "deep" happiness along the lines of a single set of criteria, and it certainly is not to be opposed to unhappiness (which would also be described as "deep").

My conclusion is that while for most of us happiness and well-being do depend in part on having "positive" emotions, these are neither necessary nor sufficient. As John Stuart Mill (1979) insisted, "better a Socrates dissatisfied than a pig satisfied." If Socrates was dissatisfied (because he knew how ignorant he was), that has little bearing on whether he lived his life well and even whether or not he was ultimately happy. To be sure, Socrates (as least as Plato depicts him) appears to have been a jolly soul, but a sour Socrates might well have enjoyed the same greatness (and, no doubt, the same fate). Struggling artists often enjoy moments of great joy, even mania, but it is not on this basis that we say that they lead happy and fulfilling lives. To be sure, one cannot be too miserable—no matter how great and meaningful one's life—and still be called happy. But this is at most a limiting condition. If Camus could assure us that his Sisyphus was happy despite his eternal meaningless suffering, there is hope for all of us more morose "philosophical" souls as well. We do not all share the often mindless optimism and expressive joy of many of our American compatriots (especially on beer and toothpaste commercials). But happiness may still be possible, for happiness is not the "opposite" of unhappiness. The emotions that make up a happy life are bound to be a lot more complicated than simple joy, an occasional thrill, and a parade of merely good feelings.

7

Self-Reproach in Guilt,
Shame, and Pride

We are most painfully aware of ourselves, of our own indubitable existence, according to Jean-Paul Sartre, when we are ashamed. In our everyday actions, we may well "lose ourselves" in what we are doing. When we are being entertained, we may well lose any sense of self at all. But in shame, we are agonizingly the center of our own attention. We feel all eyes—or at least some important eyes—are riveted on us, and we cannot escape. Indeed, even in the absence of anyone else, we may nevertheless be ashamed of ourselves just because of the possibility that someone else might "catch" us or might have seen us. So, too, in embarrassment and in guilt. But, by way of compensation, so, too, in pride. It, too, is a sense of being the center of attention, in particular one's own attention, but now in a very agreeable way. Whether we think of pride simply in terms of a sense of accomplishment, or some larger sense of superiority, as self-confidence or as self-respect or in the more questionable guise of self-righteousness, it feels good to be proud. It feels good to be oneself.

Shame, guilt, and embarrassment are three emotions that form an obvious family. In fact, they are often conflated and confused with one another. They are all emotions of self-criticism, in fact, one might say, of self-reproach or even of self-abasement. We could add to the list remorse and regret and several varieties of self-loathing. But among the "positive" self-evaluative emotions we also find pride, an emotion of self-praise (although it was for many centuries considered the deadliest of the "deadly" [mortal] sins). These are not only emotions about the self but emotions about responsibility, including moral responsibility. And so we would also expect a high degree of cultural variation, not only concerning what sorts of situations make people ashamed, guilty, embarrassed, or proud but even in the delineation of those emotions themselves. Indeed, while many of the emotions we have discussed so far have been called "basic" and have been argued to be more or less universal, even part of human nature, these emotions by contrast are generally agreed to be shaped and defined by cultural and social structures, involving what many theorists refer to as "higher cognitive" abilities, that is, learning and self-reflection. But what is worth learning, what is to be reflected on, and how it is to be reflected on depends on the particular society. At the heart of all of them is some culturally dependent conception of the self, and there are few concepts that are more dependent on social shaping and social definition.

Spanish, for instance, has no precise word for what we distinguish as embarrassment. (To be "*embarrasse*" in Spanish means to be pregnant.) French wisely distinguishes between two very different (though occasionally overlapping) types of shame, *pudeur* for the sort of shame that Adam and Eve experienced when they found themselves naked in Eden, *honte* for the shame that accompanies the disgrace of being caught in a scandal. Conflating these two is all-too-easy in English, especially in a society that feels generally conflicted and uncomfortable with sexual and more generally bodily issues. By contrast, many societies do not recognize guilt as opposed to shame. We do make that distinction, but we do not give them the same moral weight. Our society seems a bit overzealous about guilt but is disturbingly short on shame. Indeed, shame (often confused as above and also conflated with humiliation) has been rejected as a legitimate moral emotion (Nussbaum, 2004). Our Judeo-Christian heritage and also the increasing size of our cities is responsible for this, one could argue: Guilt is central to both Jewish social history and the Christian notion of sin. Shame, by contrast, usually involves relatively small groups without an overriding judge or lawgiver.

Guilt itself, however, has several very different meanings. There is legal guilt, that which follows a judicial verdict. There is mere causal guilt, that is, being involved in the chain of causes and effects that brought about some unfortunate situation. (This is the sense of guilt embodied in that dubious legal concept of "strict liability," but when it is cut free from self-acknowledged responsibility it also starts looking a lot like embarrassment.) And then there is moral guilt, guilt that clearly implies blame. (In the celebrated O.J. Simpson case, the criminal court found him not guilty but a civil court found him morally guilty nonetheless.) One can be causally guilty without any tinge of moral guilt or blame, too, for instance, when one is tricked or forced to harm another person without any knowledge or control over doing so. It is moral guilt, of course, that is so central to Judaism and Christianity, and the worst kind of guilt is the violation of God's, not man's, law ("Render unto Caesar what is Caesar's . . .").

What makes guilt particularly interesting, to Freud and the psychoanalysts as well as to novelists like Dostoevsky and Kafka, is the fact that one can *feel guilty* despite the fact that one has done nothing wrong. There are those who would like to blame this on the Catholic Church, or on Jewish mothers, or on the story of Adam and Eve, but the truth seems to be that as far back as there have been human beings living together, something like a sense of guilt or shame has been there, too. One might suppose that this feeling of guilt without actual guilt is very much like our earlier example of irrational fear, where one is afraid of something that one knows not to be dangerous. But I think that the cases are quite different, first because no one has proposed anything remotely like a brain mechanism for guilt, as has been so elegantly demonstrated in the case of fear reactions, second because there is a complexity to guilt that far outstrips anything that we saw in primitive fear. This is not to say that it does not have a neurological basis, nor is it to deny that it may have an evolutionary explanation. But as Freud and his colleagues duly noted, there is a great deal in our complex psychology and experience to account for the dislocation of guilt from its putative object, "neurotic guilt," even without the intricacy of neural mechanisms. Of course, there may be further neural complications, as guilt often leads to serious depression.

What guilt (whether neurotic or well-deserved) tends to have in common with shame is the sense of having done something wrong. Thus the self is the intentional object of these emotions, but the self under a certain kind of description, the self as seriously blameworthy. But before we get to the fascinating distinction between guilt and shame, we should take quick note of the fact that both guilt and shame (as well as remorse and regret) must be distinguished from embarrassment in that both guilt and shame presume that one has done something wrong, whereas embarrassment does not. A person is embarrassed when he or she is caught in an awkward situation, but no fault is ascribed. In these other emotions, by contrast, there is fault ascribed; blame is leveled, blame of the self by the self. To what extent that awkwardness is ascribed by the subject and to what extent imposed by others is a complex question. Sometimes it seems inherent in the situation itself, that is, the emotion is not a matter of personal feeling but a quasi-objective evaluation. Different cultures, naturally, will find different situations intrinsically embarrassing. A single orthodox Jewish woman may well be embarrassed to find herself alone with a man, while a Chinese man may feel awkward finding himself just alone. This quasi-objective appraisal of the situation is something more than a person's subjective feeling about herself. It has to do with the nature of the situation in a culture. Thus we can say to someone "you must have been so embarrassed"—when we don't know yet what they may have actually felt. (Sometimes one gets embarrassed only in retrospect, later coming to see that although one did not feel embarrassed at the time one ought to have felt so.) So, too, we can say, "you should be ashamed of yourself" even when a person doesn't feel anything at all. But just saying this may be sufficient to convince the person to see what he or she has done as shameful. Sometimes, however, embarrassment seems to have nothing to do with the particular situation. There are unfortunate people who are so prone to embarrassment that almost any social situation will do.

Embarrassment, shame, and guilt can all involve three different dimensions of self-evaluation: (1) the felt evaluation of the self by oneself (thus we can be ashamed or embarrassed even when we are entirely alone, knowing that what we have done is shameful or awkward), (2) an evaluation of oneself imposed by other people (thus we can be *made* to be ashamed or embarrassed by other's looks, gestures, and words), and (3) the nature of the situation (there are situations that are embarrassing and acts that are shameful, whatever one feels). Being caught with one's pants down is embarrassing. Not pulling one's pants up is shameful, but pulling one's pants down to make a rude gesture *should* make one ashamed, just because in most situations this will be extremely embarrassing to other people.

To say that shame or embarrassment might be dictated by the nature of the situation is not to deny, of course, that it is so only by virtue of a particular perspective, usually determined to a large extent by the particular culture and society. Thus the complexity of traveling overseas (or even within one's local subcultures). The perspectives from which bare-bellied American tourists in cut-offs and baseball caps are appraised in many countries *ought* to make any sensitive American tourist ashamed and be a source of considerable embarrassment to his or her fellow travelers, but there is nothing in the nature of being bare-bellied or wearing a baseball cap that in itself should cause either shame or embarrassment. Thus the shame *(pudeur)* of Adam and Eve, who were quite naturally naked but suddenly felt the weight of a perspective they had not considered before. It was not being naked in Eden but finding themselves naked in God's (and their own) eyes that provoked their emotion. (Of course, they were also guilty of disobeying God's unusually clear and explicit instructions and thus were liable to experience *honte* as well.)

Embarrassment, Regret, and Remorse

To put some of this in a slightly different way, embarrassment, unlike guilt and shame, is an *innocent* emotion. One might say that it embodies a disclaimer, a waiver of responsibility. One finds oneself in an awkward situation but accepts no fault. Indeed, one might even feel embarrassed for being the only one correct. Years ago, in my more reckless days, I found myself in a bar surrounded by young men who were bragging about the crimes they had committed and the time they had spent in prison. I was embarrassed, as I had committed no crime nor done any jail time. But it was not as if I felt that I *ought* to have committed a crime or done time. I just felt myself viewed disapprovingly by others (of whom I disapproved). Furthermore, whether or not one sees oneself as responsible might be determined by the group in which one finds oneself. A virgin may feel embarrassed by her status when she is with a group of "experienced" friends, but it is not as if she finds her behavior in any way blameworthy. One feels shame, by contrast, only by way of accepting fault.

It is interesting to me that embarrassment is rarely cited as a basic emotion, despite the fact that it has such striking autonomic system responses, blushing in particular. It is partly a matter of physiology, partly the peculiarity of human self-consciousness, that explains Mark Twain's wonderful comment, "man is the only animal that blushes, or needs to" (1912). (In fact, other animals do show signs of embarrassment, but blushing would be rather pointless when their faces are covered in fur.) But Twain's wonderful witticism points to an important aspect of embarrassment, that it is not even plausibly just a physiological reaction but necessarily involves a relatively sophisticated conception of self as one self among others, a self subject to others' expectations and judgments, which can then be "internalized" and applied by the self to oneself. These emotions also highlight the centrality of judgment in emotions, especially judgments of responsibility. This is one of the most profound ways in which emotions display intelligence: They acknowledge fault and responsibility, or the absence of it.

As for some of the other negative self-evaluating emotions, they also involve having done (or having intended to do) something wrong. They differ, for the most part, in the sort of wrongdoing involved. Regret is the most innocent of the lot, although, unlike embarrassment it does admit fault. But one does not regret doing some egregious moral wrong. One regrets missing a wedding reception or one's college reunion, or one regrets not marrying his high school sweetheart or going to dental school instead of pursuing a once-promising musical career. But, for the most part, the person doing the regretting suffers the damage. Indeed, regret can be merely pro forma, without any feeling at all, as when we "send our regrets" that we will miss a party or a reception (which we had no desire or intention to attend in the first place). It is not as if we are being deceptive or hypocritical. Regret does not, as such, require much of a commitment or an emotional investment. There are, of course, serious regrets, for instance, not marrying the person of one's dreams or choosing the wrong career. But the seriousness of the regret has to do with the depth of the loss, not the amount of guilt. One can usually explain and rationalize one's regrets, and when one cannot do so, a more serious emotion may be called for.

By contrast, remorse indicates this more serious sense of responsibility. One feels or ought to feel remorse for committing a serious crime or for causing grievous injury to another person. We rightly insist on much greater punishment for those criminals who show no remorse. Remorse, unlike most cases of regret, can be a debilitating emotion, depending on the severity of the offense: Having ruined *someone else's* life, one now goes about ruining one's own. Remorse, unlike regret and embarrassment, is not only filled with fault and responsibility but, like guilt, is itself a form of self-punishment. Morally, it is a very burdensome emotion.

There is the interesting case of what philosopher Bernard Williams (1993) called "agent regret," which combines a kind of innocence with causal guilt. For example, while driving, one hits and hurts a child who dashes between two parked cars. On the one hand, one could not possibly have avoided the accident (assuming that one was not speeding, was paying attention, etc.). On the other hand, one tortures oneself with "what ifs": What if I had taken another route? What if I had started out five minutes later? What if I drove a smaller more sensible car? One can hardly be held responsible for the tragedy but one can certainly *feel* responsible and *take* responsibility. (I think that taking responsibility should be distinguished from *being* responsible, a distinction often ignored by philosophers. One can take responsibility even where one can be argued not to be responsible at all, for instance, for the bad behavior of an underling over whom one in fact had no control.) Thus we begin to get a glimpse of the convoluted twists and turns of responsibility that will go into the most complex and confusing emotion of the self-evaluative family, *guilt*. But to understand this, I think we have to examine guilt's relationship to shame.

Shame Versus Guilt

Shame and guilt are both morally weighty emotions, but there are differences. They are both social emotions, not just in the sense that they involve other people but in that they both have to do with our place in the social order. One difference between them has to do with the nature of that social order. A great deal hangs on this, and anthropologists have delineated very different societies on the basis of the prevalence of one or the other emotion. Shame is a straightforwardly social emotion. Shame involves the sense of seriously failing those around you, violating their norms, falling short of their expectations, letting them down. We might even call it "tribal," so long as that term is not mistakenly interpreted as "primitive." Ancient Athens, for instance, was clearly a shame society, as is modern-day Japan. In Japan, shame has become something of an art form. Failure, whether a military defeat, a business scandal, or an outrageous act of personal mis-behavior, requires a ritualized expression of shame. That expression cannot just be an empty gesture. It requires the actual emotion. Hypocritical expressions of shame, even if performed in accordance with the prescribed rituals, become doubly shameful, as does a refusal or failure to perform the rituals themselves.

In extreme cases, such as military defeat or marital infidelity, the expression of shame might require the taking of one's own life, the ultimate act of self-censure. But shame is also the other side of honor, and to be ashamed is to show not only that one has done something wrong but to demonstrate that one still has some sense of honor and a place in society. Thus Aristotle calls shame a "quasi-virtue," because to act wrongly and not be ashamed is much worse than to act wrongly and be ashamed because one has done wrong. So, too, an old Ethiopian proverb insists that "a man without shame is a man without honor." Shame can be a very concrete emotion, geared to a specific act and context, or it can be a very general recognition about oneself and one's "character," but to be ashamed is to mark oneself still a member of the society or community one has violated. Thus the paradox: Shame maintains honor in the face of dishonor. By contrast, to be shameless is to have no honor at all.

Shame, although it is derived from one's social relations, is for the most part self-imposed. Shame might be imposed on a person, by way of public criticism or through the rituals of shaming and shunning, but what is imposed is the need for the person to take upon him or herself the blame for having done something wrong. A shameful situation is a situation in which (within the culture) one is expected or will be forced to attribute fault to oneself. Shame, accordingly, is or can be a most effective tool for moral cultivation. Because it is self-imposed, it is by its very nature taken to heart. One can to a considerable extent shrug off other people's criticism and even their contempt, but one cannot shrug off one's own. Furthermore, shame is an extremely painful emotion. People will do a lot to avoid it. They will even, if necessary, do the right thing, whether it is giving to charity or saving Jews from the Nazis, just in order to avoid shame. "I couldn't look at myself in the mirror if I didn't do it" is a powerful self-directing stimulant for doing good. Thus it is a dangerous warning sign in our society that shame is on the wane, that so many people, especially young people, seem to have become "shameless." Some social workers point to a frightening generation that does not accept censure from others, rejects the standards of society, and is not willing to self-ascribe blame. But this, I would argue, is only part of the picture. Those same young people tend to be very tribal (the current word is "gang") and feel intense shame about letting each other down and violating their peculiar norms, that is, those within the group. So I would say that they are not shameless at all, but, to the contrary, their sense of shame is itself the danger to the larger society—and to themselves. The codes they think inviolable are in fact barbaric and a throwback to a thoroughly uncivilized era of human history.

Guilt, by contrast, is a social emotion in a quite different sense and it has very different consequences. Guilt has to do with violating authority and breaking the rules. Consequently, it involves fear of external blame and punishment much more than does shame, which is more often self-imposed and may be quite distinct from any sense of external punishment. Accordingly, reactions to guilt are much more unpredictable than expressions of shame. In shame, one typically tries to make amends and rejoin the community. Or one withdraws from the community that one has failed until there is an opportunity to reinstate oneself. In guilt, by contrast, a familiar reaction is denial. Another is lashing out in anger. Still another is the vehement rejection, even hatred, of whatever authority has set the standard. To summarize the whole anthropology of moral philosophy in a simple contrast, one might say that shame is to ethics—that is, the customs and mores of a society—as guilt is to morality—that is, the basic rules of society. So a man who breaks the law is guilty (whether he is legally found to be so or not), but a man who drags his family into a scandal and into the gossip papers (whether or not he broke any law) should be ashamed. Guilt involves violating a higher authority (God, the law). Shame is betraying one's fellows and thereby showing oneself to have a flawed character.

A particularly interesting observer of guilt is Albert Camus, who in his three novels, *The Stranger*, *The Plague*, and *The Fall*, pursues the idea that we are all guilty (his version of original sin), but we just do not realize it. Thus in *The Stranger* he allows us to trace the development of the consciousness of his (anti)hero Meursault, as he first realizes how much the people around him loathe him as a murderer and yet refuses to give up his innocence. Only at the very end does he accept the guilt for his crime and hopes his execution will be greeted with "howls of execration" by the crowd. (In the description of the shooting, Camus artfully draws us a picture of an act without an actor, a protagonist who is as much a victim of the sun and his own taut nerves as the perpetrator of a terrible crime.) In *The Fall*, Camus depicts an "innocent" attorney (yes, Camus is well aware of the irony and plays on it throughout the book) who learns that his innocence is a fraud and becomes a "judge-penitent," a man consumed by guilt who then defines himself and his self-righteousness in terms of it. The idea that we are all guilty is an idea that haunted Camus in his own life as well.

He seems to accept his character Tarrou's argument (in *The Plague*) that we are all complicit in crimes against humanity, for instance that we are all murderers insofar as we refuse to reject the death penalty. Following the Bible, Freud, and Kafka, Camus sees that there is a lot more to guilt than the mere fact of having personally done something wrong.

This is not the place to get into the convoluted question of neurotic guilt, which may begin as an ordinary feeling of guilt but requires no initial guilty act. At family gatherings, it is common to get such feelings, quite apart from any peculiar intricacies of family history. Thus the essential question is the origin of such feelings, whether in repressed childhood memories (as in Freud) or collective historical or archetypal guilt (as in post-war Germany, for example, or in Jung's psychology). The allegorical account of "original sin" is a picturesque but implausible and arguably unjust explanation of seemingly unwarranted guilt. In our current moral world view, it is not fair that "the sins of the fathers be visited on the sons." More persuasive, I think, are the philosophical accounts, for example, Jean-Paul Sartre's conception of "bad faith," which we cannot by our very natures escape. As both free (we have "transcendence") and locked into our circumstances (our "facticity") we cannot evade our responsibility, not only for what we do but for what we are, what we become, and what the world is as well. It is a harsh portrait of human nature, but it displays one of many ways in which it is human consciousness itself that is deeply and irremediably flawed. And this sense of an irremediable flaw is what, philosophically, provides the foundation for that pervasive sense of guilt to which we are prone, no matter how righteously we live our lives. Indeed, the cruel irony is that the more self-consciously and righteously we live our lives, whether under the auspices of some religion or simply in the clarity of an enlightened morality, the more guilt we are prone to feel. There are always, for people who are thoughtful, good deeds not undertaken and much else that is left to do.

Defining Evil

At this point, let me digress to take a stab at defining the problematic notion of *evil*. Evil is not usually thought of as an emotion-related term, but I think that it is. The problem is that evil is too often defined in a consequentialist way; that is, evil is whatever causes catastrophic harm. That is much too broad. Philosophers and theologians who have argued about evil since Saint Augustine have distinguished between natural disasters (whether or not these can be attributed to God or gods or the fates) and human-caused disasters in which some (secular) blame can be attributed. It is only the latter, I think, that deserves to be called evil. The tsunami that took the lives of hundreds of thousands of people Christmas of 2004 was terrible and tragic but not evil. Hitler was evil. Pol Pot and the Khymer Rouge were evil. But it was neither the catastrophes that they caused nor their evil intentions alone that made them evil. I would argue that it was also their lack of guilt and remorse for what they had done.

This is, if you like, the "positive" aspect of guilt and remorse, that it partially redeems or at least lessens the blame if one acknowledges his or her admittedly evil actions. A criminal who confesses and feels remorse is not so evil as one who continues to insist that he did nothing wrong. Hitler and Pol Pot (so far as we know) expressed no guilt or remorse about what they had done. On a more domestic and civilized level, a CEO who has to "downsize" a workforce of tens of thousands might well be pressured to do so by "market forces," but his or her character will be measured by the amount of anguish and the sleepless nights he or she suffers. "Chainsaw" Al Dunlap apparently fired thousands of workers at Sunbeam with no pangs of conscience. (There were cheers of delight when he himself was fired in turn.) Robert Allen, the CEO of AT&T during its "restructuring" and massive layoffs, called the firings "the worst thing he had ever been through in his life," and we think better of him because of that. There is a special problem with those who are blinded by ideological or religious fanaticism, and another with those who are in total denial or self-deception. But without going into these special problems I would say that the lack of guilt and remorse, not just bad intentions or disastrous consequences, is necessary to understand the nature of evil in the world. As Bill Maher has recently said, evil doesn't require scheming and plotting about how to hurt people or make their lives more miserable. It may involve no more than self-interested oblivion, an unwillingness to acknowledge or an indifference to the harmful or even disastrous consequences of one's actions. I would add that it is only afterward, when one has either acknowledged or refused to acknowledge one's guilt in the matter, that the evil can be fully defined.

Pride

From evil, I turn to pride. Some people would find this perfectly appropriate, insofar as the self-interested oblivion and indifference that sometimes brings about evil might seem to be an apt description of certain forms of pride. But pride need not involve either self-interest or oblivion, nor is all pride that "false pride" that is so often responsible for foolish and sometimes malicious behavior. To put the matter simply, pride is just another self-evaluating emotion, but the evaluation is in this case praise, not blame. Right away we need to appreciate the historical changes in the status of this emotion, however, which in Aristotle's Athens was a kind of overarching virtue (*megalopsyche*, or knowing that one is excellent). In medieval Christianity, by contrast, pride was the worst of the vices. Today, by contrast again, it forms the core of such conscientious self-help strategies as "black pride" and "gay pride." Pride seems to have come full circle, from capstone of the virtues to the most damnable of sins to the boot straps by which one can pull up one's dignity.

Of course, there is overweening pride, false pride, and exaggerated pride. One can feel proud of oneself way beyond one's merits. One can feel proud of oneself while ignorant of relevant facts (the self-congratulatory winner struts around the track, not yet realizing that he has been disqualified from the race.) One can even feel (falsely) proud of oneself without any justification at all. (One wonders about all of those out-of-shape fans, who don't even go to the games or support the team, who nevertheless feel so proud of themselves because their local sports team has won a victory.) Like all emotions (and like all virtues) pride can go wrong. But most of us now reject the humiliating medieval mentality that would make any thinking well of oneself a sin even as we remind ourselves of the Greek corrective to overweening pride, the concept of *hubris*. Even for the Greek *megalopsychos*, there are limits to pride.

Pride is often opposed to humility, notably in the Christian tradition but also by that self-styled "pagan" philosopher, David Hume. Such contrasts tend to be polemical. The Christian celebration of humility dictated a wholesale condemnation of pride, while Hume's praise of pride entailed the condemnation of that "monkish virtue," humility. Humility, however, is not the same as humiliation, although humility is a lot like guilt, and the two are often linked in religious teachings. Both involve a cosmic sense of one's own insignificance whereas pride is a celebration, however limited, of one's significance. But I think a more insightful opposition is between pride and shame, both self-evaluating but differing in one obvious dimension, pride's praise versus shame's blame. But this obvious difference hides a not-so obvious kinship between the two. Not only are they both emotions of self-appraisal (as, one might argue, is humility), but they are both social, or what I call "tribal," emotions. The evaluations, although self-ascribed, are done so on the basis of one's status in the community. Thus those out-of-shape fans are oddly entitled to feel proud of their team insofar as they are part of the community, even if they have contributed nothing to the team's victory. (Those same fans, however, will probably be loathe to share the blame and the shame when their team loses.) And we can feel proud or ashamed of our parents or our children or even our congressmen insofar as we identify with them. Emotions of self-evaluation are social and interpersonal emotions, and they have a central place in our conceptions of ethics and culture.

8

Nasty Emotions: Envy, Spite, Jealousy, Resentment, and Vengeance

And finally, from the social emotions to the antisocial emotions. In the last of these chapters on various emotions, I want to discuss several rather nasty and double-edged emotions, double-edged in that they tend to be remarkably self-destructive even as they are aimed at bringing down other people. Envy is an excellent example.

Envy

Envy is rightly listed as one of the "seven deadly sins," although one might better view it as a spectacularly bad emotional strategy rather than as anything like an offense against God. Envy is well-known in its effects: It makes the subject ill, represented in myth and pop psychology with a twisted, hideously ugly face and by the noxious color green (or more accurately, a sickly chartreuse). But the immediate focus of envy isn't oneself, who does in fact suffer, but another person or other people, who may not know that they are envied at all, and some particular feature, possession, or benefit. One envies another person for some advantage, for instance, good looks, a nice house, a lottery win. At the heart of envy is an invidious comparison ("he has it, I don't"). But the key to envy is not just wanting what someone else has. It is wanting it without merit, without any intelligible claim of a right to it, without any real hope of getting it. That is why people behave and show off in such a way that they will be envied, provoking envy in others in order to enhance their own self-esteem. But the person who envies, by contrast, experiences a radical diminution of self-esteem, and that is why it is essentially a self-defeating emotion.

The target of envy is rarely a whole person or *everything* about a person. Martin Amis presents a particularly nasty case of such all-encompassing envy in his dark novel, *The Information*, but such cases provide a much more promising plot device in literature than a way of understanding envy in everyday life. The typical object of envy is some aspect of the person, usually something that is not transferable, such as their birthright, their looks, their talents, their abilities, their skills. That is part of what makes envy hopeless. When envy simply involves things—for example, if I envy my neighbor's Jaguar automobile—it is not impossible that I could have one of those myself. I am just not willing to spend the money or take out the loan to get one. That is a choice that I make and is not well characterized as envy. As the object becomes more difficult to obtain, however, especially if it is one of a kind, envy becomes more appropriate. I might envy my friend's skill at languages, his ability to learn French in a few weeks and Hungarian in just a little longer, but the sad truth is that I am not good at learning languages, so it is not just his skill but his talent that I envy. I could put in the time to learn a language, perhaps, but that is not the point of my envy. What I envy is what I cannot have, namely, the ease with which my friend can learn a language. I might also envy someone's deserved honors; for instance, I can envy Russell Crowe his Academy Award even though I am not an actor and have never displayed any acting talent at all. (I think that much of current American celebrity culture can be explained in terms of finding or creating people to envy who have no special skills or merits at all.) The key to envy is that *I do not have anything like a right or a claim to the possession or talent or honor in question.* Nor is there much of anything I can do about it. That is why envy is such a self-defeating strategy. It is desperately wanting what one knows full well one does not in any sense deserve and cannot have.

Envy has not always been treated with such disdain. About forty years ago, a conservative economic psychologist named Helmut Schoeck suggested what has become something of a mantra for television advertisers, that envy is good for consumerism. "Keeping up with the Joneses" was for many years the encapsulated theory that envy would stimulate the economy, making sure that no one was satisfied with what they had but lived in constant aspiration, if not anxiety, that their excesses may nevertheless have been less than their neighbor's. Paul Krugman writes of the laughable situation of the very rich in America today who keep investing in bigger and bigger houses even as the standard among them for what counts as a "big house" keeps escalating. In other words, there is no keeping up with the Joneses. This is not the place to discuss the economic and ecological costs of such thinking, but it may be worth a moment to consider the emotional logic here. The assumption is that people deserve to have what the Joneses have because they also work hard, occupy a similarly privileged place in society, and have the money. But it is envy insofar as the target (measured in perceived status) keeps receding and thus becomes unattainable.

Jerome Neu (2004) distinguishes between the competitive aspirations championed by Schoeck and what he calls "malicious envy," an emotion that is not merely competitive but pathetically so. The addition of the "malicious" also suggests that the envy is not just covetous but involves a malevolent attitude toward the envied person. I am not so sure whether this is a necessary ingredient in envy, but it is certainly a common one. Thus envy's double edge: It is not just competitive without hope or merit and so damaging to oneself. It can also be malicious and dangerous to the other person as well, or in this case, damaging to the general social system in which it plays a role.

Envy was not considered a sin not because of its malicious tendencies, since it is usually ineffective, but because it tends to demean one's self, whether or not it also corrupts the soul. Like shame and guilt, it involves a negative self-evaluation, but unlike those emotions, it lacks the dignity of a moral sense. One rarely envies another person's virtue. (The presumption, perhaps, is that anyone can cultivate such virtue for oneself.) One is much more likely to envy another's talents, his or her possessions, looks, or personality. But what is really damaging in envy is its helplessness. This is where Schoeck's analysis is mistaken. Insofar as one has the confidence and the ability to compete for the object in question, it is not envy. And insofar as one feels that he or she has a right to the object, again, it is not envy but jealousy (which we will discuss in a moment). What makes envy so damaging to the self is the perpetual frustration that comes with wanting what another has, having no sense of entitlement to it, and being able to do nothing to get it. That makes one ignore or discount what one already has, and so we are subjected to the pathetic sight of people blessed by good fortune who nevertheless lead bitter lives because of what they do *not* have. As the Talmud wisely counsels, "the rich man is one who is satisfied with what he has."

Spite

If envy is self-destructive, it is not intentionally so, even if self-destruction is the inevitable and usually unwitting result of envy. That is not the case with a variant of envy, namely spite. The phrase, "cutting off one's nose to spite one's face" captures the straightforward, intentionally self-destructive nature of spite, but spite, one could argue, is not just self-destructive, as that old adage would suggest. It is also willfully destructive of the object or feature envied and often of the other person as well. Envy turns to spite when the frustration has become so intolerable that the only solution seems to be "if I can't have it, no one will!" (whereas the path to wisdom is "just let it go"). Thus spite is malicious envy with an extra wicked twist. It is not only aimed at the person envied but at the object of envy itself. Of course, when the object of envy is inseparably attached to the person envied (a person's good looks, for example, or a talent that he or she has), the destruction of the object usually involves serious damage to the person as well. So whereas envy is self-destructive, spite almost always has victims. As one of the most vicious (hardly just "negative") emotions, spite is, I think, too often ignored. Hatred may fuel some of the most violent conflicts in the world today, but hate is comparatively straightforward. Spite is twisted and in that sense even more dangerous.

The aim of hatred is to destroy or at the very least humiliate the other. Spite and its emotional kin, by contrast, have a much more convoluted logic in which self-destruction is on a par with the damage to others. Suicide bombers, though moved by hate, are more immediately motivated by spite. (It is a mistake, I think, to regard the self-sacrifice as a merely tactical device.) The viciousness of spite should never be underestimated. Murder-suicides, the destruction of whole cities, even empires, are among the horrific products of spite. One reflects in horror at the scene of Medea murdering her beloved children to spite her philandering husband Jason. One imagines (with a lot of help from Eugene Delacroix) the tyrant Sardanapulus lying on his couch as his city burns around him. Tolstoy describes in ghastly detail the Russians' burning of Moscow to prevent it from falling into the hands of Napoleon and his invaders. Spite may be a self-destructive emotion, but as a matter of strategy it often carries with it a great deal of collateral damage. And the very nature of spite seems to be that it remains so focused on its object and is so self-aggrieved that it leaves no room for any moral qualms. Shame and guilt may follow (in those cases where the spiteful person survives), but it seems to be wholly absent from the emotion itself. That is what makes it so dangerous, I would suggest, more so than even raw hatred, which, because it involves moral considerations (for example, seeing the other as evil), may be open to moral negotiation and reevaluation in a way that spite is not.

Envy is self-destructive, spite is doubly destructive, and the one tends to turn into the other. But that is not the whole of it. Envy, like most nasty emotions, promotes an uncanny ability to rationalize. Thus rather than give into frustration and the humiliation of feeling unworthy, envy imagines that it does have a right and thus has been wrongfully deprived. Thus it turns into resentment. Or, envy deludes itself into the idea that the object in question is *already* in some sense one's own, and the emotion becomes jealousy. Whereas envy involves the full recognition that one has no right or claim to the object envied, resentment and jealousy do claim such a right. Jealousy differs from envy in that the jealous person feels a sense of prior *entitlement* and thus fears an undeserved loss rather than desires an unmerited gain. Indeed, the most familiar and dramatic example of jealousy is the man or woman who fears losing his or her spouse or lover. The jealous spouse does indeed have a claim, and believes this claim has the potential to be violated. I want to say more about jealousy, as its intentionality is intriguingly complex compared to most other emotions. But for the moment, let me just say that jealousy differs from envy in the fact that it claims a right—and thus is in a position to do something about its situation, to fight back—that envy lacks.

Jealousy

Jealousy is about fear of loss, but it certainly is much more than that. For one thing, we need to ask, "loss of what?" Jealousy is not grief. It is not loss as such. As I said, it is a *fear of* loss, not yet loss itself. As in envy, one could in principle be jealous of almost anything (possessions, talents, skills, personal features), but as opposed to envy, jealousy requires some sort of legitimate claim. A jealous person must have some right (or believe that he does) to the thing in question. Furthermore, the object of jealousy is usually something important, even if its importance becomes evident only with the possibility of losing it. Thus a small child becomes jealous when another child takes his discarded toy. But it is already *his* toy, as he will loudly protest to the trespasser. What is often at stake in jealousy (as in envy) is not the thing itself but rather the claim. Thus the familiar phenomenon of jealousy over something unwanted just in order to protect one's turf or status.

The most dramatic case of jealousy, of course, involves another person, or rather two other people, and a romantic situation. The premise of a romantic setting, at least for most people, is a kind of exclusivity (which may or may not be an aspect of sexual intimacy). We are not usually jealous of friends if, for example, they start to hang around with other friends. But an erotic relationship spurs expectations and these expectations are often reciprocal (which is not to say that they are either symmetrical or in agreement). (Where the object of jealousy is an inanimate object, the question of reciprocity does not arise.) But here the accounts differ wildly. Traditionally, this reciprocity has everything to do with sex and fidelity. A husband might utterly ignore and neglect his wife but nevertheless continue to assume her sexual fidelity to him. A wife might utterly abuse and humiliate her husband but nevertheless continue to assume his sexual fidelity to her. But whatever one thinks of these ugly scenarios, they point to the conclusion that sexual fidelity has some special status in sex-based relationships, although whether it is the sex or the fidelity that is the focus is an important issue that is often the source of considerable controversy.

The question "what counts as sex?" was much in the news during the national embarrassment of Bill Clinton's impeachment for a White House sex scandal, though one sometimes suspects that the scandal was nothing but a combination of political and prurient interests. It has long been a tenet of teenage sex play (intensified by recent "abstinence" campaigns) that anything short of "going all the way" doesn't really count as "sex." What sounds like lawyerly nit-picking in a seasoned politician is in fact a well-established distinction in sex lore. So is jealousy limited to cases of sexual intercourse? The answer is "obviously not." But is it really sex, then, that is at stake? Or is it fidelity? Couples who agree to an "open" sexual arrangement would insist that they do not get jealous, even if this is more often a matter of policy than practice. Thus it can be argued that it is the violation of trust that is involved in sexual jealousy, not the sex as such. (There are complicating circumstances, such as the violation of social taboos or the transmission of a sexual disease, but these provoke anger and indignation, not jealousy.)

In some societies, extramarital sexual relations are not only allowed but encouraged, but other activities, say drinking coffee or even just talking with someone other than one's spouse, are grounds for divorce—or worse. In our own society, the scenario where a husband or wife or boyfriend or girlfriend gets jealous just because the other is just talking to someone else is familiar enough, even without any real fear that this might lead to sexual activity. This suggests that what jealousy is really about is *intimacy* or *attention*, and not sexual fidelity (although sex, to be sure, usually prompts a serious shift of attention). Also, jealousy tends to have its eye nervously on the future, not the past, so while a husband might be jealous that his wife paid rapt attention to another (younger, more handsome) man, it is not that incident that he is jealous *about*, even if it is true that the incident provoked the jealousy. What he is jealous about is the possibility of further intimacy and a resultant loss of intimacy on his part. (This "zero-sum" assumption in jealousy is itself a fascinating issue, and usually turns to a large extent on the assumption of exclusivity. Indeed, if one believes that a person can only be romantically intimate with one other person then the zero-sum assumption becomes a self-confirming truth of sorts.)

Jealousy has a complex structure in that it is not just about two people but necessarily three. Thus the "romantic triangle" is a set part of dramatic lore. In fact, it has been argued to be more than that too, for jealousy often involves one's sense of pride or, in some societies, honor, and this puts it more in league with shame than with simple, pathetic, but often silent envy. In other words, there is also a fourth party to jealousy, and that is the anonymous "other" of society, public opinion. For that reason, too, jealousy is often desperate and even deadly, provoking us to do what we otherwise would never think of doing. It is not just a matter of loss but of humiliation, loss of honor. Just think of poor Othello. If we were to conceive of jealousy just as the fear of loss, his desperation is not easily understandable. But if it also involves ridicule or the violation of his honor, rendered all the more pronounced by his minority status, then we can readily understand how his violence might be not only a powerful personal urge but socially sanctioned and encouraged by the entire society. We can also understand how resistance to jealousy might be not just a matter of personal pride but a part of a social campaign (although it was surely not this for Othello). Insofar as jealousy involves a claim of entitlement and absolute right it can be not only dangerous but unjust as well. Thus jealousy turns into murderous spite (sanctioned by law in many societies, including Texas). Indeed, the idea that Othello did wrong in murdering Desdemona has only to do with the fact that he was wrong about her alleged infidelity, not because his jealousy (if valid) would not have warranted killing her.

What rights one person has to the attention, the intimacy, indeed, the body of another is a very real question. There is also the question of whether jealousy is a "natural" emotion or whether it is the product of certain sorts of social schemes and concepts. If the latter, one could argue, it is malleable and therefore negotiable in terms of those schemes and concepts. It has been argued by my colleague David Buss (2000) that jealousy is an emotion that we have inherited from our ancestors, favored by evolution for its survival advantages. The advantage has to do with the slow period of maturation of human infants (as opposed, for example, to fawns and baby antelopes, which are capable of galloping after their mothers within hours after falling from the womb). That means that our sexual inclinations should be such that in addition to being naturally impelled to the original act of mating we must be motivated to stay together for a substantial period of time, through nine months of pregnancy and at least a couple of years of child-rearing. The idea is one that has been used to explain several aspects of human sexual behavior, most importantly our tendency to pair-bond (like several species of water birds) and stay together for long periods of time. Jealousy is a highly evolved emotion that protects that bonding. But here, according to Buss, gender makes a dramatic difference. Men tend to jealously guard the sexual behavior of their spouses, wary that any other male will impregnate her (and the cuckolded male will nevertheless have to do the work to raise the off-spring). Women, by contrast, tend to be more concerned with the attentiveness of their male companions. (This difference tends to correspond, according to several older sociobiologists, to the supposedly natural promiscuity of males and the supposedly faithful nature of females.) It should be evident that such theories are and should be politically controversial, and the obvious rejoinder is that whether or not we are so inclined by nature, we have sufficient reflective and critical capacities and enough "free will" to act contrary to our natures, or at least to these specific demands of our natures. Naturally promiscuous or not, males are supposed to control their impulses. Naturally parental or not, we are rightly expected to take care of our children. But the argument has other implications that might be worth our brief consideration here.

The first is the question: To what extent we can control our emotions, especially if we inherit them from our ancestors and have no choice in the matter (or, at least, we have no choice in whether or not we are so inclined)? But as with promiscuity, biology is not destiny, and, moreover, there are good arguments that jealousy is not inherited but cultivated. In which case culture might be changed. For my generation, I should add, this was not just an abstract argument. In the 1960s, we actually did try to eliminate jealousy as a common and accepted emotion, both with regard to sexuality and material possessions. History, it must be admitted, proved us naive. Both sexual jealousy and material avarice are back with a vengeance. But whether this shows that jealousy is inherited and a matter of biology and not culture is another matter. It might have to do with deep structures in our culture or in the human condition that are nevertheless learned and shared rather than simply inherited.

The second and wider concern has to do with the problematic role of emotions in evolutionary accounts of human nature. To put the matter very briefly, just because something has become a common human trait does not mean that it has been "selected for," in the familiar Darwinian language of natural selection. To be sure, we have inherited the *capacities* to have the emotions we have (and no doubt many others besides), but whether natural selection is so specific that it selected jealousy rather than some more general sense of defensiveness, possessiveness, or territoriality is rather dubious. So, again, we find ourselves facing the question of "basic emotions," whether some emotions are "hard-wired" into the human psyche, and, again, I think we will do ourselves a big favor if we say, at least from the perspective of ethics, that it doesn't really matter. It is enough to explore what role these emotions have in our lives and what we can and should do about them, whatever their ultimate source.

From the perspective of ethics, accordingly, our questions about jealousy must be focused not on the origin or biological nature of jealousy but on its intentional structures and what it means in our society. Jealousy includes a claim of entitlement. One has a right to that which he or she claims. The hard question is, what is that? In a marriage or a romantic relationship, is it really sexual fidelity, as emblematic and central as that has become to both our sense of romantic drama and our sexual obsessiveness? Is there, as many people would insist, some sort of tacit "contract" that comes into existence when two people have sex together or, at least, have sex together with some regularity? Or are the legitimate expectations we have of one another not focused on the realm of the physical at all but extended to such attitudes as respect, concern, and intimacy? All but the most callous and perhaps self-deceiving libertine will surely acknowledge that sexual intimacy quite properly arouses interpersonal expectations of this sort, and so the question of jealousy becomes a much more general question of what we owe to each other, especially in these extremely vulnerable interpersonal relationships. And that becomes one of the central questions of ethics, not biology.

Resentment

Resentment is a particularly strategic and intriguing emotion, which is why one of the great philosophers of modern times, Friedrich Nietzsche, wrote so much about it. He diagnosed resentment as the motive for the whole of the Judeo-Christian tradition and its sense of morality in particular. The argument is straightforward if extremely contested. The creation of a morality that favored the weak and the oppressed and the invention of an almighty God were the expressions of the resentment of the weak. It was, he says, an ingenious emotional strategy. To begin with, it made the weak feel good about themselves. And they felt protected. Their resentment allowed them to rationalize their impotent and impoverished position in ancient society. If wealth and power were evil, so they were taught, then better not to have them. Besides, "the [weak] shall inherit the earth." So where envy sees itself in an inferior position, not having what it really wants and unable to get it, resentment rationalizes this inferiority as unjust *oppression*, and in so doing grants to itself a kind of moral superiority. Thus the righteousness of those who preach humility. (This should strike us as a dubious paradox.) But it permeates modern life, creating a "victim mentality" even among the very powerful (who are never, in their own view, powerful enough). It is an energizing motive, inspiring both cleverness and ingenious subversion. It rarely presents itself as it is, but always in the guise of righteousness. That gives it not only higher status but makes it much more persuasive as well.

But why, then, is resentment a self-destructive strategy? Because it is riddled with self-deception and hypocrisy, Nietzsche says, and his explanation seems plausible. In resentment we realize that we really want what we dismiss as "evil" (and the scandalous history of hypocritical religious zealots is good evidence for this), and we are (at least on occasion) smart enough to see through our own conceits. But also, the presupposition of resentment is the same as the presupposition of envy, and that is one's impotence in the face of the world. Resentment rationalizes its position, but it remains stuck there. An oppressed people that rises up and fights back is heroic, win or lose, but resentment just sits and sulks, all the while congratulating itself on its righteousness and abstemiousness, interpreted as virtue. But the result is that resentment gets us nowhere and motivates no effective action. Furthermore, dialectical movement between these various nasty emotions is evasive and insidious, furthered by self-serving if also self-deceptive strategies. In *Othello*, Iago begins with envy, turns to resentment, and, when that fails, devours himself and everyone else in spite. The aggrieved reflections of his emotions explain their unusual intelligence, even if the thinking that goes into them is evil, unwise, self-destructive, and ultimately disastrous for everyone involved. Othello, by contrast, is destroyed by his own jealousy. (There is no question in our minds of his conjugal right to Desdemona or whether or not she has been faithful to him.) But jealousy displays its own peculiar intelligence, as Othello seizes on one piece of bad evidence after another to confirm the suspicions that he would rather not have but his insecurity demands. But so, especially, does resentment, which uses such evidence to wage its own bitter war against perhaps imaginary oppressors, and thus shows itself to be among the most resourceful of our emotions.

Vengeance

Several decades ago, Arthur Lelyveld wrote:

> There is no denying the aesthetic satisfaction, the sense of poetic justice, that pleasures us when evil-doers get the comeuppance they deserve. The impulse to punish is primarily an impulse to even the score. . . . That satisfaction is heightened when it becomes possible to measure out punishment in exact proportion to the size and shape of the wrong that has been done, . . . *mida k'neged mida*—measure for measure, *lex talionis*.

There is a powerful truth here that is too often overlooked or flatly denied. Vengeance is not only a powerful motive. I would argue that it is also an essential ingredient in our sense of justice, despite the fact that people often contrast the two (sometimes at the instructions of their lawyers). (I should note here again that "vengeance" is not quite the name of an emotion as such, although it clearly designates what we would all recognize as an emotional phenomenon. The archaic word "wrath," however, captures the name of the related emotion quite accurately.)

Vengeance is the original passion for justice. The word "justice" in the Old Testament virtually always refers to revenge. In Kant and Hegel, the word *"gerechtigkeit"* refers to retribution, and throughout most of history the concept of justice has been concerned with the punishment of crimes and the balancing of wrongs. "Getting even" is and has always been one of the most basic metaphors of our moral vocabulary, and the frightening emotion of righteous, wrathful anger has been the emotional basis for justice just as much as benign compassion. Aesthetic satisfaction indicates the depth of the passion, the need for "proportion," and the intelligence involved in this supposedly most irrational and uncontrollable emotion. Our response to the many revenge novels and films is an indication of not only our deep-seated sense of vengeance but also the concept of fairness that is built therein.

This is not to say, of course, that the motive of revenge is therefore legitimate or the action of revenge always justified. Sometimes vengeance is wholly called for, even obligatory, and revenge is both legitimate and justified. More often it is not, notably when one is mistaken about the offender or the offense. But to seek vengeance for a grievous wrong, to revenge oneself against evil—that seems to lie at the very foundation of our sense of justice, indeed, of our very sense of ourselves. Even sentimentalist Adam Smith (1759) writes, in his *Theory of the Moral Sentiments*, "The violation of justice is injury . . . it is, therefore, the proper object of resentment, and of punishment, which is the natural consequence of resentment." We are not mere observers of the moral life, and the desire for vengeance seems to be an integral aspect of our recognition of evil. But it also contains—or can be cultivated to contain—the elements of its own control, a sense of its limits, a sense of balance. Thus the Old Testament instructs us that revenge should be *limited to* "an eye for an eye, a tooth for a tooth, hand for hand, foot for foot, burning for burning, wound for wound, stripe for stripe" (Exod. 21:24–5). The New Testament demands even more restraint, the abstention from revenge oneself and the patience to entrust it to God. Both the Old and New Testaments (more the latter than the former) also encourage "forgiveness," but there can be no forgiveness if there is not first the desire (and the warrant) for revenge.

Vengeance is not just punishment. It is a matter of emotion, often delayed, protracted, or frustrated emotion, and it is always *for* some offense. Vengeance always has its reasons (though, to be sure, these can be mistaken, irrelevant, out of proportion, or otherwise bad reasons). Vengeance is no longer a matter of obligation and it certainly can't claim to be rational as such, but neither is it opposed to a sense of obligation (for example, in matters of family honor) or rationality (insofar as rationality is to be found in every emotion, even this one). Vengeance is the emotion of "getting even," putting the world back in balance, and this simple phrase already embodies a whole philosophy of justice, even if (as yet) unarticulated and unjustified.

R. S. Gerstein writes: "Vengefulness is an emotional response to injuries done to us by others: we feel a desire to injure those who have injured us. Retributivism is not the idea that it is good to have and satisfy this emotion. It is rather the view that there are good arguments for including the kernel of rationality to be found in the passion for vengeance as a part of any just system of laws" (1985). But I want to suggest that vengeance just is that sense of measure or balance that Kant and many other philosophers attribute to reason alone. But, of course, it is ultimately the same old dichotomy that is most at fault here, the supposed antagonism between reason on the one side and passions on the other. Where would our reasoning about punishment begin if not for our emotional sense of the need for retaliation and retribution? And what would our emotion be if it was not already informed and cultivated by a keen sense of its object and its target, as well as the mores and morals of the community in which the offense in question is deserving of revenge?

Perhaps nowhere is the denial of what is most human about us (that is, our emotions) more evident than in the various debates and concerns that surround the problems of punishment in criminal justice. The ongoing dispute between the "utilitarians" (who believe in a "deterrence" theory of punishment) and the "retributivists" (who believe that punishment is necessary in order to satisfy the demands of justice) not only neglects but explicitly dismisses any mention of that passion which alone would seem to give some fuel to the notion of punishment, namely the emotion of vengeance. This is not to say that punishment should serve *only* to revenge, but it is to say that punishment is in part the satisfaction of the need for vengeance and punishment makes no sense without this. Several years ago, Susan Jacoby (1983) argued that our denial of the desire for vengeance is analogous to the Victorian denial of sexual desire, and we are paying a similar psychological price for it, in all sorts of displaced destructive behaviors and anxieties. As with our hunger for sex, we do not succeed very well in suppressing our thirst for revenge.

Maybe the point was overstated in the majority opinion in United States Supreme Court decision *Gregg v. Georgia* (1976):

> The instinct for retribution is part of the nature of man, and channeling that instinct in the administration of criminal justice serves an important purpose in promoting the stability of a society governed by law. When people begin to believe that organized society is unwilling or unable to impose upon criminal offenders the punishment they "deserve," then there are sown the seeds of anarchy—of self-help, vigilante justice, and lynch law.

But at least the emotion of vengeance was taken seriously and not merely sacrificed to the dispassionate authority of the law. But in the end, it is perhaps not just a question of whether revenge is rational or not, but whether it is an undeniable aspect of the way we react to the world, not as an instinct but as such a basic part of our worldview and our moral sense of ourselves that it is, in that sense, unavoidable.

Every act of revenge results, however, in a new offense to be righted. And when the act is perpetrated not against the same person who did the offense but against another who is part of the same family, tribe, or social group (the logic of "vendetta"), the possibilities for escalation are endless. Accordingly, the limitation of revenge through institutionalization is necessary. But it does not follow that vengeance itself is illegitimate or without measure or of no importance in considerations of punishment. To the dangers of vengeance unlimited it must be added that if punishment no longer satisfies vengeance, if it ignores not only the rights but the emotional needs of the victims of crime, then punishment no longer serves its primary purpose, *even if* it were to succeed in rehabilitating the criminal and deterring other crime (which it evidently, in general, does not). The restriction of vengeance by law is entirely understandable, but the wholesale denial of vengeance as a legitimate motive may be as much of a psychological disaster as its unlimited exercise is dangerous.

Just to be clear, I have not tried to defend vengeance as such, but my claim is that vengeance deserves a central place in any theory of justice and the emotions. As do all of the nasty emotions. They play a central role in our thinking about ourselves and our relationships with other people, perhaps regrettably, but that is who we are. But all of the emotions we have discussed play a substantial role in our lives and our conceptions of ourselves, and between them they provide a pretty good portrait of what it means to be human.

PART TWO

Toward a General Theory

Myths about Emotions

✤

9

What an Emotion Theory Should Do

Because the emotions are such an essential part of our lives and accompany, cause, or define the most memorable and traumatic moments of our existence, we discuss them, think about them, speculate about their nature and origins, argue about their causes, their warrant, their justification, and their appropriateness. In other words, we theorize about them. Whether the theory is as simple and straightforward as assuming that people tend to get angry when they have just been humiliated in public, as speculative as wondering whether depression might be anger turned inward, or as esoteric as mapping that part of the brain that is "responsible" for shame, we need theories because we want to understand why people (why *we*) have the emotions we do, why people get angry, feel fear, fall in love, get embarrassed or ashamed, become jealous or depressed or ecstatic.

As social beings, we urgently need to understand other people and their motives. (Even nonsocial creatures need to have some sense when a predator or a rival has malevolent intentions.) A dog looks up quizzically and a bit desperately when it has been lightly kicked or stepped on, wondering "why?" and quickly determining whether this was an intentional act, requiring one kind of response, or an accident, allowing the dog to relax again. Of course, a dog doesn't speculate, much less theorize, but even a dog has the need to understand the emotions that are directed toward it, whether they are aggressive and endangering or tender and encouraging. The need to understand and predict others' behavior usually means that we need to understand what motivates them, and this in turn usually requires recognizing and to some extent understanding their emotions.

In addition to the need to understand other's emotions, we have the ability to articulate and understand our own emotions. This, it turns out, is often more difficult than understanding the surface meanings of the emotions other people direct toward us. But there are many levels of self-understanding as well as many degrees of sophistication in our theories about emotion. We can understand ourselves in the rather minimal (but still remarkable) sense of being able to notice and name our emotions, and we can understand our general patterns of behavior that may not be at all evident in any single emotional response. We can also understand our emotions in depth, that is, understand why we should feel such-and-such in a way that is far more profound than simply identifying our emotions as they occur. It is commonly thought that we are in more or less immediate touch with our own emotions, except in cases of quasi-pathological denial and self-deception. But the truth rather seems to be as Nietzsche pointed out, that we become aware of our own states of mind only with some difficulty, and understand ourselves profoundly only in relatively rare circumstances. What we think we *ought* to feel and what we would *like* and *expect* to feel are powerful determinants of what we think we *do* feel. Theories of emotion, accordingly, meet their most personal challenges not in the explanation of other people's and patients' peculiar behavior but in understanding our own emotions. The ability to reflect is not only a remarkable ability: It also presents us with a constant and formidable task, to be in touch with our feelings, to be true to ourselves.

Explanations of emotion are almost always, if implicitly, theories of emotion. The very specific and situational question, "Why did you do that?" might be thought of as merely specific to the occasion, a quest for an explanation of *this* particular bit of behavior. But explanations work only insofar as they can to some extent be generalized. There are always implications for other situations of a similar kind, for broader explanations that cover other instances of emotion, even if this is not intended in the question and would probably be of little immediate interest to the person who asks it. If you were to ask a friend "Why did you say that?" after he or she has just insulted you, and the answer is not "because I was mad at you," which is virtually self-explanatory, but "because I love you," this would require a further explanation, perhaps a story of convoluted feelings of affection unrequited or other feelings of frustration. But this is because the straightforward hypothesis is that people tend to be nasty because they are angry. The connection between nastiness and love, by contrast, although also well-confirmed in our ordinary experience, is a bit more convoluted. But our ordinary explanations of typical behavior (our own or others') presuppose and presume such well-confirmed hypotheses, whether or not they have ever been expressed as hypotheses. Our ordinary understanding and talk about emotions is already theoretical.

In such everyday contexts, we do not expect a hypertheoretical reply, such as "people who violate interpersonal expectations are often motivated by unexpressed hostility" or "there is hyperactivation in my amygdala." We might even construe such statements as sarcastic or as pretentious evasions. This is not to say that such explanations are false or meaningless, of course, but they seem to be inappropriate within the framework of our ordinary understanding. But within that everyday framework, some explanations make almost immediate sense, and others seem to make no sense at all, and this in turn points us to more sophisticated and more abstract hypotheses and theories. The question that then confronts us is the connection between these more or less ordinary ("folk") theories of emotions and behavior and the more abstract scientific theories of psychology and other disciplines. One way of thinking about this is that the explanations that make the most immediate sense often turn out to be those that can be further explained by more powerful theories while those that make little sense violate not only common sense but psychological plausibility as well. But this also suggests why even the grandest theories in psychology sometimes seem to be no more than elaborate restatements of common sense.

In everyday life, we already operate with surprisingly observant and sophisticated theories that are built into our common experience and "folk psychology." Spelling out the relevant hypotheses would, in ordinary circumstances, be superfluous or pretentious. But when we are trying to understand more general patterns of behavior, we are not so interested in any particular piece of behavior or in the platitudes of folk psychology but rather in broader patterns and higher-level and less-obvious psychological regularities. For instance, the way resentment tends to follow perceived slights and abuses in hierarchical organizations, or the ways love and respect in a troubled marriage tend to be undermined by unacknowledged competition, suspicion, and jealousy. That is why we are intrigued by theories that contradict folk psychology, or go beyond, though never too far beyond, it.

It is folk psychology that gives us our orientation to understanding our emotions. So if a Freudian claims that depression is really a form of internalized anger, we are intrigued, but only because we understand what is being put into question, namely depression and anger, which are familiar experiences for most of us. So, too, if Freud in one of his more cynical claims insists that "love is nothing but lust plus the ordeal of civility," we can ponder that provocative claim only because we already have a pretty good notion of what love and lust are and what "the ordeal of civility" might refer to. Folk psychology, and scientific psychology too, are a curious amalgam of low- and high-level empirical generalizations and conceptual truths about emotions (and other facets of human psychology), many of them built into ordinary language and "common sense" platitudes. Accordingly, they lend themselves to conceptual analysis as well as observational and experimental confirmation and disconfirmation. That is why philosophers often appeal to ordinary language and common sense. So do psychologists. And so do we all, even the most reductionist neurologists.

It is our business, as philosophers and scientists, to analyze and at times "see through" folk psychology, ordinary language, and common sense, but we nevertheless have to start with folk theories of emotion as our home base. That is where all theorizing about emotion begins, and it is the language in which even the most radical hypotheses have to be couched. I do not deny that there are sophisticated and exotic languages that cannot be easily "translated" for the layman, in neuroscience, in physics and chemistry, in dynamic systems theory, but in order to constitute theories *of emotion*, they must at some point be translated back into folk psychology. That is the way that we know what we are talking about.

But there continue to be philosophers and cognitive scientists who speculate that "some day," our knowledge of the brain will be sufficient that we will all talk the language of neurology. Some of them argue that folk psychology and thus most of psychology as a discipline is wholly archaic, unscientific, and based on out-of-date unscientific concepts. Paul Griffiths (1997), for example, compares the current philosophy and psychology of emotions to early Greek astronomy accounts, which described apparently real phenomena (for example, Aristotle's "sub-lunar objects") that have been shown to be nonexistent by contemporary science. The current science of choice is neurology, which, according to Griffiths, renders folk psychology and much of psychology as quaint and valueless as Greek astronomy. The theory of evolution and neurology, by contrast, represent the truth about what emotions "really" are. But the theory of evolution seems too unwieldy an instrument to explain the relatively fine-grained details of our emotional life. And while we are making remarkable progress in the neurosciences we still know very little about the neural substrate of any but the most primitive emotions. Meanwhile, folk psychology, our ordinary language about emotion, is what we've got to work with—and against—in our studies of the affective aspects of life. It is and will for the foreseeable future be the basis for our discussions and theories of emotion.

Folk psychology represents the accumulated observations and experience of humanity. It is not just an archaic relic. Some philosophers draw a sharp (perhaps too sharp) distinction between the "hard" physical and biological sciences and the more commonsense social and psychological sciences. They suggest that our knowledge of the workings of the human personality have not and very likely will not ever go through the revolutionary changes affecting physics and astronomy and the like. But gung-ho advocates of the neurosciences have been promising for years that neurology will replace folk psychology. Personally, I doubt that very much, even though we could be wrong in our everyday thinking in all sorts of ways that the neurosciences might be able to correct. But if we were to take the suggested route away from our accumulated experience and ordinary understanding of emotions, it is not at all clear what would be left of our concepts of emotions.

We are so used to operating within the framework of folk psychology, however, that we do not readily appreciate just how dramatic a difference it makes to our emotional life. Animals and infants have emotions, but we adult humans articulate them, reflect on them, and try to understand and explain them. Animals and infants have emotions for reasons, perhaps (a dog gets angry *because* his territory has been violated, a baby cries in fear *because* she does not know the person who is holding her), but we adult humans can articulate these reasons and, if called on to explain ourselves, spell out our emotional reactions to other people. What difference does this make? Well, a dog or a baby might err in their emotions (if there is no trespasser, if the baby-holder is a loving friend of the family) but we adult humans can be mistaken about our emotions in a very different way. We can misidentify our emotion and we can misdescribe or get quite wrong our reasons for having the emotion. Once there is a gap between having an emotion and naming that emotion, there is room for a very special kind of error. In reflection, we can be mistaken *about* our emotion as well as in our emotional response. But in reflection we can also contrast our emotion with what we think we should or would rather be feeling, and by means of such reflection we can take steps to modify, modulate, or alter our emotional states, or, perhaps, decide that what we do feel is correct and what we think we "ought" to feel is mistaken.

Thus it is by way of reflection that we can affirm or deny our emotions and take responsibility for them. This was the position of the ancient Stoics, who incorporated reflection on an emotion into the emotion itself. I think that this is right. For us (adult humans) we have very few if any emotions that do not in any way involve and include reflection. One of the Stoic conclusions, and mine too, is that we can, through reflection, to a certain extent take responsibility for and control our emotions. But also, through reflection, we can refuse to take responsibility for our emotions and by doing so not even try to control them. Not surprisingly, some of the most intriguing theoretical claims about emotions tend to be those that allow us to blame our emotions on something or someone other than ourselves, to theorize about them in such a way that we have no need to take responsibility for them. As valuable as reflection and theorizing can be in putting us in touch with our emotions and helping us to cultivate and change them, there is enormous appeal in using the same skills to evade responsibility. Thus in trying to develop our own theory of the emotions with an emphasis on emotional integrity and responsibility it is important that we first appreciate the battalion of theoretical prejudices arrayed against us.

One kind of theory that encourages this has to do with the general thesis that all of our emotional reactions are based in the brain and central nervous system (which is undoubtedly true). Thus, to take a very simple example, there is the idea that love is the product of brain chemistry, for instance, endorphins and oxytocin. (These can also be induced by chocolate.) This is very interesting, to be sure (and allows us rationalize our love of chocolate as well as our relationships). But it becomes problematic when it becomes *reductionist*, and love is believed to have nothing to do with our choices or decisions or hopes and dreams or insecurities. Lovers were exchanging chocolates long before anyone knew of endorphins or oxytocin, of course. Neurophysiological reductionism is but the most current and most exotic of the various theories with which we distance ourselves from our own emotions. (It used to be fate, spells, and love potions.)

Another prevalent way of displacing responsibility for our emotions through theory is to transfer the determination of our emotions away from ourselves and to the situation or the institution. An excellent example is the famous Milgram experiments back in the seventies, where ordinary people were encouraged by an authority figure to physically punish supposed subjects who gave a wrong answer (or so they thought—the subjects were stooges just pretending to be hurt). The subjects involved in the experiment were understandably upset. They had been persuaded to act in a way that can only be called cruel and sadistic. But the general view was that the blame for their behavior fell clearly on the experiment and the experimenters, or, more specifically, on the situation created by the experiment. Thus the experiment is still taken to confirm a general view called "situationism," the claim that our behavior is determined by situations, for example, a situation in which an authority figure is to be obeyed and not by "character" or personal choice (Doris, 2002).

But, then, character has also been used in a deterministic way to explain away any need to take responsibility for our emotions. (Illustrious defenders of such a philosophical view include John Stuart Mill and Arthur Schopenhauer.) The idea is that we cannot do anything about our character. The findings of the Milgram experiment are indeed upsetting, but that is no reason to deny that character and personality are significant determinants of our behavior. I think we can safely say that our emotional behavior is determined in part by both the situation in which we find ourselves and by our personalities and personal choices. But despite the apparent opposition of the situationist and personality views, we should appreciate what they share in common, namely, the tendency to minimize or displace our sense of responsibility for our emotions. In either case, our emotions are said to be wholly the product of something other than our active cultivation and taking responsibility for our emotions.

A theory of emotions is not just a grand psychological hypothesis or set of hypotheses telling us how we do in fact behave. It is also—or should be—an way of understanding emotions in which our role as reflective and responsible agents retains a central place. This is not in any way to challenge the value or the authority of science in the study of human behavior. But insofar as the sciences just provide another rich source of excuses, we need to be wary.

Alternatively, the most immediate and seemingly most obvious route to emotional understanding and the best theory of emotion would seem to be by way of attention to our ongoing personal experience by way of the discipline of phenomenology. This despite our propensity for self-deception and wishful thinking about ourselves. Phenomenology is the study of the structures of experience, and a phenomenology of the emotions is a study of the structures of emotional experience. But we do not have a ready-made language of phenomenology. Some natural languages have a more attentive and sophisticated grasp of experience than others, but all languages, by their very nature, develop through conversation about publicly observable objects and events, not inner, seemingly "private" feelings. It takes a special effort to describe one's experience as opposed to (what one takes to be) the objective world. That is, we have to explain how the world *seems* to us rather than how it is. A simple example of how this might work is the "discovery" of visual perspective during the Renaissance. Of course, people had always seen things in perspective, and when they looked at (more or less) realistic paintings they understood—and artists had ways of indicating—what was closer and what was farther away. (Putting one thing in front of another was an obvious clue.) But during the Renaissance, artists discovered the techniques of perspectival representation, which in turn represented *how we actually see* in perspective. Almost every elementary school student who learns single- or double-point perspective feels amazed, as if he or she just learned a magic trick. But what he or she has learned is nothing but the nature of their own visual experience and what in some sense they have "known" but not noticed almost all of their lives.

So, too, one could make a similar example out of the Impressionists, beginning with Monet, who taught us what we actually see when we see a colored object. (Never mind that Monet himself was almost blind, and what he showed us was first of all what *he* saw.) But, again, I remember my early art lessons and the feeling of revelation I experienced when I learned that a person's skin was not just white or brown or black, that an ordinary nose was a Fauvist palette of yellows, blues, and greens, and that the sky actually came down to and touched the grass! It was not that I had never seen this before. Of course the fact that the horizon met the sky was one of the most obvious things in my life. But it was certainly not one of the most obvious things in my experience. My attention had to be drawn to it, and when it was, then it was "obvious." So, too, phenomenology. In the history of folk psychology, one wonders when it was that people started noticing that the experience of some emotions included a feeling of heat or a "sinking feeling." Such matters were already well-known to the Greeks and are evident in the amazingly perceptive writings of Homer. But we ought to wonder how much else is not yet recognized by us or captured in our folk psychology, even though it might be perfectly "obvious" in our experience.

But what, you may ask, of the emotion *before* it is described or independent of any description? Here I become a skeptic. The French existential phenomenologist Maurice Merleau-Ponty (2003) spent much of his career pursuing the question of what human experience is like when we peel off the layers and influence of language and linguistic categories. He came up with the conclusion that, for the most part, this could not be done. Language permeates our experience in virtually every aspect. Animals and infants have emotions without language, but we do not. Even in adult human beings brute sensations like pain are shot through with questions and concerns that come with language and the awareness or confusion about what is happening. Emotions, with their complex of judgments and engagements with the world, are by their very nature creatures of language just as much as they are products of biology, neurology, and psychology. That means that questions of interpretation and reflection are involved even in something so seemingly straightforward as naming or identifying a particular emotion. Whether it is anger or resentment, and precisely what one is angry or resentful about, is in part determined by how one views the emotion. This is not to say that one cannot get it wrong. (We often do.) But it is to say that there may be several ways of getting it right, and our naming and then accounting for our emotion contributes to its being the emotion it is.

But if emotions include reflection on the emotions and the very ability to reflect depends on language, then there is no separating the emotion itself (or the emotional experience) from our language and linguistic capacities and our psychological knowledge. Or, we should say, "languages," because it is obvious that there is not just one folk psychology but many, as there are many "folk" in the world and many psychological subsets of even a single society. I think it is important, as we describe in considerable detail both the emotions we name so readily in American English and as we describe the various ways in which we talk about them, that we keep in mind that other cultures (and subcultures) have other ways of dividing up and referring to the phenomena of their emotional lives and, sometimes, quite different theories about how they work. This in turn infiltrates our emotional experience and makes it implausible to suppose that every person in every culture has the same emotions. We will only begin to explore some of these cultural variations in this book, but it is important that we always keep this in mind. The (more or less) clear distinctions we make in English (say, between shame and embarrassment, hatred and contempt) may not exist or may be very different in other cultures and in other languages. So, too, the various words we translate as "anger" (Latin *ire*, Polynesian *riri*, Japanese *okorimasu*, classical Chinese *nu*) may refer to significantly different (though obviously not entirely different) emotional phenomena, depending, among other things, on the role the emotion plays in that culture and how people think about it, for example, whether it is honored or feared and whether it is highly successful in manipulating people or alternatively shameful to the person who expresses it.

For instance, anger is prized and often effective in America, but it is feared as "demonic" in Tahiti and shameful in other cultures. In ancient China, *nu* was cognate with such words as "women" and "slaves," suggesting that it represented weakness, crudeness, and bad manners. Moral indignation, by contrast, was considered a serious moral virtue (thanks to Roger Ames for this). One thing that a theory of emotions must do, even if it is wedded to folk psychology, is take into account these linguistic and cultural, and consequently theoretical, variations. We may be folk but we must strive to be cosmopolitan, transcultural folk, and an adequate theory of emotion should reflect this as well.

Finally, folk psychology is not just the accumulated wisdom and experience of humanity. It also consists of accumulated unthinking platitudes, systematic misperceptions, self-deceptions, and implausible or misleading myths and metaphors. (Neither myths nor metaphors are necessarily falsehoods, but they can be highly misleading in a variety of ways.) In folk psychology, but also in the neurosciences, we find a rich source of myths and metaphors, many of which serve as excuses to disown our own emotions. Thus I want to argue against common sense and one of the basic assumptions of much of folk psychology, the idea that we are passive to our emotions and the victim of them. So, to me, one of the things that an adequate theory of emotions should do is to make it clear to us how reflection makes possible emotional intelligence, integrity, and responsibility. It is a myth that emotions are dumb feelings, or necessarily stupid and unthinking responses, or irrational as such. As we theorize about emotions, what we should want is the best theory, that is, not just a theory that confirms our own folk psychology nor just a theory that embraces the fast-coming findings of the sciences, but a theory that we can use to understand, guide, and take responsibility for our emotional lives. A good theory of emotions, in other words, should make us not just smarter but better people as well.

10

MYTH ONE
Emotions Are Ineffable

Before we even try to put together a general theory of emotions, we will have to uproot and examine a whole series of historical and popular misunderstandings about what emotions are and what they are not. The net result of these misunderstandings is that they give rise to a system of convenient excuses to the effect that we are not responsible for our emotions and need not bother that much trying to understand them, except, perhaps, by way of pure scientific curiosity.

In the next half dozen or so chapters, I would like to use our discussions of various emotions to expose these excuses for just what they are: excuses, misinterpretations, or one-sided understandings—devices to evade both responsibility and understanding. This will not be the all-too-familiar scientific condemnation of the way we ordinarily talk about emotions and "folk psychology." As I argued in the last chapter, our ordinary experience of our own emotions—and our occasional experience of some extraordinary emotions—provides our basis for any theorizing and yields a great many insights into the ways our emotions function in our lives.

Perhaps the best place to begin is with that initial block to any intelligent discussion of emotions and emotional intelligence, and that is the refusal to talk about such matters at all. Sometimes, this is in the name of propriety and privacy. We do not like to be forced to listen to the details of someone else's emotional life and we do not like to be compelled to reveal our own. (On the other hand, we have a notorious weakness for gossip, and when we have the opportunity to eavesdrop or indirectly learn of the emotional travails of others, few of us are capable of resisting.) In academia, the refusal to talk about emotions is often a matter of neglect; philosophers, scholars, and scientists would just rather study and talk about something else. Until, that is, new scientific techniques and whiz-bang technology enters the picture, at which point there is a rush to funding to participate in the new "hot" discipline, whether or not it actually helps our understanding of emotions. But the neglect of emotions in academic and scientific life is not just due to a preference for studying other matters. When psychology became self-consciously a "science" over the course of the twentieth century, the understanding of the emotions just didn't fit very well into that aspiration.

The move to make psychology more scientific began in the late nineteenth century, most notably with the work of Sigmund Freud in Vienna and William James in America. They were both fascinated by emotions, and, not surprisingly, emotions played a central role in their theories. They also put a great deal of emphasis (and, in those days, faith) in the potential of the new neurology to reveal a great deal about the workings of psychology, though neither of them thought for a moment that the data of consciousness and experience could or would be eclipsed by the then-new discovery of the basic biology of the brain. (The neuron, the nerve cell, was only discovered in 1895.) Both Freud and James saw in the new neurology the possibility of enormous breakthroughs in science, and with this (combined with their clinical studies) came a new scrutiny about the contents of consciousness and the self-reports about those contents.

But by the time those two old masters were dead, psychology had entered its dark age. With the advent of "Behaviorism" (I capitalize it here to suggest the name of a quasi-religious movement), it was aggressively argued that if psychology was to be a science, it could have nothing to say about that mythological entity called consciousness. B. F. Skinner of Harvard, who took James's place as the premier American psychologist, had many clever and sarcastic things to say about those who still insisted on talking about "consciousness" and "mind" and "experience," but the net result was the murder of the very concept of psychology. Psychology ("the study of the psyche") became "the study of behavior" and *nothing but* behavior and its equally observable causes. (The brain was also excluded, said to be no more than a "black box.") The emotions, which were nothing if not feelings and experience, became *non grata* in psychology. As late as the 1960s, when I did graduate study in psychology, the emotions rarely got more than a mention at the tail end of chapters on motivation in major psychology textbooks. There was, presumably, nothing to study there and nothing to be said. In the 1940s, emotions were treated (at best) as "acute disturbances" (P. T. Young), as "a disorganized response, largely visceral, resulting from lack of effective adjustment" (L. F. Schaffer), as antithetical to intelligence (R. S. Woodworth). They were dismissed as mere "disruptions of behavior" by such luminary psychologists as D. O. Hebb.

If behaviorism eclipsed any serious mention of emotions in human behavior, emotion was especially ruled out of bounds in animal studies. It was not until thirty years ago, when an established but brave biologist named Donald Griffin (already famous for his studies of bat sonar) risked the censure and ridicule of his colleagues by introducing the phrase "animal minds" into zoology, cautiously and with ample caveats, the mandatory apology being made that we had no way whatever of ever "getting into" animal minds and experiencing their emotions. What was presupposed—even when it was explicitly rejected—was the "Cartesian" model of minds as private and accessible only to the subject. Bodies and behavior were publicly observable, of course, but they did little to reveal the animal psyche. (In fact, animals were assumed not to have any psyche at all, a barbaric view that can be traced back at least to Descartes, who used this assumption to justify his practice of vivisection.) Both halves of this "Cartesian" model, I will argue, are false. But on a more humane level, it is worth pointing out that many of these same scientists had cats and dogs and parrots and hamsters at home and treated them in every way as if they had very real feelings and could be made happy or hurt or even humiliated, but this, they explained, was "merely anecdotal evidence" and thus scientifically no evidence at all.

This despite the fact that Charles Darwin, the patron saint of most of today's biologists, wrote one of his best books on the emotions and expressions of animals as well as men, and Darwin certainly had no trouble ascribing to animals at least some of the feelings and emotions that we ascribe to each other. But that, say the critics, was his mistake, mere "anthropomorphism," the unforgivable error of projecting human qualities onto dumb animals that had no such capacities. It is only very recently, thanks to bold and innovative animal-loving psychologists like Franz de Waal at Emory University, that our appreciation for the emotional complexity of at least some "higher" animals, apes and dolphins most notably, has now earned scientific recognition.

I would like to tell you that the situation was different in philosophy, but during the twentieth century we were darkened by our own version of behaviorism, notably logical positivism, which began as a healthy antidote to Nazi romanticism but ended up as dismissive of all things humanistic—not only emotions but ethics, religion, and aesthetics—that were not subject to scientific verification. In fact, mid-century, there was a movement in ethics called *emotivism*, which reduced all ethical statements to mere expressions of emotion, devoid of "cognitive" value. Emotions, in other words, told us nothing about the world and had no cognitive content. One of emotivism's promoters (and the most popular English-speaking advocate of logical positivism), A. J. Ayer, insisted that calling something "good" or "bad" or "right" or "wrong" was no more than exclaiming "hooray" or "boo" (1952). Another, less crude advocate was Charles L. Stevenson, with whom I had the pleasure of studying (when he was nearing retirement) at the University of Michigan. He, too, thought that ethics was nothing but a matter of "attitude," and attitudes, like emotions, told us nothing about the world but only something about the subject. So, he said, "this is good" means "I approve of this, and I would like you to do so too" (1952). That is much more polite and more conducive to discussion and deliberation than "hooray," to be sure, but with much the same implication: Ethics was nothing but emotion and emotion was nothing at all.

Looking back at emotivist philosophy, Alasdair MacIntyre, perhaps the most important ethicist in America in the twentieth century, concluded that emotivism was much more than a dismissive view of ethics. It was a symptom of a general moral breakdown in modern society. His diagnosis and recommended corrective is far beyond our scope here, but it is worth noting that the crucial part of MacIntyre's solution was a renovation of the ancient and medieval conception of ethics in terms of *the virtues*. This conception of ethics was prominent in Aristotle and later in Aquinas, and one of its most interesting aspects, from our perspective, was its emphasis on the importance of the passions—the right passions, that is—in ethics. This puts emotivism into an odd position. On the one hand, emotivism is intended to be dismissive of ethics, at least as a serious philosophical discipline. (Stevenson used to insist that he was by no means dismissing the importance of ethics, but as a philosopher, he said, he had no more to contribute to moral debates than any man or woman on the street corner.) On the other hand, however, the emphasis on virtue and emotions (passions) puts those practical aspects of our life under a powerful spotlight. And what emerges in that light is not only the possibility but the necessity of analyzing and discussing emotions and the evident fact that emotions are our way of "tuning" ourselves into the world (a metaphor suggested by Martin Heidegger several decades earlier). The fact that ethics involves the expression of emotion does not lessen the importance of ethics but rather enhances the significance of emotions.

Philosophy has a long history, and if we look at that history we get a much more interesting, complex story than the traditional "reason versus the passions" antagonism that animates so many thinkers. Plato had his suspicions about emotions, but he fully endorsed some of them (notably *eros* or love) as essential to human aspirations. His student Aristotle, as I have several times indicated, was a champion of the passions (indeed, the word is his, *pathé*, plural for "sufferings"). He insisted that the passions, that is, the right passions, in the right amounts, at the appropriate times, were essential for living the good life. After Aristotle, this enthusiastic view of the passions dimmed considerably even as the sophistication of the theories increased. Thus the Stoics had an ingenious theory of the passions (one to which we will return again and again), the upshot of which was that all of the passions turn out to be counter to happiness and well-being and poor life strategies. But the Stoics also taught that the emotions are judgments, in other words, shot through with intelligence (although misleading intelligence, on their view). They were, accordingly, both describable and analyzable in considerable detail. Only the "first movements," the bodily feelings that provided the first step in emotions, had to be described indirectly, through such quasi metaphors as "feeling deflated" or "becoming aroused." But the judgments that constituted emotions could be discussed, analyzed, and understood in exquisite detail.

Following the Stoics (I think of Marcus Aurelius as a kind of transition figure to Saint Augustine), Christian psychology became even more subtle and creative about the passions, elevating some of them to exalted (even divine) status, denigrating others (notably, the seven deadly sins). But, again, the passions remained central to ethics and the theories of the passions became more and more attentive and thorough. Modern philosophy, with its emphasis on reason and science, again displayed schizoid attitudes of fascination, suspicion, and dismissal toward the passions, although two of the great "rationalist" philosophers, Descartes and Spinoza, put the passions at the center of their philosophies. The Scotsman David Hume was almost alone in elevating passion above reason ("Reason is and ought to be the slave of the passions"), but nineteenth-century romanticism caught another wave of enthusiasm and declared, in various ways and with increasing emotion, "passion is everything!"

But not even the romantics suggested that the passions could not be talked about. The academic neglect that became so evident in the mid-twentieth century was unusual in its severity and it was tragically successful in pushing discussion of emotion out of the academic and scientific arena and into the hands of "self-help" writers, self-appointed spiritual gurus, and others who may have had insights but also had their own axes to grind and books to market. Notably, it became one of the platitudes of pop psychology that everyone is unique and no one's emotions are truly comparable or even comprehensible to anyone else. Moreover, emotions were once again assumed to be feelings that could not as such be described. To make it worse, feelings, subjectivity, and what has become nostalgically celebrated as "the enchantment of the world" were assumed to be threatened by science, thus responding in kind to the bloated scientific opinions of the behaviorists. But these neo-Romantics wrongly believed that all science was what they disdainfully called "scientism" (or, more accurately, scientific reductionism), and this was what was responsible for our modern disenchantment with the world. It followed that the quest for a theory and systematic understanding of emotions was not likely to be part of such an agenda. Not all popular authors bought into these platitudes, but the fact that they became platitudes suggests that they worked their way into "common sense" and ordinary language, and consequently into folk psychology as well. In this and the following chapters, accordingly, I want to delve a bit deeper into the complexities of describing our emotions, putting feeling into language.

As for the idea that the emotions cannot be described without losing something essential, this is most often said of love, at least by way of complaint or warning. If anger and fear are diminished by describing them, that would, perhaps, be good because it would be conducive to self-control. There is something to this, evidently, and at least sometimes articulating even one's most basic emotions is sufficient, by way of reflection, to soften and limit them. But anger and fear can also be bolstered and further motivated through articulation, and this is something we should surely try to understand. But with regard to love, the cautionary tone is most likely due to the romantic celebration of love that overemphasizes overwhelming feeling and underemphasizes the factual, cultural, and institutional context of this emotion. Thus I have often heard it said among my students (and when I was a student) that love cannot be described. But what they/we are in fact confessing is our own poetic clumsiness and our incapacity for psychological insight and articulation. Or, just as often, just plain laziness.

But if love is described, doesn't it lose its luster? Isn't it better when it remains unaccounted for (which is not to say, of course, unexpressed)? It is as if in being exposed to the air love becomes corrupted or shows its otherwise hidden flaws. I suspect that there is considerable truth to this, at least to the part that says exposure betrays weakness. When called upon to justify one's affection (a rude thing to demand, in most instances) a person is very likely in his or her own defense to stumble upon some unflattering truths. This tends to undermine the infatuation that is so typical of incipient love and the idealization that comes with maturing love. But seeing one's beloved through the unloving eyes of one's suspicious or unsympathetic friends does indeed constitute a threat to love, and one might well not get past that experience. Of course, some people dig in their heels and become more devoted, especially if the critics are one's parents, but that is a different matter. But as for the popular idea that love cannot be described, I have countered that in my own writings on love, as did Plato and many other authors. Love can indeed be described, although it is notoriously complicated and requires much more than a simple ascription of feeling. And so, too, we can describe all emotions, and not just as feelings.

When I described love in chapter 4, I described a great many things, including the intentional object of love (the beloved), the reasons for love, the self in love, and, I would add, the cultural institutions surrounding courtship, couples, marriage, sexual and romantic expression, and much more. I also described Plato's various accounts of love, because emotions—love in particular—shift as an experience with our conceptions and ideas. Our emotions also have a history. Not only do our concepts and practices change over time, our emotions do too. *Eros* was not the same before and after Plato. Nor was the "romantic" love of the eighteenth century the same emotion enjoyed or suffered by the medieval troubadours. So, too, in discussing fear and anger I described a great many things, including the causes and expressions of these emotions, their intentional objects (danger and offense respectively), their rationality or irrationality, even (briefly) their neural pathways. But love, fear and anger and all emotions, whatever else they might be, are (at least in part) feelings. Can we describe those feelings?

Well, yes and no. William James, the great physician-philosopher-psychologist at Harvard at the end of the nineteenth century, had a theory that will come up many times in this book. His theory attempted to spell out in exact detail the nature of emotional feelings, which, he stressed, *are* the emotions. But, according to James, those feelings are of a very specific sort. They are the feelings that are caused by specifiable physiological disturbances, namely, the activities of the autonomic nervous system and the endocrine system. That has the great virtue of specificity, and as a theory it has the great virtue of verifiability. But although it specifies the feelings that constitute emotions, the theory hardly makes any attempt to *describe* those feelings, apart from the indirect method of saying "it's the feeling you get when the hairs on the back of your neck stand erect" or "it's the feeling you get when your knees start getting all wobbly." Thus the feelings that we have when we have an emotion can be pinned down to a physiological occurrence, but they cannot exactly be described; that is, the experience of the feeling cannot as such be described.

Moreover, it has seemed to many theorists that it makes little sense to try to describe or account for the more elusive feelings that make up an emotion, those that cannot be traced to a specific physiological or physical source, those that I will include more generally in "emotional experience." Here, many theorists have thrown up their arms in despair, speaking vaguely of "affect" or "affective tone" or retreating to metaphor or agreeing with the romantics that such feelings are ineffable and indescribable. But again, I would raise the rude question, to what extent is this incapacity simple inarticulateness or even laziness? It is no doubt true that our language of "inner experience" is fairly crude and undeveloped, as our public language is quite naturally geared to shared experiences and to objects and situations in the world. But it does not follow that the larger feelings involved in emotions are either ineffable or indescribable. Nor that we should limit ourselves to what I will now call the "Jamesian" feelings of physiological activity.

In a later chapter, I will attempt to provide a scheme for describing the surprisingly complex dimensions of emotional experience. But for now, I just want to understand the difficulties in doing so, and so start to understand why psychologists, in particular, have been so quick to retreat to the behavioral manifestations of emotion, for instance, facial expressions and patterns of behavior, or to turn to neurology and the burgeoning neuroscience literature. First of all, there is what I referred to earlier as the "Cartesian" assumption of the privacy of the mind and emotion. I suggested that this model is false, and I will defend this charge in a subsequent chapter. Second, there is the complex issue of language. A few centuries ago (and even last century), it was assumed that there was a more or less "natural" if mysterious connection between a word and what it referred to. That assumption has pretty much been totally discarded, even for material objects. The philosopher W. V. O. Quine, for example, argued that a word that seems to refer to rabbits, in a language that we do not know, might refer to any of a number of alternative aspects of rabbithood, and it is only from within the context of that language and its uses that such seeming ambiguities are resolved. Wittgenstein, a few years earlier, had written about what he called "language games," within which reference got fixed through the *use* of words, not by the words themselves. Today, there are many varieties of such "pragmatist" theories, but they all accept the view that reference is something complex and to a large degree contextual, not a simple "natural" connection between words and things.

Now if this is true even when we are talking about such concrete objects as rabbits, it is even more complicated when we are talking about such intangible mental entities as feelings. (Quine, a friend of Skinner's at Harvard, dutifully refused to talk about such things at all.) But are feelings discrete entities, even if they are strange entities? We often talk about emotions as if this were so. Indeed, in the first nine or so chapters I made only minimal effort to combat this impression. I talked about "anger" and "fear" and "love" as if these terms each referred to some discrete psychic entity or type of entity, and insofar as these entities turn out to be feelings, we would expect there to be some discrete feeling as well. Thus the temptation to leap to Jamesian feelings, which do seem to be more or less discrete and to avoid the much larger, more diffuse feelings that philosophers refer to vaguely as "affect" and such. But I made the point in talking about love, alluding to other emotions, that it is not a distinct and momentary feeling but a *process*, which might include any number of other emotions as well. So, too, with grief. And, I would say, anger, fear, shame, guilt, and all the rest of them. This makes the challenge of picking out *the* feeling or *the* experience of an emotion pretty hopeless. On introspection, what we find is a varied *flux*, a flow of sensory and emotional flotsam and jetsam, what James memorably called "the stream of consciousness," and consequently there is no way to pin down emotional experience in a simple or single description.

So, on the side of emotional experience, there are no discrete entities to be described. Instead, what we will find is that the language we use to refer to emotions is partly responsible for shaping and carving out the emotions themselves. But on the side of language, this makes matters all the more difficult to disentangle. If language shapes emotions and emotional experience, then it follows that one cannot simply depend on simple "translation" of emotion terms from one language to another. Thus the various translations of "anger," for example, depend on the exact use of those terms, *ire*, *colère*, *Zorn*, *riri*, etc., in the context of the language and the culture. Here, of course, an enormous debate erupts. "But surely the similarities between, say, Tahitian *riri* and American anger are such that we are entitled to say that they refer to the same thing!" But if there is no "thing," then the debate finds itself stuck for a common reference. To be sure there are similarities—facial expressions, aggressive behavior, not to mention physiological measures—but we have to be skeptical, at least, about the supposed sameness of reference, especially the assumed similarity of emotional experiences. Do we, in fact, have the same experiences? Especially if we are thinking cross-culturally? But how could we prove this, given the general problem of accurate translation from one culture (not just one language) to another?

This, in turn, makes the effort to describe emotional experience even more troublesome. When I describe love, for instance, am I describing a peculiarly American or Western experience? Or, especially, a distinctively male experience? (Simone de Beauvoir famously said that "men and women mean different things by 'love,' and that is why they don't understand one another.") Does "love" refer to a mode of emotional experience that only people who use a certain "romantic" language experience? There is that wonderful La Rochefoucault quote, "How many people would ever fall in love, had they never heard the word?" A profound insight, but in any case, we should not simply assume that what we mean by "love" is what anyone else in any other culture means by words that are, with some difficulty, perhaps, so translated. And I would be the first to suspect that my own account of love is at least colored by my American male sixties' experience. Yet I would not go so far as to suggest, as many romantics have, that "everyone's experience of love is different." (How would we verify that? Doesn't that make at least as radical an assumption as those who would unthinkingly assume that love is a universal experience?) But in our description of emotional experience, we need to be very careful and as straightforward as possible about *whose* experience it is that we are describing and what the scope of that experience might be. It is not that love or any other emotion is indescribable, but the language with which we describe our emotions may also be part of what gives them shape and form. So whereas we started by worrying whether language could describe the emotions, now we should worry whether language and the emotions are too close for comfort and can be adequately distinguished.

Emotions are not "ineffable," but I have suggested that the description of emotional experience is very complicated. I think that there is another problem at work here, however, more easily diffused. If one expects the description or the phenomenology of an emotion to capture or reproduce the actual feeling and intensity of the emotion, then, of course, one is asking much too much. Just as the explanation of a joke is rarely funny, much less as funny as the joke itself, an account of an emotion need not itself be at all emotional. Nevertheless, understanding an emotion may well be instrumental in deepening it, or correcting it, or redirecting it toward its proper object. That is what Freudian therapy has always tried to do. That is what a good deal of art and literature and philosophy attempts to achieve. A passion often becomes more and not necessarily less exciting when it becomes more articulate or refined. It often becomes stronger, better directed, more "rational," and perhaps even more exquisite when it is understood and cultivated with style and intelligence. There may be some crude virtue to dumb feeling in certain dramatic moments, but the challenge is to cultivate and articulate our emotions and consequently our culture to create a world that is not just crude but emotionally rewarding.

11

MYTH TWO
Emotions Are Feelings

In this chapter, I want to tackle the biggest oversimplification in our various attempts to talk about the emotions, the seemingly obvious idea that emotions are feelings. The idea that emotions are feelings is, as I argued in the last chapter, both common sense and plausible. Virtually every emotion includes some feelings, including those "Jamesian" sensations that accompany bodily changes. The problem is specifying and spelling out what other "feelings" constitute an emotion, over and above those sensations, and I suggested that we explore the more general notion of emotional experience in order to do this. In this chapter, I want to pursue the objection that "emotions are feelings" may be a plausible starting point but it is woefully inadequate as an analysis of emotion. It also lends itself to the "primitivization" of emotions that allows us to easily turn them into excuses. Feelings are by their nature dumb and without intelligence, whatever our intelligence may subsequently make of them (by way of diagnosis, for instance). One doesn't expect an unintelligent feeling to carry with it any sense of responsibility at all.

But I already agreed that an emotion is a feeling, didn't I? Isn't that simply a matter of definition (confirmed by many of the best English dictionaries)? Well, yes, but no. "Emotion" is a fairly recent term (as I suggested in chapter 3), but as broadly embracing as it is, it refers us to a more or less limited (though by no means homogeneous) collection of psychological states and processes. "Feeling," by contrast, is an enormously promiscuous and generous term that includes all sorts of experiences, from the feeling of cold water dripping down the middle of your back to the feeling that something is awry in the kitchen to the experience that Watson and Crick must have had when they started feeling that DNA must involve some sort of detachable double structure. Feelings, in other words, range from the simple and sensuous to the extremely complex and sophisticated (what we often call "intuitions"). Only some of these feelings are involved in what we call emotions.

What feelings all have in common seems to be no more than the fact that they are "felt"; in other words, they register in consciousness and they are not merely intellectual (like thoughts and thinking). This is not to say that they must be conscious in the sense that one can recognize or articulate them. In fact, one might not even notice them (the dull throb that becomes just routine background as one goes about one's daily business). But neither is it to suggest that a feeling *cannot* be fully conscious and articulated. Freud hit a conceptual block when he struggled with the idea of an unconscious feeling—or "unconscious affect," in his terms. He concluded that the very idea was a contradiction in terms, as opposed to an unconscious emotion, which was possible, he argued, because its idea component (its intentional object) could be unconscious even if its affect (feeling) component could not be.

Feelings, in other words, cover a far larger territory than emotions. But couldn't it be the case nevertheless that emotions are feelings? Sure, why not, so long as this is not taken as a definition of emotion, and so long as it is not thereby supposed that emotions must be inarticulate. There is also some question whether every emotion necessarily includes feelings, for there are "calm passions" (Hume) and aesthetic emotions (James) that may not display any evident feelings. But I have a deeper problem with the idea that emotions are feelings than a quibble about mapping the terrain. And that is the long-standing idea that emotions *just are* feelings, and feelings of a very primitive kind. This is an idea that pervades empirical psychology (before it was split off from empiricist philosophy) and it goes back at least to John Locke, the great physician-philosopher-psychologist in London at the end of the seventeenth century, and David Hume, his brilliant Scots follower. For both of them, an emotion was a simple sensation. For Hume, who worked this out in great detail, an emotion was essentially a sensation (an "impression") that had one of two qualities. It was pleasant (as in pride, for example) or it was unpleasant (as in hatred, for instance). Hume (1973) saw right away that this feeling (sensation, impression) analysis did not even begin to capture the full character of these emotions, so he elaborated a complex causal apparatus of "ideas" that cause the pleasant or unpleasant impression and ideas that in turn are caused by the pleasant or unpleasant impression, and it is the whole complex ("a monstrous heap") of impressions and ideas that gives the emotion its distinctive character (as pride, for example, or as hatred).

Hume's analysis is ingenious, but it gets stuck on the idea that the emotion as such is a simple sensation. We find much the same analysis in William James, who is also an empiricist, at the end of the following century. Now spelling out what we only mentioned in passing in the previous chapter, James says that an emotion is nothing other than *a feeling caused by sudden changes in the body.* James, like Hume, embellishes this simple vision with a large number of much more complex and insightful qualifications and observations. But the essential theory—the one that guided psychological research for much of the twentieth century—is that an emotion "IS" (James puts it in capital letters for emphasis) a sensation, a simple feeling caused by a bodily disturbance. It was with this theory as my target that I began my own research on emotions many years ago, as did many of my colleagues in psychology. So the idea that an emotion is a feeling is not a simple matter of definition. It is a serious matter of theory and understanding with profound practical implications. If we were to think of an emotion as a simple bodily feeling, for instance, there would not be much to be done about it and there would be no obvious role for reflection. We can put up with the feeling like an itch or a headache, distract ourselves through activity, or diminish it with pharmaceuticals or booze. If an emotion is much more than a feeling and a bodily disturbance however, then there is the need to understand it and how it fits into our lives and, indeed, what we can and should do about it. As I have insisted all along, my interest in emotions is not just scientific. It is first of all a concern about ethics and living well and what I call emotional integrity. What we *feel* is just a tiny piece of the picture.

James, like the earlier empiricists, seemed to think that the feelings involved in emotion were sensations. He firmly tied these sensations to physiology so we could rather precisely specify that these sensations are those that one feels when one's heart beats faster, one's face flushes, and so on. Thus emotional experience is not ineffable nor is it mysterious. One can easily imagine someone who has never blushed wondering what blushing would feel like. So, too, we can readily understand that many people do not recognize what is happening to them physiologically, but nevertheless we can understand what they must be feeling on the basis of measurable physiological symptoms. Thus the very general notion of "feeling" gets tightly specified to bodily sensations. To be sure, we also embellish our physiological vocabulary with metaphors, "feeling as if my heart is about to burst," "feeling as if a heavy weight is on my chest," "getting that sinking feeling," and the like. But James, much to his credit, gets rid of the vagueness and obscurity of feelings and replaces that notion with something admirably concrete and, most important for scientific study, measurable.

But James mixes together a number of very different bodily phenomena and so, too, the very different feelings that accompany them. James's primary examples involve the activation of the autonomic nervous system, that is, the more or less "automatic" system that causes hormone secretion and then increased pulse and heartbeat, harder breathing, sweating, muscular tension, and skin sensitivity. (At least some of these may be voluntary as well, for instance breathing, which we can control. Nevertheless, when we fall asleep, we still breathe "automatically.") Some of today's proponents of "basic emotions" or what they call "affect programs" still stress the importance of these "peripheral" physiological processes (Robert Levenson at UC Berkeley, for example), but most such theorists now emphasize brain functions. But in either case, the resultant feelings are pretty much confined to simple sensations. (Thus a polemicist like Le Doux can suggest that these are nothing but "icing on the cake" and of little significance for understanding emotions as neurological processes.) The ancient Stoics, as we noted, referred to what they called "first movements," those physiologically based feelings that (they claimed) *preceded* our emotions. But they, too, did not accord much significance to them. Thus that sinking feeling in the chest when one is saddened or disappointed is not yet melancholy, and the energized aggressive feeling when one is made angry is not yet anger. The feelings themselves were not particularly meaningful but the emotions certainly were meaningful. The Stoics saw that the familiar physical feelings in emotion are but a small part of our emotional experience.

The bodily sensations that James lumps together are by no means all of a kind. James mixes together a number of very different sorts of feelings. While he highlights those feelings that are caused by the activation of the autonomic nervous system, he also mentions—and not just in passing—the *voluntary* tensing of our muscles and preparation for action (for example, clenching one's fists in anger, shrinking away in shame). And James even says, rather famously, that shifting one's musculature—smiling or removing one's frown ("straightening one's brow")—actually changes one's emotions. But the feelings that go along with such behavioral changes are very different from the feelings produced by the autonomic nervous system. (I will discuss this in much more detail in chapter 20.)

What is oddly ignored in the discussion of feelings is the whole dimension of *intentionality*, our many ways of being engaged in the world. I will later argue that an adequate description of what an emotion is *about* includes a description of the emotional experience of the world engaged in the ways peculiar to this or that emotion. Thus the "feeling" of getting angry includes the experience of seeing another person as offensive or a situation as frustrating, and a feeling of shame includes the experience of oneself as offensive or as having violated certain norms or taboos. One might argue (rather pedantically, I think) that such experiences hardly count as "feelings," and I would not vehemently disagree. But that is why I prefer to talk about *emotional experience* rather than simply "feelings," which carries the implication of something simple and unstructured. The point, however, is that insofar as an emotion encompasses feelings those feelings include some sophisticated and subtly structured perceptions of the world. They also embody various evaluations or "appraisals," and not just "oh, good!" and "that's bad," as I shall argue in another chapter soon. In other words, it is not that emotions are not feelings, but rather that what is meant by "feelings" includes all sorts of experiences that are by no means so simple as sensations.

Finally, let me end by questioning a recent use of the terms "feeling" and "emotion" by two giants of contemporary emotion neuroscience, Joe Le Doux and Tony Damasio. They have suggested that the term "emotion" be restricted to the neural mechanisms they have done so much to discover (Le Doux, 1996; Damasio, 1999). An emotion, accordingly, is for the most part unconscious. "Feeling" is the term they reserve for the aftermath of emotion, which may well involve consciousness. I think that this is disastrously confused and confusing. I do not want to legislate or stipulate how these "folk" terms should be used in neuroscience (by way of stipulation, neuroscientists can, like Lewis Carroll's Humpty-Dumpty, use words in any way that they choose). But insofar as scientists are discovering something important about *emotions* (as I think they are), it is important to have the terminology make sense. To say that feelings *follow* emotions in the above sense is unintelligible. I agree that the two terms must be carefully differentiated, but not in an arbitrary way that violates our most common understanding and renders the emotions beyond the reach of reflection and any semblance of (non-drug-induced) voluntary control.

12

MYTH THREE
The Hydraulic Model

The idea that emotions are feelings lends itself to another passive image, that of a psychic fluid filling up the mind or the body. I call this the "hydraulic model." In this chapter, I want to challenge this as a misleading metaphor. To say that it is a metaphor, however, is not in itself to condemn it. Good science is filled with metaphors, often provocative, pregnant, insightful metaphors. But this particular metaphor points us in exactly the wrong direction if we are to understand our emotions. Even the illustrious Doctor Freud employed it, and it led him to some of his most-often disputed models of the mind.

The hydraulic model of mind is based on an image of fluidity, fluid under pressure, and it is this hydraulic pressure that explains many essential aspects of our emotional life, why, for example, we feel compelled to express our emotions, why we often find it so hard to restrain ourselves, and why certain emotions are marked by "sinking" and "elevated" feelings. For someone like Freud, it allows for a compartmentalization of the mind, perhaps on the model of a subterranean stream and a surface flow, a body of water with undercurrents beneath the surface, or (Freud's more civil engineering preference) a plumbing arrangement with various vessels, pipes, and channels. I have several times insisted that we should think of emotions as processes, and this, too, can be incorporated by the hydraulic model, emotions as flux and flow. It also makes good sense of such depth metaphors as "deep" and "profound," for the spatial implications of hydraulics allow for such a "depth versus surface" dimension. And, indeed, since one of Freud's early ambitions was to discover an isomorphism (a parallel form) between the mind and the anatomy of the brain, such an image was of particular value, although he continued to hold it long after he had given up his idea of a strict psychophysical parallelism.

Our own endorsement of the hydraulic model is evident in the way we talk about the emotions. Take, for example, the all-purpose example of anger. We often talk about anger in terms of cooking metaphors: "heating up," "simmering," and "boiling over." The hot fluid metaphors fit rather plausibly with both the red-faced appearance of anger and the feeling of "heating up" as one flushes and tenses one's muscles. When one gets really angry, one "explodes" with rage, or, with a lot of self-control, one can "bottle up" the anger. One might also let it out through gritted-teeth "hisses" or perhaps more rapidly (as in "having a hissy-fit"). Occasionally, the metaphor turns centrifugal (as in "flying off the handle"), but most often the images are of filling and heating up, of pressure and overflowing, of containment and explosion. William James captures it precisely in his essay "What is an Emotion?" as a feature of certain personality types:

> In certain persons, the explosive energy with which passion manifests itself on critical occasions seems correlated with the way in which they bottle it up during the intervals. . . . The sentimentalist is so constructed that "gushing" is his or her formal mode of presentation. Putting a stopper on the "gush" will only to a limited extent cause more "real" activities to take its place. . . . On the other hand the ponderous and bilious "slumbering volcano," let him repress the expression of his passions as he will, will find them expire if they get no vent at all.

Anger appears to be a particularly appropriate example ripe for such a metaphor, but for other emotions, the images are not so clear or consistent. Fear does not feel like a force or a fluid building up inside of us, nor does love (although lust does sometimes give that impression). "I'm so filled with love," in addition to being a warning sign (of probable narcissism and desperation), is an odd image. Indeed, even "overflowing" is an exceptional and not entirely innocent description of the feelings of love. Love is more of a feeling of attachment, of need, of intimacy, of affection (it might, with some effort, be described as "warmth," but hardly as pressure or boiling). Jealousy, too, is not pressure but more like a haunting. Shame, embarrassment, and guilt weigh us down or make us feel out of place, but they feel more like depletion than fulfillment. One can be "filled with joy," but joy is more like helium than hot liquid, and the similarity is not so much the hydraulic model as the image of the self as a container to be filled.

Nevertheless, these and other emotional metaphors all have something in common. Consider that one can be "paralyzed" by fear, "riveted" by fascination, "struck" by jealousy, and, of course, "felled" or in various ways "caught" or "struck by love." (The image of Cupid's arrow may have been reduced to kitsch by Bouchet, the Baroque, and Hallmark cards, but the image is indelible.) Fear and hatred "take over." Jealousy becomes an obsession. Shame and embarrassment overwhelm us. We wallow in guilt. Joy lifts us up. The images may vary but they share a significant similarity, an image of *passivity*. The idea is that the emotions happen to you, or happen *in* you, but they are beyond control of the will. The will supposedly comes in only after the emotion is fully operative, and then by way of containing or controlling it. In the case of "down" emotions like grief and sadness, the will might step in as an external prod, "OK, now, get over it." My ultimate concern with the hydraulic model, accordingly, is just this: that it too sharply separates the emotions from the self and it too radically removes the concept of responsibility from our conception of our emotional lives. It is not enough that we can *control* our emotions. The theme of this book is that emotions can be cultivated, educated, and sometimes even *willed*, not just controlled. That is what emotional integrity is all about.

The hydraulic model has a distinguished history. The medieval physiologists hypothesized that the various "humours" of the body (choler, spleen, bile) determined both temperament and specific emotional episodes. Descartes and later Hume endorsed the idea of "animal spirits" flowing in the blood as the proximate cause of the passions. Animal spirits was an apt metaphor (albeit one taken quite literally at the time) to capture both the idea that emotions were essentially biological and part of our animal natures (this was well before Darwin's evolutionary theory) and quite literally fluid, or at least contained in fluid and flow (this was, at least for Descartes, who oddly opposed the notion, before the acceptance of Harvey's discovery of the circulation of the blood). Descartes and Hume also both viewed the animal spirits as an intermediary between mind and body. They were clearly bodily but also had direct manifestations in the soul or mind. So, too, the modern versions of the hydraulic model have this appeal. They capture the bodily dimensions of emotion and make a gesture, in the case of anger a convincing one, toward direct manifestations in consciousness. Thus, in anger, we *feel* ourselves filling up and heating up. In anger, at least, it doesn't seem like a metaphor at all.

The two ideas easily work in tandem. The idea that emotions are feelings readily lends itself to the image of feeling as a psychic fluid filling up the mind (or the body). The hydraulic model, as the name suggests, concerns the disposition and discharge of that fluid. Freud took on the metaphor quite literally. In one of his earliest theoretical works, *The Project toward a Scientific Psychology* in 1895, he precociously took on the new neurology (the neuron was discovered the same year) and tried to explain all psychological processes in physical or physiological terms. So the mind, the "psychic apparatus" as he called it, took on the same shape and structure (still for the most part unknown) of the brain. Filling the psychic apparatus was psychic energy, a fluidlike substance that Freud simply called "Q" (for quantity), and the model of the mind concerned the vicissitudes of that quantity. By the time he wrote his justly famous *Interpretation of Dreams* a few years later (1900) the model was in place, and he sketches it in the theoretical pages of that great book. The psychic apparatus seemed a lot like a late-nineteenth-century boiler system, the sort that boiled water to heat the houses of the time.

In the psychic apparatus (and in the brain), as in the boiler system, the hot dangerous fluid put tremendous pressure on the entire system, found easy passage through those channels that were open to it, was blocked from others that were kept closed, sometimes with considerable force. It is not hard to see in this some of the basic terms of early Freudian psychodynamics, the notion that the unruly forces of the unconscious put considerable pressure on consciousness (something like the gauge of the system), the charging of certain ideas or urges *(cathexis)*, the strong impetus to release or discharge *(catharsis)*, the need to constrain and contain these dangerous impulses whether by redirecting them *(sublimation)* or by forcefully clamping down on them *(repression)*. As I noted, Freud's idea that the mind was isomorphic (has the same form) as the brain turned out to be fairly naïve, but the idea that psychic energy moved through the brain seeking release, and was sometimes redirected and sometimes blocked, continues to have considerable appeal. In current neuroscience, all of this gets restated in terms of nerve impulses, neurochemistry, the activation or deactivation of synapses, etc. But however plausible it may be in talking about the central nervous system, this language still causes considerable difficulties in talking about emotions, and the reason is the very virtue of the model, that is, it is mechanical, but the emotions, in their full manifestations, are not mere mechanisms.

The hydraulic model needed to be updated, as it is so obviously the product of nineteenth-century technology. The revolution in electronics —and the discovery that the nervous system works by way of electrical impulses—naturally led to a new model of the mind in terms of computer terminology, the high technology of our day. So we have added to or replaced our discussion of pressure and containment, release and repression, with talk of hardware and software ("wet-ware" is a cute but informative variation on these), input and output, programs, "delete" and "save" commands, comparisons to crashing hard drives and memory storage capacities. But this is still mechanical, and practitioners and aspirants in artificial intelligence (AI) find themselves hitting a wall when they try to move beyond calculations and strategic computations (no matter how complicated) to something so organic as emotion.

Can or could a computer have emotions? I get asked this all the time. My answer is agnostic. (Some of my friends were insisting, thirty years ago, that a computer could never beat a master at chess.) But this much is clear: It is not enough to program in the verbal expressions that are typically expressions and reports of emotion, nor would it do to make a computer face, whether a simple "smiley face" or an anatomically correct model of a human face, with the appropriate facial expressions. (It is remarkable what a range of expressions is immediately recognizable even on the prototype basis of a simple "smiley face." One can turn the upward smile curve into a downward grimace curve, adding and making only slight modifications to the eyebrows, and so on. The iconoclastic and conscientiously rude cartoon show *South Park* admirably succeeds in exemplifying a marvelous range of expressions using only such devices.) But between programmed expressions and the experience of emotions still lies a philosophical abyss.

AI is a mediating suggestion in the updating of the hydraulic model. As I said, I am agnostic about the claim that a computer might be programmed to have emotions, but the real value of the artificial intelligence model rather seems to go the other way, namely, that we might better understand human emotions if we think in terms of computer programming. As you will see when I present more of my "cognitive" model of emotions, there is an obvious linkage between the programmable intelligence of computers and the learned and evolved intelligence of emotions. But we should insist on adding one more dimension to the AI model, and that is evolution. A programmer need not care where or how a computer gets made. Indeed one of the leading proposed solutions to the mind-body problem in recent decades has been what is often called *functionalism*, the idea that the material make-up and origins of the substratum of consciousness is of no great importance. Only the structure matters. In other words, one could, in theory, make a brain out of silicon chips, or for that matter out of tin cans and string, so long as its architecture was sufficiently similar to that of a brain. But what brains have in addition to their structure is an evolutionary history, and that history includes both their development in the individual and their evolution through the historical parade of species. What this means, I will suggest, is that the evolution of emotions is not just a chance combination of brain parts that survived the ordeal of natural selection but the successful "fit" of creatures with emotions into an environment that codetermines what will count as their "success" in life. In other words, the brain is not just a mechanism but part of an organism that evolves in an environment. And emotions are not just mechanisms but evolved and learned ways of coping, dealing, and engaging with the world.

What are the alternatives to the hydraulic model? As I said, in the case of anger, at least, it just *feels* so plausible to think of that emotion as a hot fluid building up inside of us. Well, here are three alternatives. Each of them captures the "pressure" part of the model, but without the hydraulics. The first, and most primitive, has to do with the fact that *desires* are involved in the make-up of most emotions, even if, as in grief and embarrassment, the desire is to withdraw from other people. But desire is different from mechanism, and it is not so obviously cause and effect. Desire is as much of a "pull" as it is a "push," an attraction toward something rather than an impulse to get rid of something. It is what Spinoza called "*conatus*," to distinguish it from intellect, and what Freud referred to with his language of *drives*. Desires can be sharply directed, like the ravished desire for food in hunger or the lustful sexual desire of a nineteen-year-old, or they can be a much broader and diffuse concern, for instance, the concern for one's children or aging parents. Desire draws us to things, actions, situations. It is an important element in the intentionality of emotions. We do not only perceive and evaluate the objects of our emotions. We desire them, or we desire to do something with them, or we want something to happen with or to them, as in hope (or not, as in the case of fear.)

Thinking of emotions as we think of desires lessens the temptations of the hydraulic model. To be sure, we occasionally have the odd experience of having a desire that seems not to be ours but rather to be a kind of affliction (perhaps the sexual cravings of that nineteen-year-old), but I think that (a) these are for most of us unusual as we thoughtlessly identify with our desires, and (b) that unusual experience of alienation from one's desires typically involves reflection and some sort of problem in what Harry Frankfurt calls "second-order desires." Frankfurt notes (as did the Stoics) that some of our desires we affirm and want to act upon, others we do not. A smoker or an alcoholic trying to quit no longer desires to act on his or her strong desire to smoke or drink. In fact he or she desires strongly not to act on the desire, and this inner conflict creates the sense of alien desire. But for most of us, most of the time, this is not the way things go. We are quite content to want what we want, and this explains the feeling of "pressure" when there are obstacles in our way, but it is not as if our emotions are therefore not our own.

Second, there is the familiar feeling, in a conversation or a group discussion, perhaps also in class, of the need *to say something*. In class, I watch eager twenty-year-olds not only raising but sometimes vigorously pumping their hands in the air, desperately trying to get my attention so I will call on them so that they can express their insights or deliver their pearls of wisdom. Having been in that position myself (a long time ago) I can still remember the experience. It seems as if something has to come out all right, but it is nothing so vulgar or formless as hot fluid. Rather, it's words. In my privileged position as lecturer, of course, I rarely feel that powerful need, as I am doing the talking a good deal of the time. But in animated conversations with colleagues, I often struggle to "get a word in edgewise," and I want to suggest that this is a lot like the felt need to express our emotions. We all know the frustration and sense of incompleteness when, for example, the professor did not call on us and we didn't get to say our piece. We also know the sense of relief that came with getting our say, the response from the teacher and the reaction from the class not withstanding. Now one might object that this only characterizes the expression of the emotion rather than the emotion itself, but I think that we make too much of this distinction between an emotion and its expression. Except when the expression is suppressed, the expression of the emotion is one with the emotion. So, too, the idea we want to present to the class is rarely fully formed before we get to say it. To a significant extent, the saying of it is where the idea is formed. The feeling of pressure in anger, most notably, is much more like this need to say something than the need to release tension or get something out of our system. Again, our anger is an action in the world rather than an internal commotion. And so, too, all of our emotions are engagements in the world, engagements that are formed, in part, by their expression.

Finally, at an even higher level of sophistication, there is the "pressure" of *narrative*. I periodically emphasized the idea that emotions are not mental entities or events so much as they are processes, where the important difference is that they proceed in time. Love is obviously like this. That there are love stories is not incidental to the emotion of love but makes up its very fabric. The stories may differ—slightly and in details—but the general narratives are more or less fixed. They are summarized, awkwardly and in a somewhat sexist way, by the "boy meets girl, boy loses girl, boy gets girl, they live happily ever after" plot of so many "true" romances. But some such narrative is true of nearly all emotions, apart from those few (like a momentary shock of fear) that are so short-lived that they have no time for narrative, only for a causal explanation (the sudden appearance of a large black shadow or the sound of a terrifying noise). But narratives, as we all know, have a logic. It is not deductive logic or the logic of scientific discovery but it is, nevertheless, logic. When we see a film there are certain expectations that follow from the logic of the emotional narratives, and when that is violated ("No, she can't go off with *him*!") we feel strangely maimed, at least for a little while. (Woody Allen's films *Crimes and*

Misdemeanors and *Match Point* both have this effect.) When we get angry, there is a logic, both in the anger itself and in the situation that ensues once the anger is expressed. It is the narrative of the emotion as well as the narrative that follows its expression that drives emotion along. Again, it is not a matter of "getting something out of our system" but rather of completing the narrative. (That is why it is so very hard to close the novel just before the last chapter or shut off the DVD player at the climax of the movie.)

The hydraulic model captures the dynamism and energy of our emotions, which is why it so appealed to Freud and so many others. And it certainly explains the urgency of many of our emotions and the fact that some of them, at least, do feel as if they are forcing themselves upon us rather than emanating from us. Thus the hydraulic model represents an important part of the phenomenology of at least some emotions. But it is not to be taken literally nor should it be accepted as a general model of emotion. Its representation of passivity, in particular, is something that we should vigorously resist, not that we are never "pressured" by our emotions—for surely we are in any number of cases, if only because we have followed an emotional strategy so far and invested so much in it that we feel that we "cannot" back out now. But that is very different from finding oneself as a cauldron or a boiler and the victim of forces not at all our own doing.

13

MYTH FOUR

Emotions Are "in" the Mind

One of the most profound problems that goes along with thinking about emotions as feelings is the idea that feelings, and therefore emotions, are "in" the mind. The history of the idea of mind, the notion that we have a mind *in which* events and processes take place, is long and intriguing. It is not an idea that Aristotle, for instance, ever entertained. He had a conception of the soul, but the soul for him was nothing but the "form" of an animal or a person, and the form of a person was essentially tied to his or her membership in a social community. He recognized, of course, that we had emotions and other psychological states. He did not doubt that we got angry, felt afraid, had pity for others, loved our spouses and our children, and so on, and he wrote extensively about such passions. But he would have been perplexed if you had asked him whether these were entities "in one's mind."

This was not just a vocabulary problem. To be sure, Aristotle did not have our contemporary concept of an "experience" (prompting the German philosopher Martin Heidegger to comment wryly that the Greeks never had any experiences). The likelihood of Aristotle's perplexity displays a deep conceptual difference dividing us from the Greeks, and also other peoples, for example the ancient Chinese. The Greeks (and the Chinese) did not carve up the world as inner mind versus external world. The concepts of mind and soul developed along with Christianity, although they have earlier origins, one could argue, in the teachings of Aristotle's teachers, Socrates and Plato, and even before that in the ancient Egyptians and earlier Greeks. In Homer, for instance, the soul (after death) is represented as a mere shadow, a "shade," of the living original. Eventually, the mind and the soul acquired a *content*. It started to make literal sense to talk about ideas *in* the mind and as a consequence about the "external world," which became a stock term in philosophy. All of this started to congeal in the early modern period, soon after the Renaissance, and it all came together—or at least we now read as if it all came together—in a single great philosopher, the Frenchman René Descartes.

Descartes (1989) made famous the question that would obsess philosophers for the next three centuries, "how do we know that what we experience in our minds, which we know immediately and beyond a doubt, corresponds to the way the external world, the world outside us, actually is?" The ins and outs of that question and its various affirmative and skeptical answers is beyond our scope here, but we do need to focus on the first part of the question, the confident declaration that we do have knowledge of our own minds. As I said, Aristotle, who in some ways becomes a role model for Descartes, would not have understood the assertion. Nor, of course, would Freud, many years later, who would say that Descartes was simply wrong. Freud rightly insisted that we do not know either immediately or beyond a doubt what is in our own minds. Even if we hold onto the locution of "in the mind," the question of *what* is in our minds is distinct (more or less) from the questions how and whether we *know* what is in our minds. Animals, in an obvious sense, never know what they are feeling. They just feel it.

The answer to the "how and whether" questions is complex and intriguing. Sometimes, even much of the time, we do seem to "just know." But that is because we are well-practiced in the art of monitoring and knowing ourselves and there is (as Descartes pointed out) a special "privileged" access we have to our own psychological states (Moran, 2000). Yet, we do get it wrong, sometimes with remarkable consistency. Indeed, one of the most impressive and disturbing observations over the centuries is that people are often mistaken about their own emotions. (This was not, needless to say, just discovered by Freud.) People misread and misname their emotions. And, of course, they misread other people's emotions, particularly when their perception is colored by their personal preferences, prejudices, and interests. Overly enthusiastic wannabe lovers are disastrously quick to misperceive expressions of romantic interest in their intended beloved. Nervous lovers are disastrously quick to mistake expressions of romantic interest in rivals. Resentful competitors too easily detect disdain (and worse) in the victors. But the same wishful and motivated thinking that leads to the misperception of other people's emotions results in mistakes concerning one's own emotional states as well. The gap between having an emotion and knowing that one has it is enormous, and one might even argue that it is more impressive that we so often get our emotions right than it is surprising that we sometimes get them wrong.

This has terribly disturbing implications for a great deal of psychological research as well as for our confidence in our own grasp of ourselves. A standard technique for ascertaining the emotional states of experimental subjects depends on "self-reports," usually by way of questionnaires and such. But if people are so often wrong about their emotions—especially if they are college undergraduates who are both emotionally overwrought and inexperienced, self-reports are suspicious indeed. My excellent colleague Jamie Pennebaker has suggested ditching such "subjective" reports altogether in favor of straightforward but well-designed objective tests ("Did you floss this morning?" "Have you said the words 'I love you' in the past twenty-four hours?") (Pennebaker, Mehl, and Niederhoffer, 2003). But then, of course, the interpretative skills of the investigator will be under scrutiny more than ever before.

If we do not always recognize our own emotions, we do sometimes get informed by our friends, who see how we are behaving (and thus what we are feeling) more clearly than we do. Occasionally we notice our own curious behavior. Or we surmise it from what we hear ourselves saying (or what we find ourselves writing). Or we have it dredged out of us by a therapist or a psychoanalyst. All of this bears on the question of consciousness and what it means to make an emotion "fully conscious." But before we tackle that complex question, how we know what is "in" our minds, I want to look a lot harder at what we mean by "in our minds." My thesis is that old Aristotle, in what we might see as his naïveté, had a much more manageable conception of psychology than we do. The whole movement of behaviorism, after all, was an effort to get rid of that troublesome "ghost in the machine," and, in philosophy, to get rid of the dualism that gave rise to "the problem of the external world." But in so rejecting the "inner," both psychological and philosophical behaviorism only reinforced the "inner-outer" distinction, denying only that there was anything to be found inside.

Descartes's dualism of mind and body—"Cartesian dualism"—was pretty much accepted by most of the philosophers who followed him, whatever else their differences. John Locke and David Hume rejected Descartes's rationalism, but along with most of the empiricists (including the logical positivists) they held onto dualism without flinching. The most notable exception was Descartes's Dutch contemporary, Baruch Spinoza. Spinoza's view of the passions was brilliant and complex and I will come back to him from time to time. But his view of the mind was radical and for the most part it was anti-Cartesian, despite his philosophical allegiance to Descartes. Spinoza (1981) denied Descartes's dualism and in its place insisted that there is only one thing (or "substance") in the universe, namely the universe as a whole, and mind and body are simply two aspects of that one substance. In other words, he rejected the separateness of minds and the distinctness of minds and bodies. (He also rejected the separateness of God, which got him excommunicated from his Amsterdam synagogue, but that is another long, sad story.) But despite Spinoza, most philosophers and most psychologists, and consequently most of us, incorporated Cartesian dualism into our thinking and speech. There is mind and then there is body (and the rest of the physical universe). There are things in the mind that are directly accessible only to us (that is, to the individual whose mind it is) and then there is the external world, which we simply assume (unless we are philosophers) to be very much like the ideas we have of it in our mind. (Science fiction films, like *The Matrix*, *Vanilla Sky*, and Rick Linklater's *Waking Life*, play on this common assumption.) Emotions are among the contents of the mind, with the slight complication (well-noted by both Descartes and Hume as well as by James) that they also involve the body by way of those "animal spirits" that originate in the body but leave their impression on the mind or soul.

Some philosophers began to rebel against Cartesian dualism by the eighteenth century. The most thoroughgoing rebel was Immanuel Kant, who introduced the wild idea that the external world is itself a product of our mental processes. This put an end to skepticism (for those who accepted his theory) and it also seriously altered the idea of mental "contents." The contents of the mind, for the most part, were the actual things in the world, or *phenomena*, "things as they appear." Kant insisted, however, on an a priori base of sensations and concepts, the raw materials and forms that we use to construct reality. We do not just "make up" the world. But what was "in the mind" was no longer to be thought of as a representation or a mere idea of what was also outside of us in the world. Indeed, it starts to look as if *nothing* is in the mind, although Kant was not ready to make this bold leap. The apparatus of knowledge was still in the mind even if the objects of knowledge were not. Consequently, the status of emotions in Kant's theory is not very clear either, in part because he did not—as Descartes, Spinoza, and Hume had, devote an extensive study to them. But he set the stage for a movement in philosophy that would, without the crude ax of behaviorism, eliminate the need for a mind with contents as opposed to the "external world."

That movement proceeded through the philosophy of the post-Kantians, including G. W. F. Hegel, who forecasted his ambitious philosophy in the aptly titled *Phenomenology of Mind* (or *Spirit*, *Geist*, where the difference in translation indicates a significant ambiguity between a secular and a quasi-religious interpretation of Hegel's thought). At the beginning of the twentieth century, the German-Czech philosopher Edmund Husserl borrowed a key word and concept from Kant and Hegel and initiated a philosophical method he called "phenomenology." As in Kant, Husserl's phenomenology attempted to overcome skepticism without sacrificing the importance of mind. It is with Husserl that the all-important notion of *intentionality* comes to the fore (although it had been kicking around philosophy at least since the late Middle Ages). Instead of talking about mind and its contents, Husserl talked about intentional acts and objects. The mind was essentially an activity (a thesis also promoted by Kant and Hegel), and its objects were essentially the objects in the world. Even sensations, Husserl insisted, were not strange entities in the mind but rather aspects (the "material") of the various acts of consciousness. And concepts were not in the mind either. They were more like the structures of phenomena, the structures of the objects of our experience.

Husserl was not entirely consistent in his attempt to radicalize Kant and Hegel, nor did he free himself from the Cartesian position. (A famous set of lectures he gave in Paris, which attracted much attention and the attendance of several of Husserl's most famous followers, were published under the title *Cartesian Meditations*.) Nor did he have much to say about the nature and structure of emotions. But one of Husserl's students, Martin Heidegger, did make the radical break from Descartes, insisting from the start (in his monumental work, *Being and Time*) that "Being-in-the-World" was a "unitary phenomenon," not divided into mind or consciousness on the one hand and the world on the other. In fact, Heidegger was so resolutely anti-Cartesian that he refused to use such words as "mind" and "consciousness" and even "experience," suggestive as they were of the Cartesian position. But Heidegger did give a central place to the emotions, or at least to moods, which he insisted "tuned us to the world." (There is a noteworthy pun here; the German word for mood is *stimmung* and the word for "tuning" is *bestimmen*.) But another follower of Husserl (at least in his early years) was one of those young Frenchmen who were so enthused upon hearing Husserl's lecture in Paris, Jean-Paul Sartre. Sartre took the bold new picture of phenomenology, as radicalized by Heidegger, and used it directly to carry out an investigation of emotions.

In that theory (or what Sartre admits is only a "sketch" of a theory), the first target of attack is William James. The second is Freud. Both are guilty, Sartre charges, of overmechanizing the emotions. They are also guilty, Sartre says, of minimizing the importance of the defining characteristic of emotions, their intentionality. (In all fairness, both James and Freud do employ the concept of intentionality, but Sartre is right. They give it a much less prominent place than he does, and both of those great theorists end up as Cartesians in spite of themselves.) In an earlier essay and in his later tome *Being and Nothingness*, Sartre argues that there are no "contents" to consciousness. Consciousness is pure activity, the activity of intending the world. Accordingly, consciousness as such is *nothing*, and the emotions thus cannot be contents of consciousness. Emotions are rather strategies for dealing with the difficulties we encounter in the world. (You can appreciate just how beholden I am to Sartre, more than to anyone else.) Feelings play no important role in Sartre's theory. Neither do behavior and bodily disturbances play any essential role, although Sartre allows that these are typical *consequences* of emotion. In other words, Sartre allows us, through phenomenology, to eliminate "the mind." We can still talk, as did Aristotle, about anger and love and thoughts and ideas. But we are now talking about things done by (or suffered by) the person, not the contents of a mysterious inner realm.

Sartre does not share Heidegger's insistence on eliminating all talk of "mind," "consciousness," and "experience," and for this reason his phenomenology remains seemingly more familiar and more consistent than Heidegger's, who clearly drifted away from it by the time he had gotten a few hundred pages into *Being and Time*. For Sartre as for Husserl, phenomenology is the study of *the essential structures of consciousness*, but now without the cumbersome Cartesian notion that consciousness has contents. It is just activity, the activity of intending the world, and some of this activity is the having of emotions. So the phenomenology becomes the description of the essential structures of emotion, which means, in part, the description of their objects and their strategies and purposes. In his early essay on the emotions, Sartre seems to think that all emotions serve more or less the same purpose, *to escape from a difficult world*. Thus emotions all involve a kind of strategic denial: the denial of difficulty, the reevaluation of a difficult situation, or a mode of behavior that avoids, ignores, or renders one oblivious to such a situation.

An extreme case of such avoidance, Sartre contends, is fainting. I have trouble understanding this as an emotion or even as an expression of emotion, but the circumstance Sartre paints for us—a young proper lady in an extremely awkward social situation—is in its own way oddly persuasive. Much more convincing is his retelling of the Aesop's fable of the fox and the grapes and the face-saving strategy of resentment. ("Those grapes are sour anyway.") We will talk further about such strategies a bit later, but suffice it here to say that Sartre considerably expands his sense of the role and function of the emotions in the five years between the publication of his essay and the publication of *Being and Nothingness*. He also solidifies his anti-Cartesian position regarding the "contents" of consciousness. Not only does consciousness not have a content. It is literally "nothing," and as such is not part of the causal order of nature. His ultimate aim, beyond our scope here, is to defend an "absolute freedom" in which we are responsible for everything we do or think or become. But his first accomplishment, of great relevance here, is that he solidifies phenomenology as an anti-Cartesian enterprise. There is no mind apart from body and consciousness is necessarily embodied, but consciousness is utterly irreducible to body.

If this sounds paradoxical or self-contradictory, that is part of Sartre's point, that there is something paradoxical or self-contradictory about the very existence of consciousness ("being-for-itself"). Sartre does not want to ignore the bodily manifestations of emotion, but he prefers to recast these neither as symptoms nor as expressions but as part of the strategy and activity of having an emotion. And he does not deny that the emotions are psychological but he does not equate the psychological with what is "in" the psyche. The psychological is a distinctive set of activities directed at and in the world.

But what of the obvious? What of the fact that we do know our own emotions (even if we can be wrong about them) in a way that is different from the way that anyone else—a friend, a voyeur, a psychiatrist, a neuro-scientist—knows of our emotions? Don't we have some sort of "privileged access" to our own emotions, thoughts, and feelings? That is, we typically do know what we are thinking or feeling without having to look at our facial expressions or watch our behavior or listen to what we say (much less look at our brains), as we do when we try to read the thoughts and feelings of other people, even those with whom we are most intimate. Moreover, we can keep our thoughts or feelings "to ourselves," without making them evident to other people, even those who know us best and with whom we are most intimate. And it is a good thing that we can, one might add, for who knows how much damage we would do to each other if our every thought and feeling were transparent to others. How does phenomenology, in eliminating the mind, account for this, the seeming "privacy" that Descartes took as one of his primary data? What about what he called "subjectivity," the unique (even if not total) transparency of oneself to oneself, which seems so obvious for each of us who is self-consciousness?

The reply to this is that phenomenology does not at all try to eliminate or dispense with subjectivity, our unique perspective from the first-person standpoint. Rather, it highlights and celebrates it. I am indeed aware of my own thoughts and feelings in a way and from a perspective that is mine and mine alone (leaving aside certain alleged "psychic" skills and wild brain hook-up experiments that are still in the purely speculative stage). There is no need to deny this and considerable absurdity if we do so. What we can and should deny is that this peculiar perspective indicates a mysterious private space, accessible to me alone (and so, too, in each of our cases). There are not different realms, only a great many points of view.

Subjectivity, with all of its peculiarities, remains very real. Consciousness, that is the fact of subjectivity, is captured in Thomas Nagel's now famous colloquial expression "what it's like to be [a bat, a cat, a Thai, a Native American, a white Christian man, an African American Jewish woman . . .]." Subjectivity is an essential property of a *person* (or a creature) who necessarily has a body and therefore a place and thus a distinctive perspective. But there is no consciousness, which is why Kant denies that there is any "soul-thing" (despite his belief in the immortality of the soul), and why Sartre rather bluntly insists that consciousness is no-thing or nothingness. In fact, even William James has his doubts. In a famous article entitled "Does Consciousness Exist?" his answer is a cautious "no," although there are still perceptions and thoughts and various acts of consciousness in addition to those pesky bodily sensations that remain at the heart of his analysis of emotion.

So how does emotion fit into this phenomenological picture? Quite simply, emotions are *acts* of consciousness. They are not entities *in* consciousness. They can also become objects *for* consciousness, through reflection, as we become aware of the fact that we are getting angry or falling in love. But the model is now very different from the model we discussed in the previous chapter, the image of feelings in the mind analogous to fluid in a boiler system occasionally bursting out in more or less controlled expressions and behavior in the real world. The mind—or better, consciousness—is more or less continuously active in its engagement with the world. Some of those engagements involve behavior and expression so restrained that they are not at all evident to anyone else—except, perhaps, to someone who knows you very well or has been specially trained to perceive such things. Our emotions, when we are infants, exist as an unconstrained continuum from experience to expression. As our emotions get more refined and specific, so, too, does our ability to constrain our expressions. (Some people, needless to say, learn this much better than others, and some cultures are much more thorough than others in teaching it.) So the privacy of our emotions and other mental states is not a matter of metaphysics but of learning. We *learn* to keep our thoughts and feelings to ourselves.

Furthermore, every culture has what Paul Ekman calls its "display rules." Even if some emotions are "basic," hard-wired, and universal (as Ekman believes), there is nevertheless enormous cultural diversity in teaching which emotions should be displayed and how, and in what circumstances. And each individual, too, on the basis of his or her experience and social position learns in remarkable detail how he or she ought to express his or her emotions, and which emotions ought to be expressed. Of course, many of us get it wrong, or we might begin with an unfortunate endowment of either temperament, upbringing, or environment. So, too, perhaps, we may sometimes be justified in saying that whole cultures get it wrong, for example, when continuing ethnic rivalry and hatred or widespread greed and selfishness destroy nations and even whole civilizations. But all of this happens in *our* real world, not a world "external" to the mind, and nothing happens in the inner reaches of the mind. There simply are no inner reaches of the mind. There are just the peculiarities of the first-person standpoint and of particular people and personalities.

So once again, we are thrown back to the ancients and to Aristotle. Sometimes, there are philosophical advantages to arriving early on the stage of history. There is no doubt that the invention of subjectivity and the spirituality (among other things) that culminated in Cartesianism contributed a great deal to modern life and philosophy. But they also introduced some obstinate problems and obstacles to the progress of both ethical and scientific understanding. The idea that emotions are ineffable, subjective, and private, immune to ethical scrutiny and scientific investigation, is one of them. What Aristotle and even the Stoics recognized is that our emotions are not "in us" and private but out there *in the world*, in *social* space. Our emotions arise, for the most part, in the nexus of our interpersonal relationships. Thus we might say that emotions are *political*. This is not just to say that they can be used to manipulate other people. They also originate *with* other people, and their structure is virtually always some sort of social or interpersonal structure. Looking inside, "introspecting," is looking in the wrong place for them.

14

MYTH FIVE

Emotions Are Stupid
(They Have No Intelligence)

I have insisted since the introduction that emotions give us insight and have "intelligence." It is time to start making good on that claim. First, it has been necessary to get rid of those conceptions, metaphors, and primitivist theories that would make emotions out to be mechanisms that, no matter how well functioning and convenient for survival, would not even count as candidates for intelligence. A simple thermostat, although it may be precisely designed and well made, is not intelligent, no matter how many dramatic shifts in temperature it may have to regulate during a normal week in a climate of extremes (the Arizona desert, for example). A computerized thermostat, which might be programmed with many more variables and set to vary over a course of a day, weeks, or months, is no more a candidate for intelligence than the simple thermostat. Again, I do not want to enter into the still-speculative debate about when we might be willing to say that a computer or a robot or a manmade android is or could be conscious or intelligent or have emotions, but it is clear that certain sorts of mechanisms do not raise such issues. Daniel Dennett, possibly the cleverest and in any case the most entertaining writer on these subjects, somewhat confuses the issue by insisting that even the simple thermostat can be described via "the intentional stance," *as if* it had intentionality (1991). But the question then becomes, as we move from thermostats to computers to flowers to bees to apes to humans, when are we justified in moving from the "as if" to a literal ascription of intentionality? And the unhelpful answer seems to be, whenever the creature in question is conscious and has intentionality and intelligence.

Human physiology is a marvelous mechanism and the human body is wonderfully complex and remarkably efficient most of the time. There is, to borrow W. B. Cannon's wonderful phrase, the "wisdom of the body." (Cannon, instructively, was one of the first and most profound critics of William James's theory of the emotions.) But physiology, no matter how well designed or evolved, does not have intentionality or intelligence (nor does it literally have "wisdom"). Of course, the body and its organs can be described as having purpose or function, as in the "the purpose or function of the heart is to circulate the blood around the body." But it is one of the long-running debates in the philosophy of biology whether any such functional descriptions should be taken at face value as "teleological" or purpose driven, at least in science. A hard-headed physiologist might well insist that "no, the heart pumps because it is a muscle that is stimulated by electrical impulses and when it contracts the result is that blood courses through the body and the organism lives. But the purpose is not intrinsic to the organ itself." And this, of course may all be true. Nevertheless, it is not to deny that the heart has a purpose and a function in the life of the organism. Emotions might be describable in detail as neurological mechanisms, but that is not to deny that they have purposes and functions in our lives that cannot be described mechanically. Thus I argued that the intentional language of folk psychology is at present indispensable for talking about emotions. (The behavior of animals is, in some quarters, still in dispute, but there, too, the rejection of intentional language is now a rather eccentric position.)

Intentionality is the key to emotional intelligence. Engagement with the world requires having knowledge about the world, even if—often—this knowledge is imperfect, incomplete, or just plain mistaken. But the fact that emotions are *about* the world, engagements *in and with* the world, also means that feelings, especially the bodily feelings that James talked about, do not have intentionality. (The fact that we can use them to find out about our own bodies is important, but it does not mean that the feelings themselves have intentionality.) Anthony Kenny, in one of the first books on emotion in English-speaking analytic philosophy (*Action, Emotion, and Will*, 1963) struggled to distinguish two kinds of feelings, nonintentional and intentional. Among the former were bellyaches and pains in the side, itches and flashes of color. Most of James's sensations are clearly nonintentional. Among the latter were the emotions, and Kenny took great pains to insist and explain that emotions were *necessarily* intentional.

By insisting that emotions are intentional Kenny also suggested that they involved conceptually grasping and evaluating the world in distinctive ways. And these ways could be evaluated. Often, an emotion got it right. The world (or some particular aspect of it) really is dangerous or infuriating.

Sometimes, the emotion got the world right but it was shortsighted or narrow-minded, ignoring the larger implications or the history of the incident in question. A parent who gets angry at a young child may well find reason to be angry, but the age of the child may be such as to make such anger (and the blame and ascription of responsibility that go with it) utterly inappropriate. And sometimes the facts are right but the evaluation is wrong or unfair. A man or woman who gets jealous just because his or her spouse politely talks to a good-looking stranger at a party (assuming there is no hint of actual infidelity) may be right about what has happened but completely off base regarding the warrant of the emotion.

Sometimes the emotions get downright confused. They operate on the basis of the wrong information, false intelligence. Often, and especially when the emotion is more or less urgent or spontaneous, our knowledge of the facts is incomplete or inadequate, and there may have not yet been the opportunity to learn more about the situation. An under-pressure boss gets angry because he too quickly assumes that his assistant has lost some important papers when in fact they are in his own briefcase. His anger is wholly unjustified, and one certainly hopes that when this comes to light his anger will not only cease but it will be followed by a bit of embarrassment and a sincere apology. In the case of a faulty evaluation, the parent who gets angry with a child or the boss who fires an employee for a simple minor mishap may be right about the facts but they are nevertheless unintelligent in their anger. But if emotions sometimes go wrong and if their evaluations are sometimes unfair or contrary to reason, that is to say quite clearly that they have intelligence, because being wrong presupposes being capable of being right. "Being stupid" already presupposes having some (just not enough) intelligence. Intelligence involves grappling with putative facts and values, even if ineffectively, and not just blindly reacting to the world.

Kenny further argues, also borrowing from the Scholastic philosophers, the idea that every emotion type, that is the *kind* of emotion rather than any particular instance or instances of it, can be defined by its *formal object*. This is in a nutshell the intentional structure of the various emotions. So that the formal object of fear is *something dangerous*, the formal object of anger is *something offensive*, and so on. What it is that is dangerous or offensive is, of course, dependent on the situation, the circumstances, and the psychological make-up and subjective state of the individual. But what is built into the very concept of an emotion is that it has such a structure, a formal object that is defined in terms of the *kinds* of things it picks out or perceives in the environment.

To say that emotions have intelligence, in short, is to insist that they involve concepts and conceptualization, values and evaluation, what many psychologists call "cognition" and "appraisal" respectively (although the relationship between these is not always clear). Thus one of the favorite methods of philosophers in coming to understand emotions is *conceptual analysis*, unpacking the precise nature of the formal object that, in effect, defines the nature of the emotion. This is by no means a simple matter. The variety and variations of emotions make such a task difficult, and language, while it is the basis of conceptual analysis, can also be confusing. For instance, in chapter 7, I point out that the seemingly single emotion *shame* has two quite different and distinct meanings in French. So are there two emotions or just one? I would say two—at least. Then there are the extended or derivative uses of emotion terms, for instance in our tendency to personify things in the world. Thus we get angry at the stubborn bolt or the recalcitrant jar lid as if they are *trying* to make our tasks harder. Does this indicate a lack of intelligence or is this a perfectly rational extension of concepts that are normally reserved for actual agents? (One can easily imagine ways in which such behavior would clearly become irrational, for instance, if one started pleading with the bolt or jar.) The moral contexts within which we discuss the emotions also involve concepts and evaluations that one might argue are not necessarily intrinsic to the emotion. This is not to say, of course, that our emotions (or emotion types) are unanalyzable. It is just to suggest that conceptual analysis may be tied to context and to particular languages more than philosophers would like to think, and what conceptual analysis yields may therefore not be an understanding of the emotion as such but only of an emotion as understood in a certain context, culture, and language. (That is why Paul Griffiths, among others, insists on getting "beneath" the language and seeking the emotion as such, which he construes as a neurological phenomenon.)

But to make things much more interesting (and complicated), emotions also have the power to *constitute* reality in a certain way. They *bestow* value as well as appraise it. (The verb "constitute" comes from Kant. The notion of "bestowal" I borrow from Irving Singer, *The Nature of Love*.) To say that an emotion constitutes reality (from the first-person point of view) is to point out that being angry, for example, *makes* the person at whom one is angry appear as *infuriating*. The hated person appears as *hateful*. The beloved appears as *lovely*. This last is a good example of bestowal, for the lover bestows charms and virtues on the beloved. That is to say, the lover sees good things in the beloved that are more than just the virtues that might be ascertained by anyone else, or by some "objective" study or survey that identified this and that feature of personality. A misleading way to say this is by way of the old cliché "beauty is in the eye of the beholder," but what is important is to note that this does not deny the beauty of the beloved, it only shifts its point of origin. The lover bestows beauty on the beloved. It is not there to be merely discovered but neither is it merely imaginary or delusional. It is neither in the eye nor in the beloved but in the connection between the two.

This point about love is worth repeating. Cynics (sometimes Freud and his followers) offer the harsh view that the person loved is not the beloved at all, but rather a projection or a phantom of wish fulfillment that may have remarkably little to do with the actual flesh and blood human being. And, to be sure, there are those pathological cases where the fantasy does take the place of any real relationship, and the best way to maintain such a fantasy is to keep a substantial distance from the beloved. Thus long-distance relationships are sometimes prone to such fantasy-building. (There is a wonderful but awful example in Terrence Malick's spiritual World War II film, *The Thin Red Line*, where a soldier dreams a fantasy version of his lovely faithful wife for most of the picture, but then is driven to despair and suicide when he suddenly receives a "Dear John" letter.) Even long-distance commuting couples are subject to such fantasy. As they all know (or come to find out), spending weekends together is not the same as spending everyday life together, and when the two modes of rela-tionship are confused, we are probably right in diagnosing the problem as one in which one or both people loved more in fantasy (of what might be) than in reality. So, too, unrequited love naturally lends itself to such unre-alistic projection, whether by way of absurdly enhancing the beloved ("she's really the most beautiful woman in the world") or, when love falters, by way of demonization ("she's such a succubus, a total tease, an utterly despicable person"—when all she did was to say "no" to the continu-ation of a disintegrating relationship). But love in general is not so fantasy driven. Love may focus more intensely on the beloved's virtues than other people might, and it generously bestows charms on the basis of fairly ordinary features, but there need be no distorting projections, no phan-toms, and no fantasy.

To take a rather mundane but I think significant example, I adore my wife's nose. She has not done anything to it, I should say, in the fashions that too many young women these days feel compelled to follow. It is, "objectively," a not-atypical Irish nose, thin with a small rise near the bridge. If I saw it in a picture book, say a *National Geographic*, I would not think twice about it. One might say I bestow charm and beauty to my wife's nose, but it is not as if I add anything to or falsify my perception. One might say that I "idealize" her nose, but this wouldn't be quite right either. I love her nose because it is *her* nose.

This example adds a dimension to the notion of intelligence, which I have thus far mostly described in the rather cool terms of information and evaluation. But there is also aesthetic intelligence, intelligence regarding not only the reality and warrant of emotions but also of their tendency to enhance and enrich our lives. Thus a cynic (a "realist") who rightly sees everything that is corrupt and rotten with the world may be correct, but he or she will have a miserable life. By contrast, a Buddhist who insists on seeing the good (or at least the ultimate "indifference") of everything might be less accurate about the state of the world but will probably live a better life. So, too, I could dismiss my wife's nose as "just another nose." But that would not be at all intelligent, even if it might parade as "realistic." I would miss one of the wonders of my world.

The notion of "emotional intelligence" hit the public and the publishing world in a best-selling book by science writer and journalist Daniel Goleman in 1995. I have not said much about Goleman's book, but I do think that it was important in that it put the topic of emotions and intelligence on the public map and gave voice to the concerns that many of us have had for several decades. But it was a secondary work, and the concept of emotional intelligence already had substantial scientific credentials. Moreover, I found Goleman's treatment of the topic still mired in the old tradition of emotional *control*, which is just what I want to get away from. To me, as I have already suggested, emotional intelligence is not so much concerned with emotional control as it is about intelligence *in* emotions, that is, the essential conceptual and evaluative components of emotions, their insights, and not just their "regulation." To say that emotions have intelligence is thus to insist that they *essentially* involve and require the abilities to conceptualize and evaluate and that they often employ these abilities to excellent effect.

Again, we may well have evolved with these abilities (as did many of our animal brethren) and they may sometimes be more or less "hard-wired" into us. Or they may just be modifications or by-products of features that were selected by evolution. But the fact is that we do have and regularly exercise these abilities, and they are what make our emotions *emotions* and not simply bodily feelings or physiological reactions triggered by disturbing environmental stimuli. It is our emotions that make us human, and this is not in contrast to our much-touted intelligence but in intimate conjunction with it. We are, putting various bits of Aristotle together, rational-social-intelligent-emotional (as well as featherless bipedal) animals. All of these features are both important and interconnected (except, perhaps, for our featherlessness).

The concept of "emotional intelligence" was originally suggested and investigated by Peter Salovey and J. D. Mayer (2004), who suggest that there are at least four "branches" of emotional intelligence. The first had to do with *perceiving* emotions, that is, recognizing emotions both in oneself and in others. These are two different but evidently related processes.

Traditional Cartesian wisdom says that we learn to recognize emotions in ourselves first and then learn to apply the same labels to other people. But convincing arguments and research since the nineteenth century suggest that it may be the other way around, that first we learn to recognize emotions in others, particularly when they directly affect us—Mom's losing her temper or crying in despair when, as an infant, you threw your food on the floor—and then we learn to identify similar emotions in ourselves. Or, more likely, these are two parallel tracks that cross over and interact at many points. There may well be a kind of immediate and intuitive way of knowing what others feel. (Neurologists these days talk about "mirror neurons" that make such immediate empathy plausible.) But, even if there is (sometimes) such immediate awareness of other people's emotions, the recognition of their emotions is not a simple process, and perceiving emotions—one's own or others'—is not merely "natural" in the reductive sense that people often employ. We *learn* to identify our emotions, and it may be no easy matter to learn to recognize, not to mention empathize with, those of other people.

As I have said before, having an emotion is one thing. (Animals and infants do that.) But recognizing *that* we have an emotion involves much more than this. This is what we must learn to do, using language. But there is no "natural" connection between a word and an emotion. (Even such expletives as "Ouch" are more culture and language bound than we think.) And given that there is a difference, as we saw, between ascribing emotions to ourselves and ascribing emotions to others, the "parallel tracks" are nevertheless quite different. Moreover, in addition to the specific recognition of specific emotions (though whether an emotion is hatred or resentment, say, is not always easy to ascertain), there is the ability to recognize the gross fact that someone else or even oneself is in *some* emotional state. But there are people who have trouble even with this. Autistic children, in particular, have a great deal of trouble learning to recognize emotions in others. Sociopaths also lack this ability because they lack not only empathy but the willingness to acknowledge any emotions other than their own. And some people seem pathologically incapable of recognizing that they are in any emotional state.

The recognition of emotions, in short, is no simple matter. It is not as if emotions come with labels on them. Nor are emotions readily identifiable entities that are always the same. Anger in one context (say a boss at an employee) and in another (the same boss at her husband) may be so different as to evade easy identification. Add in the likelihood of self-deception, especially where strong emotions are involved, and you have a recipe for confusion, conflation, and outright denial. This is also true of recognizing emotions in others. Some husbands are famously "insensitive" or oblivious to even the most dramatic changes in their wives' emotional states (perhaps rationalizing these away with reference to distinctively "female" feelings and physiology). Such oblivion is rarely because of an autistic or sociopathic personality (although it may seem as such sometimes). Rather, overwhelming self-interest and the desire to preserve the peace at any cost militates against the recognition of anger (which might require a vigorous defense) or upset (which would require uncomfortable commiseration, at the very least). What this means, again, is that emotional intelligence is indeed *intelligence*, in the full sense of that word. It requires learning a valuable set of personal and interpersonal skills without which our emotional lives and, especially, our emotional lives together would be much more troubled than we can even imagine.

Second, Salovey and Mayer describe emotional intelligence in terms of being able to use one's emotions to facilitate thought and direct thinking. This is a thesis that has been dramatically argued and illustrated by Antonio Damasio on the basis of his clinical and neurological studies. The folk tradition and philosophers and social scientists as well are fond of drawing a distinction between the different and often opposed "faculties" of reason and emotion, but what Damasio has shown is that people with severe emotional deficits (because of stroke, tumor, or other lesions) suffer enormously from *not being able to make rational decisions*, despite the fact that their other "cognitive" faculties (in other words, what is usually called "intelligence") seem to be functioning fine. They can calculate consequences and compare options but because they do not really *care* about either consequences or options they have no basis for making a decision. A few iconoclastic philosophers have argued the same thesis for years. Nietzsche, for instance, argued that every passion involves its "quantum of reason" and it is by way of our passions—and the strength of our passions—that we can make any decisions at all. Salovey and Mayer also mention one's ability to use emotions in imagination and memory, noting that when we are sad or depressed, we are much more likely to remember other occasions when we have been sad or depressed, and when we are happy, we are more likely to remember other happy occasions. (Have you ever noticed how much good restaurant conversation is devoted to the memory of other good restaurants? Or how scenic drive conversations tend to include reminiscences of other scenic drives?) They also talk about using changes of mood to understand other points of view. When one is sad or depressed, that may be an apt time to reflect on the sad fate of others, and it is not because "misery loves company."

Third, there is the general ability to *understand* one's emotions. Again, this is not a simple matter, for if not even the name of an emotion is automatically forthcoming then the *meaning* of an emotion is bound to be even more evasive. Understanding one's emotion is not just identifying or recognizing it, of course, but rather seeing and appreciating its causes (including its not-so-obvious underlying causes) and understanding its history and significance both in one's own life and, perhaps, in the life of one's family or the larger community. The ability to understand one's emotions also means understanding an often conflicting mix of emotions, for not only do emotions not come with a ready-made label, they often appear in confusing combination. The urge to simplify or to insist on a single and simple emotional response is yet another kind of denial. Andrew Ortony, Gerald Clore, and Allen Collins (1988) give the cute example of one's long-lost dog bounding across one's fresh-laid cement sidewalk. How could this emotional mix be captured with a single name?

Patricia Greenspan argues that the very possibility of "mixed emotions" militates against an overly "cognitive" or "judgmentalist" understanding of emotion, as such cases often seem to involve outright contradictions. When one's best friend wins the prize that one coveted for oneself there is bound to be a mix of vicarious joy (for your friend) and envy, and most likely much else besides (anger? humiliation? embarrassment? intensified *philia*?). Coping with any emotion can be difficult, but coping with conflicted emotions may sometimes seem impossible. Satisfying or even expressing one emotion may stultify satisfaction or expression of others. Add to this the complexity of "display rules" and all of those cultural demands and expectations, for instance, that one should be happy for one's friends' successes, and we have at least a recipe for deep confusion and unhappiness, not to mention denial and hypocrisy. (Just look at those cruel television close-ups of the faces of Academy Award nominees who did *not* get the award.) I do not think that such cases involve contradictions, but neither would I deny their extreme complexity.

But mixed emotions should not be thought of according to the simplistic "hydraulic" model of two streams or currents running against one another. A good part of the complexity of our emotional life has to do with the complexity of the emotions themselves. I have already suggested that emotions are structured by judgments, but these judgments are of radically different kinds and sometimes involve quite sophisticated concepts and appraisals of the world. In chapter 18, I will attempt an abbreviated survey of some of the judgments that are involved in our emotions, but we have already seen most of these in the discussion of the various individual emotions in Part I. For example, there are judgments of responsibility in anger, shame, guilt, and pride. These might even include moral principles, as in moral indignation. There are judgments of relative merit and status, for instance, in contempt and resentment. There are judgments of entitlement, notably in such emotions as pride and jealousy. There are judgments as well as desires for intimacy, as in love, and for distance, for example in such emotions as scorn and loathing, and perhaps in certain modes of awe and admiration as well. Thus there is a great deal to understand in our emotions, not just in terms of their causes and contexts but in terms of their constitutive structure. This is the heart of emotional intelligence, the considerable intelligence that we find *in* our emotions.

Fourth and finally, Salovey and Mayer say that emotional intelligence involves *managing* one's emotions, one of the main themes of this book as well. I will have much more to say about this in what follows. I have already hinted at what I take to be the distinctively human element in emotions, reflection and our ability to identify and spell out our emotional engagements in the world, and this remarkable ability allows us not only to understand but "work on," modify, and, in exceptional cases, radically alter our emotions. A good deal of this "work" has to do with understanding and evaluating the judgments that constitute our emotions. We might think of this as a second level of emotional intelligence, the intelligence we bring *to* our emotional lives, trying to put it all in reasonable order, guiding our good sense to make sure our emotions are fair and accurate in their judgments and engagement in the world. Thus managing our emotions is not an issue of control, as Goleman too strenuously insists, but literally a matter of intelligence and good sense.

The question comes up, needless to say, what kind of intelligence emotional intelligence is. Is it just a variation of other forms of intelligence? Is it *sui generis*? Here I tend to side with Howard Gardiner, who has written extensively about "multiple intelligences." Here, as elsewhere, the urge to simplify and unify is powerful, and it would indeed be easier if one could say, in line with the traditional measure of "IQ," that there is one set of skills that counts as intelligence and any suggestion of alternative forms of intelligence is parasitic or metaphorical at best. Certainly the test makers would like to make that point. But the whole of human history points in the other direction. Good intellectual problem solvers may be socially incompetent or hopeless when it comes to fixing a lamp or changing a computer ribbon. Genuinely dumb or inarticulate politicians may nevertheless display a remarkable savvy for leadership. Salovey, Mayer, and Goleman (2004) have codified an important mode of intelligence that, although it often works best in conjunction with the others, is distinctive and different. Indeed, it may well be that there are different kinds of emotional intelligence as well, perhaps one sort of intelligence that is more intuitive and built into the emotions themselves and another kind of intelligence that is more thoughtful, reflective, and managerial. The most intelligent emotions will, naturally, tend to partake in the wisdom of the world that is learned through reading and study, but we all recognize—and we philosophers with considerable embarrassment—that this is never enough. Recognizing what wisdom is and practicing it in one's emotional life are two sadly distinct aspects of character and personality. The point and challenge of this book is to bring them together, and persuade you that knowing about and understanding our emotions in theory can be an important step to living wisely and well.

15

MYTH SIX
Two Flavors of Emotion, Positive and Negative

Among the many different evaluative judgments that enter into an emotion, the most straightforward are judgments of approval and disapproval, liking and disliking, approach and avoidance. This is so obvious that I barely thought it worth mentioning. But this obvious fact leads to a natural and commonsense distinction between two kinds of emotion, "positive" and "negative," where the idea is that some emotions are good and good for you (love, for instance), while others are bad and bad for you (anger and hatred, for example). But this seemingly simple distinction is actually many distinctions masquerading as one. Once again, the conflation of these many distinctions is another instance of primitivization of emotions, another way of making them seem much more simple and one-dimensional than they are. Thus another excuse rears its head, that is, another reason for taking emotions less seriously than we ought to.

This distinction between "positive" and "negative" emotions—or what psychologists prefer to call by the chemistry term "valence"—has become central to not only common sense but to serious social science as well. The American psychologist Andrew Ortony and his colleagues (1988) have written,

From a global perspective, it seems that past research on emotion converges on only two generalizations. One is that emotion consists of arousal and appraisal. The other, emerging from the scaling literature, is that any dimensional characterization of emotions is likely to include at least the two dimensions of *activation* and *valence*.

To say the obvious, some things are judged favorably, other unfavorably. We are evaluating creatures. When we are emotional, few things seem indifferent to us. But obviously this is not peculiar to emotions. Simple judgments of taste and comfort are like this, and so, too, far down the phylo-genetic scale of animal species. One-celled organisms approach and devour some substances while avoiding others. Many philosophers and psychologists have claimed that pleasure and pain (or displeasure) lie at the heart of all emotions and provide an excellent means for distinguishing them. Hume thought that all emotions were essentially pleasant or unpleasant sensations ("impressions"). Spinoza, at one point, says that there are only three "basic" emotions (out of which all others are constructed), and those are pleasure, pain, and desire. (We would not count desire as an emotion, although it is an ingredient in virtually all emotions.) The globally esteemed contemporary Dutch psychologist Nico Frijda (1986) has also argued that pleasure and pain form the basis for all emotions. And in everyday parlance, of course, we often employ the idea of "positive" and "negative" emotions, the most evident example being the polarity of love and hate, which are thus said to be "opposites."

While I would not disagree with the obvious, that we do take pleasure in some things and find other things distasteful or painful, I think that the common tendency among both ordinary people and highly sophisticated scientists to think that all emotions are either "positive" or "negative" is one more example of how we fail to appreciate the richness and subtlety of emotions. Emotions are sometimes *defined* by having just this sort of "valence," for example, by Louis Charland (2002). But most emotions are "mixed" in terms of their constituent judgments, even those of a straightforward pro or con nature. Hate, to take a prominent example, may well combine intense dislike with grudging respect. In this chapter, I would like to cast serious doubt on the distinction between "positive" and "negative" emotions and suggest, as my old teacher Frithjof Bergmann used to say, that thinking in such simple-minded terms is like going into an art museum and being allowed only to say "good" or "yuck" while looking at a series of wonderful paintings. My argument is not that there is no such thing as valence or no such polarity or "opposites" but rather that there are *many* such polarities and oppositions. I summarize some (but by no means all) of them in the following chart.

"positive"	"negative"
that is good	that is bad
that gives me pleasure	that gives me pain
that makes me happy	that makes me sad

that is right	that is wrong
this is a virtue	this is a vice
approach	avoidance
approval	disapproval
innervating	enervating
that is healthy	that is unhealthy
that makes me calm, comfortable	that makes me "upset"
this is conducive to happiness	this is conducive to unhappiness
positive attitude to object	negative attitude to object
positive attitude to self	negative attitude to self
positive attitude to relationship	negative attitude to relationship
this object has high status	this object has low status
I have high (or higher) status	I have low (or lower) status
You have high (or higher) status	You have low (or lower) status
It is your responsibility (praise)	It is your responsibility (blame)
I take responsibility (and praise)	I take responsibility (and blame)

In brief, the judgments that make up the various emotions evaluate quite a variety of matters. For instance, the "positive" emotions, love, for instance, tend to be favorable toward their objects. But love is also commendable to have and express, indeed, it is often presented as a passion that ought to trump all others. Furthermore, love is also said to be healthy for the lover, although I expect that here the benefits of a happy marriage and a healthy relationship are too easily confused with the trauma of courtship and romance. But even if love is good for you, the fact that an emotion is good for you is not usually what the term "positive" means (unless coming from the mouth of a physician). Good health is rather something of a fringe benefit. (Most people do not get happy or fall in love in order to live longer.) Moreover, love can also make the lover feel enhanced and even ecstatic, but this is certainly not to be glibly equated with health and physical well-being. The sad truth is that love can sometimes be very bad for you, especially if it is the *wrong* love, and it gets no better as it gets more intense and obsessive.

So, too, anger (a notoriously "negative" emotion) displays a negative attitude toward its object, but whether it is appropriate to feel angry or express anger is a matter of context and subject to ancient disagreements. For many people, anger feels bad too, but whether this is because of the unpleasantness of the emotion or expected bad consequences or because of years of moral and religious warnings against it would be hard to say. Indeed, I pointed out early on that many people actually enjoy getting angry, whether or not they can admit this to themselves or would announce it to other people. Indeed, most people find anger energizing and, I suggested, a temporary boost to self-esteem. We all know about medical research that shows that anger tends to cause stress, increase the likelihood of heart attacks, and make one vulnerable to a broad variety of diseases. But it may be that it is *unexpressed* anger that does this, not anger as such. ("*I don't have heart attacks, I give them!*" screams the irate boss man.) So is an emotion positive or negative depending on how it views its object? Or how it makes one feel? Or how it is valued in society? Or whether or not it is good for your health? These are very different considerations and it would be stupid to run them all together.

I suggested above that the positive or negative evaluation of the emotion's object is too easily conflated with the benefit or harm done to the subject of the emotion, at least where these effects are reasonably evident. But these are very different, to say the obvious, and in most emotions the link with health just isn't very clear, if there is one. But other differences are more subtle. An emotion may involve a positive attitude toward its object, pride regarding oneself, for example, and yet the emotion itself may be harshly evaluated. Thus the inclusion of pride as one of the seven deadly sins. So, too, an emotion may have a negative attitude toward its object, again the self but this time in humility, but this is an emotion that invites high praise, certainly in Christian societies, at least with respect to God. Fear is a supposedly negative emotion (insofar as its object is a danger), but I argued early on that it is an emotion that is absolutely essential to our well-being. Moreover, although it is often the case that fear involves a tendency to flee (a clear example of avoidance behavior), it may also lead to aggressive confrontation. An emotion may be positive both in its attitude toward its object and toward the subject (as love enhances both the beloved and the lover), but an emotion may be positive in its attitude toward its object but quite negative toward oneself, or it may be negative in its attitude toward its object but quite positive toward oneself. Contempt, for instance. In short, there are very few emotions that can be characterized in terms of simple valence. (Simple disgust might be an exception, but there is serious question whether this is even an emotion.)

Positive and negative valence have long been and are still invoked in the psychological literature with different ends in mind. For example, those polarities that have to do with health are (obviously) featured more prominently in the medical literature while those that have to do with virtue and vice are more likely to appear in ethics and moral philosophy. Insofar as there is a meaningful correlation between the two (for instance, envy and resentment are both vices and bad for your health), the connection is clearly empirical and not merely dictated by the "negative" status of those emotions. So, too, whether an emotion is positive or negative in ethics depends on the ethics and the culture. Pride is a "deadly" sin in Christian ethics. It is one of the virtues in Greek ethics. Anger is another "deadly" sin in Christian ethics, but Aristotle proclaims in his *Ethics* that a man who does not get angry (at the right person, at the right time, in the right way) is a "fool." What counts as positive or negative from an ethical point of view depends on one's ethics.

In a moral context, the evaluations built into "positive" and "negative" have a lot to do with good and bad, with right and wrong, with virtue and vice. But good and bad, right and wrong, and virtue and vice do not share the same moral scale, and huge turf wars in moral philosophy have led to their dramatic separation and even opposition. To summarize this complex literature very simply, good and bad have to do with the satisfaction of needs and desires, right and wrong have too do with obeying certain impersonal (universal) rules or principles, while virtue and vice are attributes of personal character. (I will not introduce or discuss here the contentious polarity of *good and evil*.) So to talk about good and bad, right and wrong, and virtue and vice is to talk about three quite distinct matters (though often correlated in their results). A "positive" emotion, in one interpretation, has to do with satisfaction. (Thus love is a positive emotion because it makes us happy and satisfies an enormous number of personal and social expectations.) On another, a "positive" emotion is one that motivates us to obey the rules. (Thus love and respect make it more likely that we will act morally, while anger and hate make it more likely that we will act immorally.) A "positive" emotion, on the third interpretation, is one that exemplifies the virtues. (Thus love can be interpreted as a manifestation of a giving, sharing personality, while envy and resentment suggest a petty and vicious character.)

Given the ethical origins of all of these notions, the most obvious interpretation of the positive and negative emotions polarity is the mundane but relatively nonmoral contrast between good and bad. There are good emotions and there are bad emotions. But this is highly ambiguous. Good and bad can refer to the various consequences of emotion—whether it leads to health or illness, happiness or unhappiness, or (being more broadly considerate) whether it results in good or bad consequences for all concerned. It can also refer to the causes, context, and circumstances of the emotion, which are all too often confused with the emotion itself. For example, fear is typically considered a negative emotion, that is, a bad emotion, on the grounds that the circumstances provoking fear tend to be threatening to one's well being. (Indeed, many theorists would take this to be a matter of definition.) But it does not follow from the fact that the circumstances that provoke fear are bad for us that the emotion of fear is bad for us. The circumstances may be bad for us, but fear, as I argued, is good for us, at least when it is appropriate fear.

People seek out fear if it is safely contained. They court danger and place themselves in vicarious if not precarious situations. Thus Aristotle had to face up to the question why people would willingly go out of their way to feel fear and pity (another "negative" emotion) by going to the theater and viewing a horrible tragedy (a question typically addressed today by reference to horror movies). Part of Aristotle's answer was that the feeling of fear in such contexts was a cathartic experience that was very good for us. Leaving aside the epistemic complexities of the theater (having to do with the nature of fiction and "acting" and "the willing suspension of disbelief") we can say that the circumstances provoking emotion may be bad but the emotion itself may not be. Or, still looking to Aristotle, the release of the emotion may be a good thing, even if the emotion itself is not. And, more generally, an emotion may have moral or immoral consequences, it may be satisfying or frustrating, it may be provoked by desirable or by undesirable circumstances, it may be socially accepted or discouraged or culturally praised or condemned, and these lead to very different kinds of conclusions about the value of the emotion.

Consider again one of the most basic emotions, anger. It is typically listed among the "negative" emotions. In fact, along with hate, it is almost always the paradigm example. Why? Because anger is a notoriously hostile and dangerous emotion. It breeds violence, or in any case dissention and bad feelings. Repressed, it is famously bad for one's health, and freely expressed it is a danger to one's immediate physical well-being as it inspires both punch-ups and murder. But let's slow down here. I have listed a number of very different "negatives" about anger, and they are not all the same nor are they obviously correlated. Anger is a hostile emotion, which is to say that it has a negative attitude toward (or appraisal of) its object, the other person. Anger also tends to have negative consequences, at least when it is expressed in a crude and inappropriate manner, time, or place. Anger may cause health problems, depending on its duration, its intensity, and its disposition (repressed, expressed, and expressed *how*?). But anger is, at least sometimes, *righteous* anger. It is directed at a fault or offense that requires correction, and it is often instrumental in making that correction. One of the most powerful aspects of the women's liberation movement back in the 1970s was its recognition that women had both a right and a reason to get angry, and that anger (as opposed to the infantile rage that was sometimes exhibited along with it) was instrumental in getting women's voices heard and changing laws on their behalf (Tavris, 1982; Spelman, 1984). Is righteous anger—or moral indignation—a negative emotion? It is hostile for a very good reason. The world needs changing. And indignation often brings about a very good outcome. I am not aware of health studies specific to righteous anger as opposed to just plain anger, but in terms of overall well-being—including moral well-being—I would venture a good guess that Aristotle was right, that it is sometimes much better for a person's overall well-being to get angry than not, at least when it is right to get angry. So, is anger a negative emotion? Well that depends. Who is angry at whom and why?

One upshot of this attack on simple-minded polarity is that even the example with which we began now comes into question. Are love and hate really "opposites"? We can appreciate how much they have in common. They both involve a status of equality, they both involve a kind of intimacy and recognition of mutual importance. That is why they are so readily transformable, one to the other. They differ, obviously, in the "valence" of their attitude toward the other. But what if we were to say, as is often said, that the opposite of love is not hate but *indifference*? There certainly is some truth to that. Or what if we were to say that the opposite of love is envy or resentment or contempt? There is some truth to that too. One of the more celebrated campaigns of the postmodern "deconstructionist" movement is its rejection and often ridicule of "oppositional" thinking, thinking in terms of polarities, good-bad, white-black, male-female, up-down, and God knows what else. This rejection of oppositional thinking goes back at least to Nietzsche (who engaged in a good deal of oppositional thinking himself), and it is utterly central to the yin-yang of Chinese philosophy, but the idea has a good deal of merit in combating the dogmatic moralizing in today's politics and some of the lazy thinking that goes on in the social sciences. Thinking and talking in terms of positive and negative emotions, I have argued, is an example of such lazy thinking in the name of an easy organizational principle. The insistence on oppositional thinking is of the same genre. In discussions of love, for example, it is an old debate (going back to Plato) whether "opposites attract" or "like loves like," reducing the multiplicity of features and interactions that bring two people together to a supposedly single dimension of similarity or differences. So, too, in our thinking about the emotions in general we should be much more attentive and receptive to the richness of emotional intelligence.

One obvious way of making out the distinction between positive and negative emotions is by focusing in on just the distinction between pleasant and unpleasant emotions, although I hope by now it is obvious that this does not begin to capture the broad range of considerations that usually go into estimations of an emotion's "valence." I would not deny that there is a distinction between pleasure and pain, but this, too, is much more complex than it is usually made to seem. So let me end this chapter by discussing what is usually taken as the core of the positive-negative dichotomy, explicitly by the two Dutch theorists Spinoza and Frijda, and that is the supposed polarity of pleasure and pain.

Are pleasure and pain a true polarity? In what sense can pleasure and pain be compared as well as contrasted? The widespread assumption in both philosophy and psychology is that pleasure and pain are quantifiable features of an emotion. Two hundred years so ago the English Utilitarians, and in particular Jeremy Bentham, tried to develop a "hedonistic calculus." The idea is that pleasure is positive and pain is negative and both come in degrees or quantities ("hedons"). Thus pleasures and pains can be juxtaposed and compared on a single measuring scale. Bentham ingeniously laid out a list of dimensions of pleasure and pain, such as intensity, duration, certainty, proximity, fecundity, and purity, and the result would be a single value on a single scale with cumulative pleasure at the top end and aggregated pain at the bottom. (The obvious analogy is a thermometer, with the highest temperature at the top and the lowest at the bottom.)

Thus, according to the standard utilitarian calculations, the short-term pain of going to the dentist could be weighed against the longer-term pleasure of having healthy teeth (or, if you prefer, against the longer-term and much more severe pain that is sure to follow the neglect of one's teeth). Presumably the interests of the dentist would be accounted for as well, also one's partner (or whoever would be the brunt of one's complaining). An emotion, getting angry, for example, might be pleasurable in the short run but (given the consequences of expression) painful in the long run. One might seriously question whether the short run and the long run are psychologically comparable, and this in itself is a hotly debated issue in value theory and social choice theory. But let's just look at more or less immediate pleasures and pains, leaving aside questions of delayed gratification and such. (Goleman [1995] makes a good deal of such questions in his account of emotional intelligence.) The idea is that positive emotions maximize pleasure, negative emotions multiply misery.

Are pleasures and pains comparable? Consider the "positive" end of the supposed hedonic scale. Bentham's erstwhile pupil John Stuart Mill not only talked about "happiness" as opposed to mere pleasure but he insisted that pleasures were *qualitatively* as well as quantitatively different, that is, they differed in *kind* and not just in degree. So much, then, for the single scale, the "happiness calculus." The pleasures of doing philosophy and the pleasures of bowling are different *kinds* of pleasures and so cannot be quantitatively compared. Moreover, is pleasure the same as enjoyment, and doesn't *what* we enjoy determine the quality of the enjoyment? A young boy who enjoys ripping the wings off of flies can hardly be praised for his pleasures, and a young Socrates brooding over the meaning of life is neither to be faulted nor pitied for causing himself so much pain. There is something delicious about the emotions that constitute vengefulness, but that hardly makes them positive emotions. There is undeniable joy in *schadenfreude* but that does not mean that *schadenfreude* is a "positive" emotion, however pleasant it may be. *What* one enjoys is as important as the fact that one enjoys it. Pleasure is not just a free-standing feeling.

Consider, then, the bottom end of the supposed pleasure-pain happiness meter. Is physical pain comparable to mental anguish and suffering? To be sure, a person might be willing to tolerate just so much physical pain to avoid just so much suffering (say, humiliation), but it is by no means evident that the two are being weighed or compared, much less quantified. I might prefer going to the dentist for root-canal work to attending a departmental meeting, but it does not follow that I literally believe that one will be more painful than the other. Pain, strictly speaking, is a more or less specific, physically localizable sensation. (This is not to deny that the localization may be precise or diffuse, and there may be no identifiable physical cause of the pain.) In this strict sense, no emotion is painful, and in this strict sense, pleasures and pains cannot be compared. Physical pain is not in any sense a "negative pleasure," and there are no physical pleasures (no, not even the pleasure of orgasm or ecstasy) to compare with physical pain. For one thing, such pleasures are nonlocalizable. There are also the pleasures of a sweet taste, or a good tune, or a soft caress, but these sensations are not comparable (in part because they are so dependent on context and circumstances) to physical pains, even if they are localizable sensations.

Suffering, by contrast, is not a sensation (although, to be sure, it may involve all sorts of sensations, particularly those that are catalogued as "affective feelings"). Suffering involves context, meaning, and interpretation. One can (and usually does) suffer without suffering actual pain. Thus, strictly speaking, pain and suffering are not two of a kind and therefore not items on the same scale. But matters are still more complicated. Can a physical pain be measured merely by its intensity as a sensation, or must it, too, be measured by reference to its meaning? A pain in the chest, for example, "hurts" much more if it is believed to be a symptom of a heart attack than if it is thought to be only indigestion or a bruised rib. Thus even physical pain is not simply pain "in itself." It depends on its context, its meaning, its interpretation. There is, perhaps, a level of sheer physical *agony* that is shorn of context and interpretation, but this is not the sort of pain that can plausibly be attributed to any emotional experience, no matter how "painful." Thus it makes sense (as above) to say that we "suffer pain," and this suggests that pain, too, is subject to interpretation. But suffering an emotion seems to me not to be literally construable as pain.

So are different kinds of suffering, and suffering and pleasure, comparable in the way that "valence" suggests they should be? That depends. The suffering involved in a protracted illness may be compared to the suffering involved in a protracted misfortune, being unemployed, for instance, but that is because the two situations have so much in common. So, too, the suffering involved in a protracted illness might readily be compared to grief, with which it also has much in common. But the suffering involved in a protracted illness is not so easily compared to the suffering involved in jealousy, envy, guilt, shame, or even the suffering of humiliation or the suffering of frustration or failure. So we might say that different sufferings can be compared, but only insofar as they have many features in common, but it is not just the feelings that are being compared. There is no one kind of experience called suffering.

Can enjoyment and suffering be weighed against one another in the same sense? We often seem to do so, for instance, when we are comparing two sensations (a sweet taste and a disgusting taste), two sufficiently similar experiences (bicycling through France in the Tour de France in first place versus finding oneself humiliated in the local charity race), or two kindred emotions (not love and hate, perhaps, but pride and shame). But as for lining up all emotions on a scale from joy at the top to utter humiliation or the profoundest grief at the bottom, that just doesn't make any sense. If there is no one kind of phenomenon called suffering, there is certainly no common measure between all of the different kinds of suffering in emotion and the various joys and comforts of emotion.

So, against the restrictive view that all positive and negative emotions come down to the polarity of pleasure and pain, I want to suggest that pleasure and pain do not form any sort of polarity and are in no singular sense "opposites." Nor does the rich texture of most emotions allow us to assign a single "valence" on the basis of pleasures and pains, even "all things considered." Anger can be very pleasurable, especially if it is righteous. Anger can be very painful if it concerns an offense by a loved one. Anger can be very fulfilling on the one hand and nevertheless very painful at the same time, such as when one is winning a heated argument with a spouse or a friend. Love is among the most pleasant of emotions but it can also be the most painful. This is an essential datum in the study of emotions, this phenomenon of "mixed feelings," but this does not just mean one emotion contingently coupled with another. Within an emotion, there can be a number of different "valences," even in terms of the no longer simple dichotomy of pleasure and pain. So, are love and anger "positive" or "negative" on the basis of pleasure and pain alone? I think the question is simple-minded and there is no simple set of answers. And to defend one's behavior by simply appealing to the valence of an emotion is another excuse that bypasses the critical point, that the complex evaluation of an emotion is our responsibility. The value of an emotion is rarely so simple.

16

MYTH SEVEN
Emotions Are Irrational

If emotions are as intelligent as I claim they are, how is it, then, that they are so often and so rightly accused of being irrational? Our anger often gets us in trouble and is counterproductive to getting what we want. Hatred between nations and ethnic groups causes wars and disasters so terrible that they stand as a bloody tribute to the irrationality of our species. Love is as often foolish as it is wise, and it is sometimes downright desperate and destructive. There are indeed things to be afraid of, but, as we discussed in an earlier chapter, there are many fears that are irrational, unwarranted, exaggerated, unnecessary, humiliating, embarrassing, and sometimes self-destructive. Roosevelt's celebrated warning, "we have nothing to fear but fear itself," points out the self-inflicted damage of excessive caution when it goes against our better interests. And even the best of loves can outlive its appropriateness, hanging on long after the mutual affection and even respect is gone. It may have begun as the best of times, but it eventually can turn into the worst kind of humiliation with a devastating loss of self-respect and self-esteem. Where, one might well ask, is the intelligence in that?

"Emotions are irrational" can mean many different things. It can be a blanket judgment about emotions. All too often, this is just a thoughtless platitude, a gross generalization on the basis of a too-small set of examples or an uncritical residue of the old but now discredited distinction between rationality and the passions. One of the arguments for this position, however, is very sophisticated, namely, the Stoic argument that all emotions (passions) presume an unreasonable estimation of our own importance and our interests in other people and things. We have already argued against such notions as "emotions are irrational" insofar as this means that emotions are *non*rational, that is, dumb feelings or mere physiological disturbances. Such reactions might be fortunate or unfortunate, pleasant or painful, but in any case they are not subject to the kinds of evaluation that we routinely apply to our emotions. It should be tediously obvious by now that I completely reject any such conception of emotion. Emotions are structured by judgments that can be wise or foolish, warranted or unwarranted, appropriate or inappropriate, or right or wrong, and therefore they are at least candidates for rationality. I agree with the Stoics that emotions are (at least in part) judgments, but I disagree with their view that these judgments are always irrational and unreasonable.

To say that an emotion is irrational is to say that it is not rational, in the sense that it has in some way seriously missed its target. From this perspective, it is clear that some emotions are irrational, others are rational. The latter are right on target. Righteous anger is anger that is, as Aristotle recommended, aimed at the right person, for the right reason, at the right time, in the right proportion. "True" love is love that has found its (more or less) ideal beloved, has come to appreciate the precious role of that person in one's life, and has mustered all of one's resources to feed and maintain both the love and the relationship. If "emotions are irrational" just means that *some* emotions are irrational, or even that emotions *tend* to be irrational, then there is no need to raise a fuss. It only remains to debate how frequently and how seriously emotions (and *which* emotions) are off target as opposed to on target.

But what is the "target" of an emotion? That depends, of course, on the emotion. But, in general, we can say that the target of an emotion is getting its object *right*. That means getting angry at the right person, first of all. And if I get angry with someone, thus judging that what they have done is offensive, it had better *be* offensive, and not just seem offensive to me. Even more basic, they have better done what I accuse them of doing, otherwise my judgment is factually mistaken and my emotion unjustified. Now here we must make an important qualification, which we anticipated earlier. It may be that the person did not do what I thought they did, but I had every reason to think that they did so, and so while my judgment is wrong it is not unreasonable, and so my emotion is not irrational either. In other words, that important notion of *subjectivity* comes into play here and serves much the same function that notions like "warrantability" and "reasonable conclusion" serve in epistemology and the philosophy of science. To say that an emotion is rational is not necessarily to insist that its component judgments are *true*. It is enough that they are warranted by the evidence. If I am angry at my friend for making a rude gesture because

I am sure that I saw him do so, but then it becomes evident that he was only shooing a fly from his nose or demonstrating a gesture he recently saw in an Italian movie, it would be clearly irrational for me to continue being angry with him. (Or at least, it would be irrational for me to continue being angry with him *for that*. I might well have other reasons to be angry at him.)

In the larger picture, however, it is not just that the target of our emotions is to get it right. The emotions play a larger role in our lives than just that. The aim of our emotions, and the reason we have emotions in the first place, is to enhance our lives, to make them better, to help us get what we want out of life. In terms of evolution, there is the minimal standard of adaptivity and survival. But we want more out of life than survival and passing on our genes. That is why, in my earlier work, I insisted that all emotions have as their aim the maintaining or the maximizing of *self-esteem*. I now think that this is too simple, but I think it points to one of the important and complex themes of this book. We do not just have emotions. Emotions are strategies. They are instrumental in getting us what we want (and helping us to avoid what we do not want), and sometimes they themselves may be (or seem to be) what we ultimately want: true love, for example, and especially that all-embracing grand emotion (insofar as is it an emotion), *happiness*. But this gives us a larger picture of rationality and the rationality of emotions. Rationality is maximizing (or together, optimizing) our well-being. Our emotions are rational insofar as they further our collective as well as personal well-being, irrational insofar as they diminish or degrade it. Again, we have to qualify all of this with the factor of the subjectivity of emotions. Noble, intelligent, and virtuous emotions may in fact end in disaster, but they may be fully rational nonetheless insofar as they have to do with living our lives as we really believe they should be lived. By contrast, stupid and vicious emotions may turn out to have admirable consequences, but they are stupid, vicious, and irrational nonetheless.

This said, we can now go on to understand the relative rationality and irrationality of various emotions and emotion-types. Rarely is an emotion-type (love, anger, guilt, jealousy, sadness, joy) either rational or irrational across the board. It depends on the particular occasion and its circumstances. Much less does it make sense to say, "Emotions are irrational," as if all emotions fall into the same unfortunate category. Even the Stoics loved their virtues, and no doubt much more as well, despite themselves. But there are a few candidates for emotion-types that may be reckoned to be rational or irrational as such. One of these is envy. Of course, there are many reasons why one might want something that someone else has. Perhaps one desperately needs it while the other person does not. But it would be odd to say that a starving man *envies* a bourgeois diner the food on his plate. He might resent the wealthier man's extravagance, or the inequities of income distribution in the modern world. But in cases of dire need, envy is probably not the emotion to have. Envy is an emotion that concerns not desperate needs but comforts and luxuries (granted that many luxuries many of us simply take for granted). And then the psychological cost may be much greater than the value of what is envied.

Shopping (aside from the basics of our weekly groceries and such) is a peculiar modern indulgence. ("When the going gets tough, the tough go shopping.") Shopping has become a leisure, and thus a luxury, activity. But when the conservative German theorist Helmut Schoeck suggested that envy is an excellent emotion because it turns the wheels of consumerism and capitalism (and many advertisers would no doubt agree), he ignored the arguments against envy. Its inclusion on the list of the "seven deadlies" is no mistake. Envy is not just wanting what someone else has. It is wanting *undeservedly* and usually *without recourse* what someone else has. That means that it is almost always a strategy for making oneself miserable, if not bitter, frustrated, and unhappy. It is, in short, a bad strategy. At least where our material comforts are concerned, it is almost always better to be satisfied with what one has, however that may annoy the defenders of consumerism.

Of course it makes good sense to *work for* something one wants or aspires to, but that is not envy. (That is where Schoeck gets it wrong.) It even makes sense to *hope for* (or pray for) something one wants or aspires to, but that is not envy either. Envy is a competitive desire devoid of desert and without recourse. That is why the "evil eye" of envy (often colored a sickly green) is both so vicious and pathetic. It is desire, often pointless desire, without the possibility of satisfaction. Thus envy is one of those powerless emotions that easily fantasizes voodoo and occult forces that might gain what neither hard work nor personal worth nor even prayers will obtain. Accordingly, envy is a bad strategy for happiness and so it deserves to be called irrational as such. Which is not to deny, needless to say, that we are often, despite ourselves, irrational in this regard. We are, as Schoeck correctly argued, envious creatures, but I do not think that this has benign social consequences.

It is sometimes said, for example by the Stoics and some of the Taoists in China, that grief is another example of an emotion that is always irrational. The loss of a loved one is just a part of the natural order, says Chuang-Tsu, and it is therefore as irrational for him to grieve his wife's death as it would be to regret the time before she was born. The Roman Stoic Seneca displays a half dozen ways of rationalizing grief away, from the callous "I wasn't really that close to him" to the quasi-spiritual "there is reason and order in all of this." All of this presumes that what we take to be a grievous loss is in fact no loss at all, but if what I suggested in chapter 6 makes any sense at all, to think of a life without the potential for grief means thinking of a life without love, and if love can ever be rational (which of course it is) then grief at the loss of love must be rational too. (This is not to say that all grief is rational, of course. The loss must be both personal and substantial and the grief constrained by the circumstances.)

To be more positive, on the side of the virtues instead of the vices ("sins"), an emotion-type that is a popular candidate for rationality as such is *joy*. In America, especially, there is a high premium on cheerfulness, so one is normally expected to be joyful, even without a specific reason for being so. (On the other hand, one better be able to produce a reason for despair.) Some romantics of the "better to have loved . . ." school might say this about love, too, but I have already thrown some cold water on this upbeat thesis, and I will do so again shortly. Joy, unlike love, seems pretty uncomplicated and is usually without problematic consequences. There is considerable controversy, however, about what joy is. On the one hand, there is the well-known and familiar fact that something like joy, perhaps call it exultation or ecstasy, can be induced by a variety of pharmaceuticals, both legal and illicit, prescription, over-the-counter, and passed from friend to friend. Such joy (ecstasy) may have nothing whatever to do with circumstances, although clearly such experiences can be enhanced in the right situation, say, at a party or an otherwise delightful scenario. But joy so conceived is barely an emotion, more of a giddy feeling, and the question of rationality hardly even arises.

On the other hand, there is joy that is clearly *about* the world, or at least, about one's immediate situation, and then the question of rationality does come up, even if it is sometimes impolite. Is the joy warranted, or not? Winning a contest or a race is usually a good reason for joy. Losing one's job is usually not (although losing a job that one hates may have the unexpected consequence of great relief if not joy as such). And so often, the more or less pure experience of exultation or ecstasy tends to project itself onto the surrounding circumstances, perhaps even the world as a whole, so "pure emotional experiences" may be hard to come by. But the question we are raising here is whether joy, insofar as it is (more or less) a judgment about the world, is always rational. This is not a simple question. Part of the reason is that joy tends (its "action tendency") to withdraw from—or rather "lift itself above"—the world. Thus one can feel joy in circumstances that do not seem to warrant it. And, of course, one can fail to feel joy even in those circumstances that would seem to call for it. (Is *this* irrational?)

Displaying one's joy in inappropriate circumstances, say at a funeral, will no doubt breed considerable resentment and social condemnation. This makes such joy irrational, whatever reasons it may have otherwise. (Going to a friend's funeral after having just been told that one won a major prize puts one in an emotionally awkward situation, to put it mildly.) So, too, certain expressions of joy, gleefully breaking your neighbor's best china, for example, are not only irrational but very expensive. In such cases one might insist that it is the public expression of the emotion, not the emotion itself, that is the problem. But most of the time, feeling joyful is a fine thing to do and an exuberant if restrained expression is appropriate. Thus it is at least plausible, in a society that insists on "looking on the bright side of things," that joy in the world should be considered a rational way to feel, at least a good deal of the time.

There are people, however, who feel joy in most joyless circumstances. Extreme examples were those rare prisoners in German concentration camps who managed to remain joyful despite their ultimate degradation and the constant threat of death. More power to them, I would say, but their joyfulness may well seem inappropriate to many people. Nevertheless, inappropriate joy can be a powerful mood elevator for others in similarly miserable circumstances, for example, in Roberto Benigni's movie *Life Is Beautiful,* and if some people are offended or resentful one could argue that the overall effects of this social affect (a kind of "emotional contagion") is laudatory and therefore rational, whether warranted by the circumstances or not.

Not all rational emotions require active engagement with one's immediate circumstances. Sometimes a rational emotion may be one of detachment or distraction. The wonderful thing about joy—and the horrible thing about its "opposite," depression—is that it can remain aloof from everything even as it takes great joy in the details. In depression, to the contrary, one feels utterly detached and abandoned rather than aloof and one finds considerable reason for despair in the details. But the example of depression here is instructive. One might argue that it, like joy, is more of a mood than an emotion. True, and I have been running these together. As I suggested in an earlier chapter, the difference between them is a topic for further discussion, but, briefly, I noted that the objects of emotions tend to be specific and determinate while the objects of moods tend to be general, amorphous, and indeterminate. A mood turns into an emotion as its object becomes more focused, for instance, when a temperamentally angry man fixes his rage on one unfortunate victim. An emotion turns into a mood as its object becomes more generalized, as when a specific set-back, say getting fired from one's job, gets generalized from "being depressed about getting fired" to "being depressed about my whole life and everything about it." But depression (and I am here again talking about garden-variety depression rather than the clinical kind that brings in all sorts of more medical questions) is not necessarily irrational. Quite to the contrary. What makes moods rational or irrational, much like emotions, is whether they fit the realities of the world, whether they function as an adequate "tuning" to the world, since, as moods, they don't have either proper object or, therefore, targets. But one can surely appreciate the irrationality of depression in the midst of an enviable and admirable life. Indeed, it may be just this irrationality that is the cause of reflective despair.

Depression may be a bad strategy for well-being in life, but consider this. An important researcher named Martin Seligman has done extensive research on what he calls "positive psychology," that is, the nature and effects of the "positive" emotions. Despite my misgivings with such terminology, which I expressed in the preceding chapter, we all know perfectly well the sorts of emotions he has in mind. He summarizes several of them (hope, joy, and such) in the familiar term "optimism," and he asks the question, "do optimists perceive the world as accurately as nonoptimists (pessimists, or as they prefer to refer to themselves, "realists")? The answer is "no." People who take a dim view of life and its possibilities tend to see things more "realistically." They tend to recognize real dangers, real tragedies, and real scandals and not rationalize them. So, too, those of us who do not hold very adamant religious beliefs concerning the presence of a caring all-mighty protector and the hope of a wonderful afterlife quite naturally have difficulty sharing the confident joy of those who do so believe. But I would add that we nonbelievers have a more accurate, because less hopeful, view of the dire state of the world right now. Which view and which emotional stance is more rational? I would not dare say. But that certainly throws the question of the rationality of emotions wide open.

Most of the work to be done in ascertaining the rationality of emotions has to do not with emotion-types but with particular instances of emotion. Anger, notably, is sometimes rational, sometimes not. When is anger rational? When it is right on target, that is, when it recognizes rightly that an offense has been committed, is proportionate to the seriousness of the offense, and is appropriate to the offender or to the relationship. It is irrational to get angry about something that one merely imagines might happen or might be offensive. Some emotions, however, are rational or not regarding mere possibilities. Fear is the obvious example. The rationality of fear depends on the probability and seriousness of the potential threat or danger. So, too, hope, whose rationality depends on the probability and worth of the potential boon.

It is irrational to get very angry about something trivial, or to get only mildly angry over something very serious. It is irrational to get angry at an infant or at an infirm, incompetent, elderly patient. And for a very different reason, it may be irrational to get angry (or at least to express your anger) at your supervisor, at the judge who is about to decide your case, at the professor who is about to give you a grade, or at the customs officer who is picking his way through your luggage. So sometimes the anger may be rational but the expression may not be. The rationality of anger is very much a matter of details, the particularities of the situation. And even those who think that anger is *never* the best strategy, because love and forgiveness are always more conducive to harmony and happiness, would have to agree that there are degrees of rationality. In some situations, their judgment would still be "yes, you are quite right to be angry, *but . . .*" Given the nature of the current social and political world, however, I would withhold even such qualifications. Perhaps it is my Old Testament upbringing, but I think that righteous indignation and its straightforward expression are all-too-often mandatory in contemporary social life. And this is to say, echoing Aristotle, that righteous anger is not only rational but *not* to get angry when one is righteous is irrational because such an omission ultimately contributes to the injustice in the world.

But let us bring this discussion to a close by talking again about the most talked about emotion, love. Again I will concentrate on romantic love. I mentioned that some romantics would say that love is always good and therefore always rational, but then, too, there are other romantics who would insist that love is irrational, and that, of course, is supposed to be its charm. But we recognize that both positions are rather wacko, first because there are obviously instances of love that are horrendous and have no justification or warrant, for instance, the erotic love of a child, especially one's own child, and second because many cases of love, to use the same expression as before, are right on target. The beloved is appropriate, the relationship is harmonious, and both people are happy and flourishing because of it. So why do so many people say that love is irrational? First of all, because love so often seems to happen by chance. Two people meet at a reception that neither planned to attend, or they just happen to bump into one another on a train, start a conversation, and lifelong love commences. But serendipity isn't irrationality. If the alternative is an arranged marriage, based on the best science of the day or on the match-making skills of the wisest person in the village, then romantic love might well seem irrational. (I have heard it so described by young women who live in Iran, where arranged marriages are still the norm.) But more to the point, it is not *love* that happens by chance but rather the meeting. Love is something that is mutually cultivated over time, and there is nothing irrational about that. When two people "were meant for each other," that probably gives as much credit to their ability to work together as it does to their mutual compatibility from the start.

A second reason why love is often thought to be irrational is because of our old friend *subjectivity*. "In the eyes of the beholder," that is, for the lover, the beloved—who is just one of a million, after all, may well seem like the most beautiful person in the world. Is this irrationality? From some neutral, "objective" view, perhaps. But why should we give priority to such a viewpoint? In science, we do, of course, by definition. In jurisprudence, certainly, as a matter of justice. In the professions and skilled trades, neutrality is to be much preferred to bias. The fact that I think that you are an excellent accountant or urologist or airplane mechanic because I love you so is no recommendation at all. But my belief that you are beautiful is a subjective truth of a very different kind. One might well say that this is one of those realms that Kierkegaard called "objective uncertainty," where an objective viewpoint—if it exists at all—is of merely secondary concern. My love is not irrational because I see beauty and charm in you while strangers on the street might not. On the contrary, my *bestowing* you with personal charms and virtues seems in the case of love to be an essential part of its rationality.

But what about foolish love? Certainly love goes wrong in all sorts of ways. People often choose partners who are impossible, and they know this is so before the relationship even begins. Women who make a habit of dating married men may bet on the longshot of a permanent relationship, though then again, they may date married men just in order to ensure that they do not end up in a permanent relationship. Men who are charmed by neurotic, even sadistic, women are surely making irrational choices, assuming, that is, that what they really want is a stable loving partner who will love and respect them in return. (But again, I marvel at the enormous variety of ways that couples work such issues out and the many ways in which they feed off one another.) Love is irrational, one might say, when it knowingly goes after what it cannot have. But this underestimates both the significance and the rewards of unrequited love. To be sure, driving oneself insane in hopeless pursuit of the impossible is a paradigm of irrationality. But the secular worship of what one perceives as ideal beauty can be uplifting and inspiring. (Dante supposedly saw his beloved Beatrice only once, inspiring a lifetime of genius and creativity.)

Love is rational when it is with the right person, at the right time, in the right kind of relationship, carried on in the right way. (What "right" means in each of these cases is, of course, up to individual preferences and negotiation.) But love can also become irrational even when one is together with the right person, in the right kind of relationship, and carried on in an elegant and harmonious manner. There is such a thing as loving too much, for instance, when one's identity is so wrapped up in the other person that independent action and judgment becomes impossible, or when jealousy poisons the relationship and suffocates the very beloved who is loved so much. There is also loving someone too long. It may have been right once, but it is no longer. One's friends will no doubt say, "let go" and "move on." And they are right, but we all know that this can be tremendously hard to do. In any case, it takes time. But one of the virtues of love is its tenaciousness, and before we jump to the unwarranted conclusion that love is irrational just because we cannot simply stop loving when it is no longer in our ultimate interest, just think for a moment what love would be if it were not so tenacious, so thoroughly entwined with our own self-identity, and consequently so hard to "get over." It would be fickle, flighty, undependable, and insubstantial, hardly love—and hardly a candidate for rationality—at all.

17

MYTH EIGHT

Emotions Happen to Us
(They Are "Passions")

It sometimes seems to be one of the phenomenological "data" of our experience of emotions that emotions happen to us, and sometimes, they do. Even in Aristotle's naming of this intriguing set of phenomena, *pathé* or passions, the idea is clear that these are things that we *suffer* in life. Thus we talk about the passion of Christ, meaning his suffering, and we often talk about passions using variants of what I called the hydraulic model, images of exploding, erupting, being struck, being invaded, being felled, and "falling." We talk about being "paralyzed" by fear, "smitten" by love, "struck" by jealousy, "overwhelmed" by sadness, and being "made mad" with rage. But as we give up the hydraulic metaphor and its variants in favor of a more rational, more cognitively and evaluatively rich model of the emotions, we find ourselves less enamored of this "passivity" conception of the passions as well.

Or else, we might want to hold onto some conception of "passion" to cover just those instances of emotion that really do get out of hand and beyond our control, cases of obsession and compulsion and neurosis (not to mention psychosis), but with the clear understanding that these are not the usual but only extremely deviant instances of emotion. Most of our emotions, most of the time, are not entirely beyond our control. They do not just happen to us, but we are responsible for them. We practice them, cultivate them, and in many cases *choose* them, even if unconsciously. Thus I have described the emotions as strategies, strategies for living well, even if a great many emotions are rather short-sighted and thus not very good strategies. But to say that emotions are strategies, as Jean-Paul Sartre suggested more than seventy-five years ago, is to say something very much at odds with the current and traditional view of emotions. It is to say that our emotions are to some extent our "doing," and not just something that happens to us.

To put it a different way, how much control do we have over our emotions? Does it even make any sense to say that we choose them? Psychologists talk about "emotion regulation," leaving it open to what extent and in what ways the languages of control or of choice might apply. Philosophers have long taken the position, in part because of their celebration of reason, that we can control (but not choose) our emotions only by constraining them, or by controlling their expression. But is the question of control and constraint perhaps the wrong question? Or a much-too-limited question? Is controlling an emotion something like controlling a wild animal within? (Horace: "anger is like riding a wild horse.") Is it like controlling one's blood pressure, or one's cholesterol level, something that (certain Yogis excepted) we can do only indirectly? Or is it rather like a boss controlling his or her employees by way of various threats and incentives, the "boss" being reason? (Plato's model in *The Republic.*) Or is controlling an emotion like controlling one's thoughts, one's speech, one's arguments, putting them into shape, choosing one's mode of expression as well as one's timing? Consider the difference between spontaneously "blurting" out a comment and giving a considered response. Or is it like coordinating one's actions through practice, like riding a bike, which may be "mindless" (that is, wholly unreflective and unselfconscious) but is nevertheless voluntary and both very much within one's control and a continuous matter of choice?

Now, to be sure, to say that we choose our emotions is not to say that our emotions are sheer instances of "will." We do not just "do" them. Circumstances often impose our emotions on us, and the nature of emotions in general is such that we certainly do not have entirely free and unconstrained choice in which emotions we will have or whether we will feel—or allow ourselves to feel—any emotion at all. With the possible exception of joy and depression, and other moods that for the most part float free of the particular circumstances of our lives, we are "captive" to our circumstances. I did not choose to be in this bar at the same time as this offensive thug who is now making fun of my clothes, my height, my moustache, my accent, and my behavior. But now he has deeply offended me, and I have to decide what to do with it. I did not choose to be in this situation with this offensive thug, but I might well have chosen it. Indeed, I may resolve to come back at the same time tomorrow night to repeat the encounter and show or tell him a thing or two. So I am not completely the victim here. Even if I did not know about this particular thug, I did know about the reputation of the bar, and of the proclivities of my friend who brought me to the bar, and of the dangers that lurk in bars in general. Here I am repeating a point often made by Aristotle, that even when it seems that we have no choice or responsibility in the matter, we may well be responsible for putting ourselves in this situation, or, more importantly, for cultivating the character who would put himself in such a situation and thus be provoked or tempted to act this way.

But here I am, and here he is, and here is this situation. I feel myself getting tense (the Stoics' "first movements"), but now, do I just get angry? I have a number of choices, though none of them is very pleasant. I can walk away, and shoulder what abuse and ridicule may follow. I can answer him in kind, an unwise choice given his size and evident disposition. I can pretend to ignore him. I can really try to ignore him, for instance, by engaging my friend in a lively discussion of university politics. I can get angry at my friend for bringing me to such a place. Meanwhile, in all of these responses, I sense in myself a rising anger (note the hydraulic metaphor). I grow more tense and irritable (Jamesian physiology). I find myself thinking of all sorts of insults and defensive responses to throw at the thug—or more likely to share with my friend after we have safely left the bar (here the judgment components of my anger are fully articulated). But my choices are real choices, with real consequences, some of which further the anger (notably by aggravating the situation that initially caused it), while others tend to shift the anger (perhaps toward myself, perhaps toward my friend), and others tend to diminish it.

Distraction is often a good way of diminishing an emotion, especially if (though not in this case) the offensive situation is not continuing. An effective way of dealing with anger is going with your grandmother's advice, to "count slowly to ten" before doing anything. During that time, the situation may clarify. The guy is a thug, whom I will never see again. The evening is young, and it's been a good day. Why let him ruin it? It should be obvious that it is not simply a decision to be angry or not, but it is equally obvious that I am not simply a victim of anger. Once again, I would want to remind us of the distinction between the emotion and the event or situation causing it. Even if I may rightly consider myself a victim of the thug or the situation, I am nevertheless something like the coauthor of my anger. But as with any demanding coauthor and a dictatorial editor, I cannot write anything that I want. I have to start with what there is (or, at least, what I think there is).

One problem here is that so much of the emotions literature, and our popular talk about emotions, focuses on single instances and often very short bursts of emotion. In such cases, the idea that we are the author or coauthor of our emotions seems implausible indeed. But expanding the scope of our observations, we do come to see to what extent people cultivate their emotions and emotional responses. They discover, for example, that anger is an effective way of intimidating people, and so they allow themselves to get angry at the slightest provocation. I say "they allow themselves," but this does not imply that there is any conscious decision at the time of the outburst. It is rather a pattern of behavior that is cultivated over time. So, too, some people cultivate sadness, perhaps because they earn sympathy that way, or because "feeling sorry for themselves" allows them to withdraw and be irresponsible or unsociable. Others allow themselves to fall in love frequently, possibly just because they find it invigorating and fun. We resist calling this love, looking instead for signs of insecurity, manipulation, utter irresponsibility, or deep neurosis. Of course, we may also be morally critical, insofar as such a person tends to forget about the feelings of the transient victims. Indeed, I would say that failure to take into account the feelings (and especially the "hurt" feelings) of one's supposed beloved is definitive proof that the emotion in question—whatever it may be—is not love. Which is not to deny that it, too, whatever it is, consists in part of choices as well.

But most significant emotions are not single episodes, much less "bursts" of affect. They are processes over time. Then we can see quite clearly our role in getting angry, for example, as we willfully remind ourselves of a previous slight, over and over again, embellishing and elaborating the offense, perhaps generalizing one's thoughts to include other, similar offenses, imagining ways of getting even, until one literally "works oneself up" into a rage. For those of us who have studied emotions —and by now all of you—this angry recitation might well be joined by an interlocutor, one of those small voices of prudence in our heads that resembles the voice of one's parents or rabbi or preacher, the "Superego," nagging "Do you really want to do this?" or "Wouldn't you be much better off if you just let it go?" But there seems to me to be little doubt, in such cases, that anger does not just happen to us and it is not simply dictated by the circumstances. Our anger is, at least in part, our responsibility, and so we should *take* responsibility for it.

So, too, love. There is such a thing, I acknowledge, as being "smitten." In fact, it still happens to me on occasion, despite my happy and faithful marriage. But that is hardly love, despite what crude males may say in moments of desperation, sexual enthusiasm, or harassment. The truth is, it passes, usually quickly, and it is an experience not much more significant than catching a whiff of a delicious dish being carried past my table at a good restaurant. Sometimes, two people meet and there is "chemistry" between them. There is an exchange of mutual glances, mutual appreciation, mutual attraction. But that, too, is not love. It is just that, mutual attraction and appreciation. Now I am willing to admit the idea that, without such "chemistry," love may be less likely to develop, or in any case will be slower in coming. It is not, to put it clumsily, "love at first sight." But we all know how getting to know someone allows mutual appreciation to develop, and with it, the likelihood of mutual attraction and mutual glances that slowly transform themselves from a friendly wink to a longing gaze, from acquaintance to friendship to love. But love, let us say it explicitly, is always a process, not a momentary emotional episode. It does not make sense, except in very rare circumstances, to say that "I fell in love for fifteen minutes," or, for that matter, even three days. One might object that Romeo and Juliet were madly in love for just three days, but it is not irrelevant that then they were dead. Had they lived, and Romeo bolted back to Rosalind, we would certainly have revalued their romance. It would have been one more irresponsible teenage crush, and no more.

"Falling in love," I have argued for years, is a matter of choice, of multiple decisions. Love may begin with a meeting, which may be wondrous and magical and all of that. The eyes might lock and the gaze becomes transfixed. The most casual of conversations quickly demonstrates mutual interests, mutually exciting backgrounds, mutual compatibility. But then there is a series of choices and decisions, both mutual and individual: Should I stay or leave? Should I see him again? With or without my friends? Should we have lunch or dinner? In a romantic setting or not? Should we kiss goodnight? "Should we meet the parents? And every such decision is also a decision whether or not to further or hamper the growing relationship and the feelings that constitute it. And then there are the more straightforward and usually silent modes of emotional preparation. One thinks, "what a charming thing to say," "what delightfully intelligent eyes!" "I wonder what it would be like on a romantic vacation together," "I wonder what sort of lover he/she would be." And then the imaginative, hopeful, fanciful thoughts: going over the conversation in immediate retrospect, including an embarrassing critical analysis of every word and nuance, rehearsing follow-up conversations. And then we entertain the images, perhaps repeatedly: walking on the beach together, making love together, making babies together. Love is a process of willful escalation, and we don't "fall" into love. We *work* our way into it. As I heard it well said in the recent movie *Closer*, the lament by the Alice (Natalie Portman) character, "there is always a choice point [in falling in love], where you say to yourself, 'go ahead, or don't go ahead.' I don't know what that choice point was, but I know that there was one."

Sometimes decisions are so easy to make that we don't think of ourselves as making them at all. But the most important decisions, for instance, to say "I love you" for the first time, are dramatically transformative. This is no mere confession. It is an explosive speech act, a bomb dropped at the

feet of the relationship. With some luck and insight, the explosion is mutually delightful, a happy moment indeed. But sometimes it is not, and
friendships and work relationships are ruined forever. But every decision
involving the beloved enriches and advances or endangers the growing
feeling of love. So are we responsible for love? In the case of romantic love
and despite all of the traditional "swept away" metaphors and excuses, I do
not see how one can insist otherwise.

The decisions involved in love (and other emotions too) are not all
forward looking. Some are retrospective as well. My favorite example sup-
plies an answer to the not infrequent question, "do you believe in love at
first sight?" My answer, you might be surprised to learn, is "yes, I do." Two
people meet and their eyes lock (or, less romantically, one person spies
another, and he or she is transfixed). They get together, make the right
decisions, their love grows, they live together, and perhaps get married.
Several years go by. They look back at their relationship or the first time
they met and they agree, "I loved you the first moment I saw you." And
that's right. But alter the scenario. Two people meet, their eyes lock (or one
person is "taken" by another), they spend a few passionate days together,
but then they get tired or disgusted with one another. Sometime in the
future, one of them looks back at the brief relationship and concludes,
"that was some infatuation" (or "crush," or "wild weekend") but the word
"love" will certainly not be part of the description. (This was my point in
my unromantic retelling of the Romeo and Juliet story a moment ago.) But
here is the interesting part: The initial experience in the second case may
have been exactly the same as the initial experience in the first one. What
has changed is the retrospective interpretation of that meeting. In other
words, love at first sight depends on how the relationship works out. So,
too, it turns out to have been rational in retrospect, but there may have
been no telling at the time.

A much more terrible instance of the same retrospective reinterpretation
is the disclaimer, "I guess I never really loved you," at the end of a long
and for all intents and purposes genuine love relationship. But does such a
denial mean that the love was never real? From a third-person point of
view (of a mutual friend or a relative) it may be the denial that is both
untrue and cruel. But from the point of view of the unceremoniously
dumped lover, this will probably prompt a wholesale reconsideration of
not only the entire relationship but of one's own identity and existence,
possibly with devastating consequences.

When I insist that emotions can be strategies rather than mere reactions,
I do not mean to say that emotions are *deliberate*, the results of overt plans
or strategies. We do not think our way into most emotions. Nor do emotions fit the philosophical paradigm of intentional action, that is, actions

that are preceded by intentions—combinations of explicit beliefs and desires and "knowing what one is going to do." Insofar as the emotions can be defended in terms of a kind of activity or action, it is not fully conscious intentional action that should be our paradigm. But the realm of semi-conscious, inattentive, quasi-intentional, habitual, spontaneous, and even "automatic" activity and action have received little attention in philosophy, despite the efforts of such seminal figures as William James and Maurice Merleau-Ponty. But between intentional and full-blown deliberate action and straightforward passivity—getting hit with a brick, suffering a heart attack or a seizure, there is an enormous range of behaviors and "under-goings" that might nevertheless be considered within the realm of activity and action and (more generally) as matters of responsibility.

Consider thoughts. Emotions are a lot like thoughts, and not only in the sense that emotions typically involve thoughts. Jerome Neu, following Spinoza, suggests that emotions simply *are* thoughts. Some thoughts are carefully and conscientiously cultivated, as when we "think our way through" a problem. On some occasions, it may make sense to say that the thoughts are "invited," for instance, when after mulling over a philosophical puzzle, we give up on it for the day, and find that the answer "comes to us" in the middle of dinner or the middle of the night. But thoughts also come to us unbidden, even unwanted, and such cases support Nietzsche's famous observation that "a thought comes when *it* will, not when I will." Nevertheless, I have always thought that Nietzsche's observation served mainly to throw the whole idea of agency open for closer examination, not (as it is often interpreted) as a rejection of the notion of agency as such.

The fact is that most of us take full responsibility for our thoughts, no matter how unbidden, so long as they fit into our personal agendas, particularly if it is an original or particularly brilliant thought. But also, more generally, we accept responsibility and take a thought as "our own" if it fits a problem we are working on or an issue in which we are engaged. This might suggest to some (as Nietzsche is taken to argue) that there is no need for such concepts of "agency" at all, but I think it rather relocates the question. It suggests that our sense of agency is far more expansive than the limited realm of "the will," that is, what we conscientiously *try* to do, and so, too, is our sense of responsibility.

Thoughts, whatever else they are, are tell-tale symptoms of emotion. When we find ourselves having certain thoughts, for instance, momentary homicidal or sexual fantasies, even in the absence of any other evident signs of emotion, that is some reason to accept the attribution of the relevant emotions (fury and eros, respectively). If the thought is sufficiently horrifying, we may well dismiss it as nothing but fleeting and insignificant, but if it comes back, again and again, mere dismissal is no longer plausible.

Freud may have been wrong when he early on insisted that all such thoughts are manifestations of a wish, but he was surely right that they are usually manifestations of *some* desire or emotion. But are thoughts a kind of action? Are we responsible for them? Thoughts as products of thinking, certainly. Invited thoughts, perhaps. Thoughts uninvited, no. But it is not always easy to tell the difference between a thought that appears in the process of thinking and an invited thought, or even if uninvited.

So, too, you cannot "simply" decide to have an emotion. You can, however, decide to do any number of things—enter into a situation, not take one's medication, think about a situation in a different way, "set oneself up" for a fall—that will bring about the emotion. Or you might *act as if* you have an emotion, act angrily, for instance, from which genuine anger may follow. There is William James's always helpful advice: "Smooth the brow, brighten the eye, contract the dorsal rather than the ventral aspect of the frame, and speak in a major key, pass the genial compliment, and your heart must be frigid indeed if it does not gradually thaw" (2003). But this does not mean that we simply "manipulate" or "engineer" our emotions, as if *we* perform actions that affect or bring about *them*. The question of what we can control, and what we cannot, is much more complex than the usual distinction between activity and passivity would suggest.

Different aspects of emotion require very different sorts of arguments regarding the voluntary-involuntary, active-passive status of emotions. Moreover, there is a broad range of claims regarding such status that might be made regarding emotions, from the relatively innocent view that one can always do something to not only control but "set-up" (or prevent) particular emotions to the insistence that we are responsible for our emotions (whether or not we can control or choose them) to the view that emotions are active and do not just "happen" to us to the very strong claim that an emotion is a matter of choice, something voluntary and even willful. And since different aspects invite very different conclusions, the discussion of the passivity of emotions is no simple matter and yields no single conclusion. We sometimes hold people responsible for what they think. We usually hold them responsible for what they do. Some expressions of emotion are voluntary, but not all are.

In what sense are we responsible for what we believe, think, judge, and appraise? Does it make any sense at all to say that we are responsible for what happens in our brains (leaving aside the willful intake of mind-altering substances)? Or that we are responsible for we feel? What does happen when we choose or force ourselves to have an emotion? Arlie Hochschild (1983) did a fascinating study many years ago of airline stewardesses who have to smile and be cheerful for hours on end in the face of often irate, unruly, and sometimes rude customers. They succeed,

Hochschild says, by retooling their thinking. But is the resultant emotion therefore "inauthentic"? We usually think that "manufactured" emotions are thereby phony, but I think that is a presumptuous conclusion. There are, of course, "fake" emotions, easily detected. But cultivated emotions are not therefore phony, any more than the very real, even if totally planned, emotions that can happen when we knowingly get ourselves into a heated situation (for example, a confrontation with one's ex-wife's new boyfriend).

Which brings us back to the critical role that reflection plays in our emotional lives. So far in this chapter, I have been discussing the voluntariness of our emotions but without emphasizing the fact that much of this is due to the fact that we can think about them, weigh their warrant and justification, reconsider their strategies and/or consequences, distance ourselves from our own emotions (if only by virtue of the passing of time), and come to see ourselves as others might see us. Nevertheless, virtually everything that I have said presupposes this remarkable ability and would not even be intelligible with out it. Getting angry has a lot to do with our "building a case," our looking for and bringing in more evidence, our deciding that "yes, I'm right to be so upset and he was really wrong to do that!" Falling in love has a lot to do with entertaining thoughts of the beloved, rehearsing upcoming conversations and remembering, fondly or with distress, past meetings, reaffirming one's love of the beloved, and thinking in terms of the word "love." I said that we need not think of emotions as deliberate, but I certainly do not want to rule this out either. We do sometimes plan strategies, and while there is something odd about explicitly planning how to feel, we do just that whenever we put ourselves in situations that we know or hope will inspire emotion.

We also talked about thoughts and their peculiar role in our sense of agency, but reflection consists, to a large extent, of thoughts. (We do not want to forget, however, that much of reflection consists of other ["second order"] emotions as well.) But thinking about our emotions is fascinating both insofar as such thinking is more or less automatic—it just comes along with many of our emotions, often as a key component of those emotions—and is voluntary and cultivated. Reflecting on our emotions is something we learn to do, because we have to learn to control our emotions, and because we want to refine our emotions. But when we reflect on our emotions we often feel compelled to consider the alternatives, and this raises the question of choice and control, even when we are quite pleased with our emotional reactions and, in the terms of the Stoics, are happy to affirm them. But the key to overcoming the passivity view of emotions is to appreciate the power and pervasiveness of reflection in our emotional life. If we continue to feel passive with regard to our emotions, then that is something that we choose to do.

I do not want to overstate my thesis (that we are to a certain extent responsible for our emotions and, sometimes at least, we actually choose them), since, to be sure, the situations that provoke emotions often hit us unawares. Even where we do have a hand in setting up the circumstances that provoke us, in most cases it is not even plausible to say that we planned it that way. Of course, sometimes this is true, despite the vigorous denials. People do "set themselves up," knowing the probable emotional consequences. And their being aware of what they are doing is not a necessary part of the charge. But, typically, our emotions are both unplanned and more or less dictated by circumstances and it would make little sense to insist that we are responsible or ought to take responsibility for our emotional responses. But even so, there is a self-fulfilling prophecy involved here that cannot be easily denied. It is, I think, a Hegelian insight. When we look into our emotional lives with the idea that we are or might be responsible and ask ourselves those probing questions, "what am I doing this for?" "What am I getting out of this?" we often see aspects of our strategic behavior that would otherwise escape us. By contrast, if we look into our emotional lives with the idea that our emotions are forces beyond our control that happen to us, we are prone to make excuses for ourselves and resign ourselves to bad and destructive behavior that otherwise might be controlled. As Jean-Paul Sartre wrote in one of his most popular essays, "The existentialist does not believe in the power of passion. He will never regard a grand passion as a destructive torrent upon which a man is swept into uncertain actions as by fate, and which, therefore is an excuse for them." In other words, being an existentialist with regard to our emotions is *good for us*! Even if it does not allow us to take our lives in our hands, it lets us make our lives our own.

The voluntariness of emotion, if I may call it that, has been an under-explored theme in emotions research and in the everyday "folk psychology" of emotions. The extent to which we "choose" our emotions and are responsible for them is an almost invisible topic in the history of emotions. (Alva Noe [2005] has suggested a similar thesis for perception in general.) But at least this much is clear. No matter how fervently one believes that we are all victims of circumstances, or in God's hands, or subject to mysterious Fates of one sort or another, we are not just victims or pawns. We are essentially agents, and we have responsibilities. Our emotional lives are part of that domain. But this also leads me to an offensive suggestion about why people have been so long wedded to thinking about emotions as hijackers that render us victims instead of thinking of them as strategies we cultivate and put into play. Sartre, in his tome *Being and Nothingness*, famously develops the notion of "bad faith" *(mauvaise foi)*, by which he means our tendency to evade responsibility whenever we can. Our favorite way of evading responsibility is to make excuses. ("I know I was supposed to be here at nine, but I was stuck in traffic.") In other words, "it's not my fault. I was prevented by forces beyond my control." So it would be very convenient to think of our emotions, which motivate a great deal of our behavior, as themselves beyond our control.

If we do, then we could blame our silly outburst at the meeting on our anger, and not take responsibility for it ourselves. Or we could blame our foolish behavior on the fact that we were in love, and not take responsibility then either. But Sartre sees through the excuses, and we should too. I once summed up Sartre's philosophy and existentialism in general with the simple statement, No Excuses! And that is how I would like you to think about the emotions, too. Not that they don't have their causes. Not that they aren't often dictated or circumscribed by circumstances. Not that there are not sometimes passions over which we really do have little control. But instead of shrugging off responsibility, thinking "I am not responsible for my emotions," I want to urge you to ask, whenever you can, "why am I doing this? What am I getting out of this?" And you may well find that by taking responsibility you will no longer feel like the victim of your own emotions.

PART THREE

The Ethics of Emotion

A Quest for Emotional Integrity

✂

18

Emotions as Evaluative Judgments

Since the beginning of this book, I have tried to focus our attention on the emotions from an ethical point of view, that is, how our emotions fit into and function in our lives, their *meaning*. Accordingly, I have not paid as much attention to the new neurological and biological discoveries about emotions as many of my colleagues would like, but I hope that I have also made it clear that I do not think that these perspectives are necessarily at odds or in competition. They complement one another, face different kinds of questions, but they also inform one another. So, too, the social sciences appear to have a very different agenda than ethics and the humanities, but that opposition is illusory, the product of an overemphasis on the *science* of these disciplines and a sometimes studied neglect of their ethical origins.

After all, the question of how our emotions fit into and function in our lives needs to be understood in a number of different but obviously related ways. Looking for the meaning of emotions is one way. Studying their neurological substratum is another. Speculating on their evolutionary histories is yet another. And then there is all of that rich literature in the social sciences. Finally, there is the study of emotions in literature, in the arts, and in music. A philosophical perspective, with its emphasis on ethics and self-knowledge, is in no way opposed to these but can benefit from them in all sorts of ways. Because ethics, in one sense, is a thoroughly *natural* discipline and not at all dependent on the commands of a super-natural God or some mysterious notion of conscience. It has to do with our natural endowments and propensities, our lives in society with other people, our personalities and character, our personal itineraries and choices in life. Everything we can find out about human life, whether from science or through literature and the arts, is of importance to us.

The perspective I have been following dictates that the aspects of emotion that will be the focus of my treatment are those that have to do with an emotion's meaningfulness, which in turn means that an emotion's intelligence will be my primary concern. I intend this, as I have insisted, in several related ways, among them the ways in which emotions give us insight and understanding, the ways in which emotions shape our world, the ways in which emotions are strategies through which we manipulate and manage our world, and the ways in which we are responsible for our emotions. In other words, I take an emotional intelligence to be primarily an ethical imperative, which is why I take what I call emotional integrity, the aim and ultimate achievement of emotional intelligence, as the center-piece of our emotional-ethical lives.

In these final chapters, I would like to work my way toward an account of emotional integrity and with it the central ethical concepts of the good life, happiness, and spirituality. But first, I want to go explore in more detail just what emotional intelligence is and how it provides insight and information into our engagements in the world. Then I want to go back to some of those other disciplines, especially biology and anthropology, and see what they have to offer our naturalistic ethics. Penultimately, I want to take on the complex topic of emotional experience and the problem of consciousness, and then, finally, I want to say something more about the good life, happiness, and spirituality.

In chapter 14, I insisted that the emotions essentially involve the abilities to conceptualize and evaluate, and this is what I mean, first of all, when I speak of the intelligence of emotions. It also explains how it is that emotions have meaning. They do not just "fit" into our lives but shape our lives through their conceptions and evaluations of the situations in which we find (or could find) ourselves, of the people we deal with, and of our-selves and our place in the world. I have insisted throughout the book that emotions are *engagements with the world*, not mere self-enclosed feelings, and accordingly I have tried to pin this perspective down by insisting, in somewhat sloganeering form, that *emotions are judgments*. I mean by this, of course, that emotions are *evaluative* judgments, thus incorporating the insights of Richard Lazarus and others who speak rather of "appraisals" in their analysis of emotions and "core relational themes" (which are very much like what we called the "formal objects" of our emotions). But I shifted my thinking to the more existentially explicit conception of emo-tions as engagements with the world because I now see my former emphasis on judgments suggests more intellectualism in emotions than I intended, despite twenty years of qualifications and explanations (for instance, that the judgments involved in emotions are not necessarily articulate or "propositional" and are more like bodily "kinesthetic" judgments than deliberate and considered judgments). Nevertheless, I still think that evaluative judgments, so construed, are essential to the emotions.

In the earliest versions of my work, I was quite polemical, as are most young philosophers when they are trying to promote what seem like new ideas. My aim was to reject William James's well-established arousal theory and consider a new way of thinking about emotions, neither as feelings nor as dumb bodily reactions but as judgments more akin to moral and aesthetic evaluations than to physiological reactions or animal impulses. In retrospect—and in light of many years of debate and criticism—I have come to see my view as too much of a lurch to the other extreme, overemphasizing the more intelligent aspects of emotion but then simply dismissing the "noncognitive," feelings and the body generally. But the vision that I have held onto since those early days is one that I had already learned from Aristotle and Hume, not to mention my more intimate associations with Jean-Paul Sartre. Aristotle reminded me, against the disparagement of so many contemporary philosophers, that the emotions were an essential and indispensable part of civilized life. Hume encouraged my polemicism with his view that "reason is and ought to be the slave of the passions." But it was Sartre's little book and his larger philosophy that put me on the existentialist track, convincing me that there remained a great deal to be said, in the wake of James and Freud, about our *responsibility* for our emotions.

This was not a thesis that made much headway in the philosophical culture of mid-century. Several chapters ago, I briefly waxed nostalgic about studying with Charles Stevenson, the American logical positivist who was one of the founders of "emotivism" in ethics. But in response to his dismissal of ethics as "noncognitive" and "just a matter of emotion and attitude," I decided even as a student that this had it all wrong. Ethics was largely a matter of emotion, that much seemed true, but to say that ethics is a matter of emotion was not therefore to dismiss ethics but rather to insist on our appreciating and understanding the wisdom of the emotions. Ethical judgments are emotional judgments, to be sure, but this gives them their depth and their meaning. And it is the nature of those judgments that must be understood if we are to fully appreciate the nature and importance of ethics and achieve anything like emotional integrity.

I claim that judgments are essential to emotion, although I no longer say, as I did those many years ago, that feelings and physiology are irrelevant. I now agree with the neo-Jamesians that they are also essential to emotion, but I still insist that no feeling and no physiological response even counts as emotional unless it has the property of intentionality, *aboutness*. An emotion is an engagement with the world. I explain this by insisting that emotions are *structured* by judgments, but it is important to be clear what I mean by "judgment." I am not talking about *deliberative* judgments, that is, judgments that necessarily involve a lot (or in fact any) thought. The recent "Blink"-type emphasis on intuition and snap judgment is much more what I have in mind (Gladwell, 2005). Nor need the judgments that structure emotions even be *articulate*, that is, "spelled out" (either to ourselves or others). Nor are emotional judgments what some philosophers call "propositional attitudes," that is fully conceptual depictions of the world in "*that* . . ."—type clauses, taking as their objects propositions rather than concrete objects or people or relationships. I have sometimes compared emotional judgments to *kinesthetic* judgments, in that our awareness may be merely tacit and unspoken (even to oneself). Think about walking down a set of steps outside of your house or apartment. You are making judgments every inch of the way, but you certainly don't think about them, much less deliberate or say to yourself, "now lower your right heel a little bit more." After a bad fall you might well do this, but not in the normal course of things. So, too, we thoughtlessly make our emotional judgments and have our emotions, but this doesn't mean that doing this does not involve learning and detailed knowledge about the world and our place in it.

If an emotion is structured by evaluative judgments, this means that understanding an emotion is understanding its constitutive judgments, whether or not there may be much more to understand as well. And in thinking about emotions and ethics together, as emotivism taught us to do, the first thing that I want to do is to reject those sharp distinctions between beliefs and attitudes, reasons and emotions, facts and values. (In psychological terms, "cognition" and "appraisal" refer to the same set of operations.) Evaluative judgments are both based on beliefs and express attitudes. They also have their reasons (often good reasons) and they constitute, not just accompany, our emotions. The distinction between facts and values has often been challenged in philosophy ever since Hume sought to turn the distinction into a logical wedge between statements of fact and value judgments. But facts are often circumscribed by values (why else would a fact be of any interest to us?) and value judgments virtually all presuppose some factual basis, even where the value judgment in question seems to be "a priori" and independent of any actual state of affairs. But what would "abortion is wrong!" mean if fetuses were not in fact vulnerable to medical procedures, if they did not in fact grow to become human babies, if there were not in fact real dangers and serious financial and life-plan difficulties for human mothers. Imagine if babies were born after a short, riskless gestation period, and then were, like reptile offspring, independent from birth with nothing further demanded from the parents.

With reference to emotivism, the structure of moral emotions is already moral in its nature. So the idea that ethics is an expression of emotion is clearly correct, but that is because the emotions already have a moral structure. Take as an illustrative example the emotion of moral indignation, say, moral indignation at the very idea that a military authority has sanctioned the torture of possibly innocent captives. Such an emotion definitely involves not only factual information but also strong evaluative judgments, at least some of which are clearly moral in their structure and their semantics. They are suprapersonal and arguably universal, and they unquestionably include the claim that something is *wrong*, a violation of some principle or rule. And yet, there is no denying that it is an emotion, not a dispassionate legal claim. (Adam Smith and David Hume both get into some difficulty when they try to overcome provincial and personal viewpoints by introducing an "ideal observer," someone not moved by merely personal preferences and prejudices. But since they both insist that ethics is a matter of "sentiments" they cannot go all the way to pure dispassionate reason, like Immanuel Kant later in the century.) It might be objected that the judgment is just an *expression* of emotion, but the emotion already contains, as part of its conceptual structure, the moral judgment that *this is morally wrong*. So to say that the emotional utterance is just an expression of emotion is to get it backward. The emotion is already an assertion of a moral judgment, without which it would be unintelligible.

But compare moral indignation with just being angry, and then compare that with being irritated or annoyed. The difference between these is not merely their comparative "intensity." (In fact, one can become annoyed to the point of distraction and even desperation, while one can on occasion be rather cool in his or her moral indignation.) The difference is rather in their evaluative structure. Against the emotivists, I would insist that the evaluative judgments that structure our emotions are rarely limited to those minimal attitudes of "yeah" or "nay," the emotivists' "Boo" and "Hooray" suggested by A. J. Ayer in the name of positivism. (Thus my objection to the simplistic positive-negative dichotomy in chapter 15.) They rather involve a wide variety of very different kinds of evaluative judgments. Moral indignation, in particular, embodies a special kind of evaluative judgment embodying a moral principle. A moral principle, without my trying to take on the whole of ethics and moral philosophy, is one that tends to impersonality and generalization. When I am indignant, I believe that *"This is wrong!"* I am not just saying that I don't like it, or that it offends me. When I say that something is immoral, I am decidedly not just saying "I disapprove of it" nor am I simply urging others to do so as well (Stevenson's analysis). I am saying, with a good deal of emphasis, *"this is wrong!"* and its wrongness need not have anything in particular to do with me, my tastes, or my personal values.

The idea is that moral indignation therefore has weight that most emotions do not have. Anger, by contrast, although it is also a judgment that something is wrong, is a judgment that someone has wronged *me* (or one of my friends), but it has no evident suprapersonal meaning. (If it does take on such meaning, it tends toward indignation.) But anger is an accusation of *personal* offense. I may be offended that I have been publicly insulted, but this need not appeal to any moral principle. Indeed, I may even recognize the validity of the insult and so I can make no moral claim. ("Yes I am indeed a clumsy person, but I am nevertheless offended that you pointed it out.") Anger is for the most part "just personal." Of course we are all too prone to rationalize and elevate our personal judgments to the status of moral judgments, but this familiar piece of self-deception does not put into question the important distinction between moral indignation and anger.

Irritation and annoyance, by contrast again, not only involve no principle but they even lack any judgment of offense. They just register dissatisfaction or discomfort with the situation at hand, without blaming anyone, though again, irritation and annoyance may well slip into anger, if we look around for somebody to blame for our dissatisfaction or discomfort. Many psychologists, reasonably enough, would want to say that all of these emotions belong to the same basic "family," and, indeed, they all do share a hostile or "negative" view of the world or their objects. They may also share certain physiological features and have shared evolutionary roots, but that is not something I would want to assert here and should in any case not be used for a reductionist agenda, simply conflating anger, indignation, annoyance, outrage, fury, and any number of other related but distinct emotions. But what I do want us to appreciate is the subtlety and the importance of the differences between them. They are not just "different degrees" of the same emotion. They are profoundly different, with very different meanings, depending on the nature of the judgments that constitute them. Understanding those differences is a function of emotional intelligence, using the right words to "label" the appropriate emotion.

The idea of an emotion embedding within its structure a suprapersonal moral claim may sound odd to our ears, especially if we have been brought up to think of emotions as mere feelings and so without any "structure" at all. So, too, it may seem odd to talk about moral principles in our emotions if we have been brought up to think of morality as something handed down from on high. It would then look as if we have made a serious "category mistake," confusing what is "objective" and transcendental with something merely personal, conventional, or natural. I have already said that I am interested in a "naturalistic" ethics, but this already brings within its embrace the fact that we are social animals and need to get along and work with others, thus accepting together the personal, the conventional, and the natural. Indeed, I am not ruling out that the source of morals might be religion or rather, religious beliefs, but the "springs of action and feeling" must still be our emotions. Thus we all accept the idea of "internalizing" moral principles, whether they are the customs of our culture, the dictates of reason, or the commandments of God in Heaven. This is all I am really claiming here. But the idea of internalizing suprapersonal moral principles gives us a good start on seeing just how sophisticated the judgmental-evaluative structure of emotions can be. The same sort of analysis, with lots of other twists and turns, applies to other moral emotions such as shame and guilt, regret and remorse, pride and vanity. I tried to show the complexity and differences between these, without making a big deal out of it, in the first part of the book. But now I want the general structure of these differences to become our main topic of attention.

So my claim is that emotional intelligence, in one of its most prominent meanings, requires that emotions are constituted or structured by judgments, and these judgments can be surprisingly precise so we can make a bewildering number of subtle distinctions as well as the rather ham-fisted distinctions among "emotion families." An understanding of emotions thus involves an understanding of the judgments that structure them, and the differences may be very fine-grained and even exquisite.

It is the nature of these judgments that determines the type of emotion. William James sought to find a unifying theme that held all of the emotions together, and he claimed to find it in bodily upset. But when it came time to explain the enormous variety and specificity of our emotional responses, he failed. (It was Cannon who first argued that the variety of emotional experience was such that bodily upset could not possibly account for our many different emotions.) It was only years later that most psychologists began to realize that the "cognitive" aspects of emotion could do this. At first, this was restricted to the "labeling" of emotions, how we choose to identify them. Thus the psychological research took a sudden but significant lurch toward the complexities of language. But researchers soon realized that the identification of an emotion depended on the context in which it was experienced, which in turn determined the sort of judgments that defined the emotion. Meanwhile, psychologists following Magda Arnold and Richard Lazarus were developing a rich theory of the central role of "appraisals" in the determination of emotions. My own account, that emotions are (or are structured by) judgments was parallel to this discovery in psychology (although I had not read much of this literature at the time [Arnold, 1960; Schachter and Singer, 1962; Lazarus, 1994]). But between us, this "cognitive" turn in emotions research opened a whole new area and methodology for talking about and analyzing what had been for the most part dismissed as cognitively vacuous and of little philosophical or psychological significance. If emotions were constituted by evaluative judgments or appraisals, then conceptual analysis had an important role to play in understanding them.

Consider the family of self-abasing emotions that we discussed several chapters ago, in particular, the pair of embarrassment and shame. How do these differ? We have already answered this question informally, and the difference is not, to be sure, any dramatic or detectable difference in Jamesian bodily feelings. Embarrassment is based on the judgment that one is in an awkward situation but also on the judgment that one is *not to blame* for this. Shame, by contrast, is also based on the judgment that one is in an awkward situation but that one *is* to blame. One takes responsibility for doing something wrong, for letting down one's community, for violating public mores, for betraying a trust or a friend. But notice that at least one of the judgments here is of a particularly sophisticated kind: that of taking (or not taking) responsibility. The main argument for emotional intelligence is not just that emotions involve evaluative judgments (which might be rather simple, like "that tastes good" or "I dislike blondes"), but that they often involve very sophisticated, conceptually complicated judgments, such as judgments of responsibility.

One might argue that although this is clearly true of shame, it may not be true of embarrassment, which may involve only the *absence* of feelings of responsibility rather than the *denial* of responsibility, and I think that this may be correct. But I would say that it can go either way. If I am in a self-conscious position of responsibility, say, I'm in charge of a bunch of students on a field trip and one of the students does something utterly disgraceful and contrary to my explicit prohibitions, I might be ashamed precisely because I do "take responsibility" for his behavior. Or I might be simply embarrassed by his behavior and thus deny any responsibility on my part. On the other hand, if I am just going about my business, singing (very badly) in the shower, and I suddenly notice a crowd outside of my window, watching and listening with amusement, it probably never occurs to me that I am or am not responsible. Nevertheless, I am clearly embarrassed. But the idea that responsibility can be an ingredient in our emotional judgments enriches the sophistication of our emotional lives enormously and is unintelligible on any more primitive conception of emotions. It also suggests that these emotions are deeply dependent on cultural as well as ethical presumptions, and whether the prevailing emotion of self-blame is shame or guilt depends in particular on the ethical structure of the society.

Another dimension of emotional judgment, again unexpected on traditional and more primitive theories, has to do with what I call judgments of *status*. Consider the three emotions contempt, resentment, and hatred. All three have profound ethical implications and consequences, and all three are hostile emotions that involve a harsh view of other people (or at least of one other person). But what distinguishes them? We are not animals that merely growl when threatened. Our emotions are much more refined. Contempt is an emotion that interestingly lends itself to a certain vocabulary (studied in detail by many anthropologists and linguists). That vocabulary has two dimensions. First and foremost, it is the vocabulary of "*looking down*" at someone. We look down with contempt. (We also find someone really despicable to be "beneath contempt.") A familiar expression of contempt shows the face tilted up in order to literally look down at the person held in contempt. (This gets more awkward as the other person gets taller, but the usual solution to this is to increase the distance between the two of you or find a staircase or an elevated platform.) The second vocabulary, much richer than the first, involves the identification of the person held in contempt with "lower" animals, preferably vermin or, even worse, offensive organic matter. So we call a person we loathe (a variety of contempt) "a rat," "a snake," "a worm," or "scum," "slime," "sleaze," and we employ various crude terms for human waste. (The cultural variation and ingenuity in such matters is fascinating.) But you get the idea. Contempt involves an essential judgment of marked *superiority*. It is not just hostility or harshness.

It is quite otherwise with resentment. Nietzsche (1967) captured a real insight when he characterized the resentful man as "neither upright nor naïve nor honest and straightforward with himself. His soul squints . . ." As I explained in an earlier chapter, Nietzsche diagnosed resentment as an emotion of the weak. The weak resent the strong. In history, slaves resented their masters. Resentment is always on the defensive, and it is always *looking up* at those considered oppressive. Nietzsche captured the spirit of resentment, too, in a lowly animal, the tarantula, which he described in terms of its venomous but not very harmful bite and its quick, backward retreat into the safety of its private hole. Thus we can appreciate the enormous difference between these two bitterly hostile emotions, contempt and resentment, again not as mere differences in feeling but as an ethical matter, a matter of polar opposite judgments of *status*, the one superiority looking down at inferiority, the other inferiority looking up at superiority. These different judgments, of course, lead to dramatically different modes of behavior and very different emotional experiences.

Hatred, to complete the triad, is an emotion of equality. Our typical metaphor for hatred and its supposed opposite, love, is black and white. The good guy in the classic black-and-white western (for example, the Lone Ranger) always wears light outfits, the bad guy (Lee van Cleef, for instance) almost always wears black. But just as love seeks out equals (or, as Stendhal writes, when it does not find equality, it creates it), hatred, too, seeks out equals. Colloquially, we can easily understand why people so readily label so many of their negative emotions "hate" (as they label a promiscuous number of their preferences "love"), because it casts a person in a bad light when he or she admits to resentment or, for that matter, even contempt (in our supposedly egalitarian society). But to wrap up the point, among the judgments that structure our emotions are comparative judgments of status, whether this be moral or social, in terms of power and influence, or simply by virtue of one person being bigger or feeling superior to the other. Thus emotions often embody moral and social intelligence and play a central role in our interactive relationships. We may not want to say that all such comparisons are "ethical" in nature (and they certainly need not be "moral"), but it should be clear that in the ethical perspective that I am advocating matters of status are anything but a matter of evaluative indifference to us.

There are also judgments of what I would call *distance*. The idea here is metaphorical, to be sure, but in much the same way that the "looking down" image is metaphorical in my characterization of contempt. It often translates into a very real effort to maintain or close up physical distance from the object of one's emotion. Love, for example, is an emotion that is famously "close" or intimate. And when we feel close or intimate, we obviously try to be literally, spatially close or intimate and close the distance (whether physical, conversational, or emotional) between us. Indeed, love involves, I suggested, a kind of identity, a merging or fusion, with the other person, the ultimate closeness. Contempt and disgust, by contrast, are emotions that keep their distance. And in fact we distance ourselves from that which disgusts us. Other emotions aim to keep an "arm's length" from their object. Anger is typically like this. (Of course there is "in-your-face" anger, but this, I would argue, is a distinctively different emotion from the more usual being angry *at* someone, and different again from being angry at a great and impersonal distance (fuming, say, at the latest government policies). In-your-face anger adds a generous dose of aggression to anger, not to mention a very effective strategy for intimidating the other person.

Now you might question my seeming to multiply "types" of anger here based on what would seem to be mere matters of metaphor and expression, but the point I want to make and have been making is that the subtlety and variety of emotions is not limited to the minimal judgmental structure that an emotion may well share with other emotions of the same "type" or "family" (such as, all angry emotions are hostile). The emotions are neither discrete entities nor distinct types but complex multijudgment processes that engage any number of different ingredients along different dimensions. Expression is not just an "outward" manifestation of an emotion but an aspect or a continuation of the emotion itself.

Thus emotional distance is not just a metaphor: It manifests itself in both emotional expression and in other behavior that accompanies or follows the emotion. Thus in contempt, we expect someone to keep their distance, perhaps even with a facial expression—head pulled back, chin up—to incrementally increase that distance even more. In love, we expect caresses and a virtual compulsion to make contact, no matter how surreptitious or, in some contexts, rude. And in anger, I suggested that there may be any number of stances, depending on the precise nature of the anger and its emotional context. Being angry with the one you love usually dictates an "in-your-face" stance, coupled with an ambiguous move of slightly distancing oneself. Being angry with the registrar at the university, by contrast, usually involves a letter of complaint rather than a shouting match, and not just because of the logistics of the situation. To think that personal face-to-face abuse (or worse) is the more "natural" expression of anger is to wrongly assume from the outset that anger as such is essentially crude and violent. But even insofar as there is some "basic" form of anger (or rage) that is as near as can be to a straightforward physiological reaction, this is by no means the normal or for that matter even the usual form of that emotion. Most anger in civilized society is in fact a subtle affair whose expressions consist more of looks, glances, and sarcastic words, and the differences between the different forms of anger, including differences based on judgments of status, may be exquisite indeed.

Moral clout, responsibility, status, and distance are just some of the dimensions of evaluative judgment that constitute emotions and provide them with their considerable intelligence and relevance to our moral lives. There are also, needless to say, a variety of judgments of a more straightforward "yeah" or "nay" nature, but as I argued earlier, these may be concerned with many different aspects of the emotion and in virtually no cases pertain simply to the emotion as a whole. Thus anger includes a sense of hostility toward its objects, of elevation regarding the subject, propriety regarding the issue, pleasure or pain in anticipation of consequences, and so on. Thus while "valence" plays many different roles in any given emotion, it does not characterize the emotion as such. So, too, I have been speaking of judgments as multiple ingredients in the various emotions. Even without going back into the role of feelings and physiology, I need to say that virtually no emotion consists of a single evaluative judgment. Rather, most emotions are complexes of a dozen or more converging judgments. Anger, for example, combines accusing judgments with status and distance judgments (it is inappropriate to get angry with children or dumb animals, blasphemous to get angry at God). Anger involves judgments of blame and various judgments about history and context, but anger also arises in frustration where there may be no blame to be laid. Love consists of judgments of closeness and intimacy, to be sure, but it also includes any number of judgments about the virtues and special charms of the beloved, and these are not just *reasons for* love. They are the judgmental structures of love. So love does not only have its reasons, it consists of reasons. An emotion such as jealousy is a bewilderingly complex system of judgments, involving not just another person but a rival and thus judgments of status, blame (including self-blame), and distance (fear of losing intimacy, the thought that she is getting closer to him than she is to me!). Guilt, too, and many forms of hatred, are to be understood only in terms of a complex of historical and cultural peculiarities. Hatred, like love, could be argued to be quite different in all of its instances, and guilt too (as the Catholic Church has long recognized.) And this is even before we get into the labyrinthine realm of mixed emotions.

And yet, many of the most brilliant philosophers of the past (Thomas Hobbes, René Descartes, and Baruch Spinoza, just to start) tried to analyze the differences and distinctions among emotions in one-line character- izations (for example, Descartes (1989): "Love is an emotion of the soul caused by the spirits which incites the soul to desire to be separated from the objects which present themselves as hurtful."). These were rarely adequate, and the reason is not hard to see. An emotion is rarely a simple judgment but, as above, a combination of several and perhaps many dif- ferent kinds of judgment. It is much less, as I argued earlier, a simple "pro" or "con" attitude toward the world. A few emotions, for example, disgust, might be readily conceived in terms of a simple judgment, but just because the judgment is so simple, we would be justified in denying that disgust is an emotion at all. (That is, physiological disgust, the elemental taste of something rotten; if it is *moral* disgust, then that is a very different story.) What's more, again, the judgments that converge to constitute an emotion are going to be dependent on and to some extent follow from the sur- rounding culture and context. So shame and embarrassment involve all of those judgments that add up to "finding oneself in an awkward situation," but this is obviously going to vary with the context, the culture, and the particular people around you, as well as the sophisticated and localized judgments involved in taking or not taking responsibility.

I will not try to show you the quasi-mathematical matrix that can be generated indicating the enormous number of possible emotions, only a small number of which we carve out and name. I will simply present that as a mind-blowing possibility, that there may be an unlimited number and range of emotions, depending on how fine-tuned we are to the specifics of our world. To be sure, one can always retreat to the crude idea of basic emotion families, most of them expressed by a grunt, a roar, or a whimper. But the idea is that emotions can be highly refined as well as crude. They can be exquisite and sensitive as well as blunt, and articulate and even poetic as well as "basic." The ancient Indian aestheticians were clear about this, and they distinguished between crude *bhavas* and *klesas*, on the one hand, and refined *rasas*, on the other, where only the latter were steps to enlightenment. Unfortunately, in their obsession with categorizing the *rasas*, they sometimes tended to underappreciate the delicate differences between them (see, for example, Bharatamuni, 1967). But so, too, my thesis here, and my conception of emotional integrity, will be totally misunderstood if it is thought that the emotions that I am talking about are only of the "basic," crude, unrefined variety. The idea is that we can create better lives for ourselves only if we create better emotions as well.

This is one of several reasons why I reject the current emphasis on "basic" emotions, the idea that emotions are discrete physiological syndromes with minimal intelligence and refinement. In fact, I argue that there are no such emotions, at least in adult humans, but only a small number of seemingly clear but embarrassingly crude examples that we somewhat arbitrarily choose to emphasize because of their supposed universality and "hard-wired" simplicity. But why should the most primitive emotions be more "basic" than the most exquisite, or the most stupid emotions more essential to human nature than the most refined? What makes us human is our collective emotional imagination and our individual ability to learn and cultivate our emotions. I am not for a moment denying that there are primitive physiological responses that may well be more or less universal across our species, but what makes us human is our ability to embellish, refine, and arise above such "basic" responses, which is not to deny that, even in the most refined and civilized context, these crude emotions may have a very powerful and impressive effect. But like profanity in a play, it is their rarity that accounts for their power. A steady diet of crude emotions makes a person hardly worthy of our company, and this has nothing to do with manners.

Which brings us back again to the Stoics, those brilliant, perverse philosophers of ancient Greece and Rome. As I said earlier, it was the Stoics, more clearly than anyone else, who insisted that the passions should not be confused with their "first movements," the feelings of physiological upset and arousal that immediately follow one's initial perception of a situation. The passion itself is what comes next, an "affirmation" of those feelings as legitimate or illegitimate, as wise or foolish. Thus for the Stoics the passions are judgments, and judgments can be true or false, wise or foolish, warranted or unwarranted, and they are not just painful or pleasurable but definitive in ascertaining just how we live, how virtuous we are, how happy we can be. So far so good, in my view. But then, the Stoics make an unfortunate move, in my opinion, though it is the move that gives them their name. To be "stoical" is to stand strong against adversity, even against tragedy, and the strategy of the Stoics was to avoid being affected or at least to avoid "affirmation" of suffering by refusing to "affirm" what they considered misery-causing attachments and investments.

For example, getting angry presupposes the judgment that the offensive behavior of others is something to get upset about. But a good Stoic will "see through" this. What is one offense, in the larger scheme of things? So, too, one loves one woman above all others, perhaps even feels that he "cannot live without her." But what is the special significance of one woman, in the larger scheme of things? And can one really not live without her? So the Stoics advised avoiding love and marriage, children, material possessions, ambition and career, or, at least, they tried to distance themselves from these. (Most of the Stoics did in fact get married and have children. Whether they were loving husbands and fathers I do not know. It is interesting, however, that there were so few female Stoics.) So, too, with regard to public life. Some of the Stoics lived as virtual ascetics, but others in fact aspired to and achieved the pinnacles of power. Seneca was a Roman senator under Nero. Marcus Aurelius was one of the last great emperors of Rome. But reading both of them, one is struck by how seriously they tried to remain unaffected by the conflicts and treachery around them. This is all extremely admirable, to be sure, but their advice, to "see through" the foolish vanity of our judgments about the world, is one that I, at any rate cannot accept. More philosophically, I would say that the Stoics deny the special status of subjectivity—that one woman can mean the world *to me*—even as they defend what is an extremely insightful subjective theory of emotion as personal judgments about the world.

Now, someone might object to this whole campaign of analysis on the grounds that what I have shown is not that emotions are judgments and therefore intelligent but rather that emotions, which are rather primitive, have *cognitive preconditions*, namely beliefs and such, but that they themselves are not cognitive. (One of the most impressive defenders of this point of view today is Jesse Prinz, who in his book *Gut Reactions* offers us an innovative reconstruction of the Jamesian position and makes the cognitivism of emotions a secondary rather than a primary characteristic. Also to be mentioned in this regard is Jenefer Robinson and her book *Deeper than Reason*, although she has other ends in mind, notably the expression of emotions in art and [especially] music. Clearly a "noncognitive" view of emotions has special appeal in the understanding of music [without words or literary theme, that is], a fascinating topic which I will not try to tackle here.) I used to think that this was much more of an issue than I do now.

First, I don't see that there is a significant divide between an emotion and its preconditions, but mainly, it doesn't seem to matter whether the emotion *is* the recognition of (or an engagement with) a certain state of the world or if it recognizes that a certain state of the world is appropriate for such and such an engagement and therefore for a certain emotion. Wittgenstein suggested that we do not recognize an emotion (that is, a private feeling) but we rather name an emotion on the basis of its context. So it is not the judgment or feeling of violation that constitutes shame but rather we call it "shame" if it takes place in a situation in which the person is worthy of blame. (This is an argument that was persuasively put forward by Errol Bedford in one of the first important analytic essays on emotion, "Emotions.") This view tends to ignore the first-person (phenomenological) viewpoint (as any neobehaviorist would) and consequently does not account for the fact that a person *experiences* shame. But it does recognize, as too many "introspective" philosophers and psychologists did not, that emotions and context are not easily distinguished or separated. But shame is not just concocted by disinterested observers. Emotional intelligence is intelligence *in* the emotions, and it is not just our spectator appreciation of their functionality and significance. The emotions have ethical significance not just because they take place in ethically charged situations but because they are constituted by judgments that are through and through value laden. They provide our basic orientation to the world and to one another.

19

Emotions, Self, and Consciousness

As adult, language-using, reflective human beings, we do not just have emotions. We have thoughts about our emotions, and we have further emotions about our emotions. We approve of them or disapprove of them. We are proud of them or embarrassed about them. We can be angry at ourselves for having an emotion (say, getting jealous) or for getting emotional when we had resolved not to. And even before we gain our full linguistic-reflective abilities, before we form thoughts about our emotions or evaluate them, we learn to recognize that we have them. We name them, even publicly. "You are making me very angry!" "I hate you!" and "I love you." But even when we do not do this, we often identify them to ourselves. We know that we are embarrassed. We know that we are filled with admiration, whether or not we apply the explicit labels to our feelings.

Animals and infants do not do this. They do not have even this minimal reflective capacity. But for us, it has become an essential part of our emotional life. Our emotions and emotional experience typically include our thoughts about our emotions and our emotions about our emotions. And this is why our emotions become so central to ethics, not just because there are evaluations and appraisals already built into our emotions, and not just because our emotional behavior tends to have ethically significant consequences, but because we are continuously evaluating and appraising our own emotional responses. As the Stoics taught years ago, our passions may begin with primitive "first movements," but they fully manifest themselves only once we "affirm" or "deny" them. And what we affirm and deny is not just the emotion. It is the emotion as a reflection of one's *self*. It shows or betrays who one is. Thus a man becomes ashamed because he is afraid and thus shows himself to be timid or cowardly. A woman is proud of the fact that she actually stood up for herself and got angry at the supervisor who had been harassing her. It changes her very conception of herself as a "take-charge" person. Even before we learn to analyze it, we experience our emotions as profoundly indicative of the kind of person we are. Our emotions make us *self-conscious.*

Throughout this book, I have not said much about the self or self-consciousness, at least not very straightforwardly. And yet the self and the sense of self permeates virtually everything I have talked about, from the most "basic" emotions to our most complex emotional judgments and engagements in the world. This is not to say that all emotions are *about* the self, nor is it to say that all emotions are self-conscious in anything like the same way. Many of our emotions are about other people or about a situation, and our emotions can be altruistic, totally caring, and they may engage in tasks of no self-interest whatever. And there is an important difference, we will see, between those emotions that are self-conscious and those that are not. But the self is implicit or complicit in almost every human emotion, even those that are essentially physiological syndromes or affect programs. Thus neuropsychiatrist Tony Damasio speculates that there is prototype of self and self-consciousness in all living creatures. We have seen the self appear again and again throughout this book, not only in such obviously self-directed emotions as shame, embarrassment, and pride, where the self is clearly the center of focus, but also in anger, where it is not the focus. Anger is nevertheless all about an offense *to* the self and so necessarily involves a sense of the offended or frustrated self. Furthermore, as we saw, anger often involves strategies to salvage self-esteem in which the self plays a magisterial role (as "judge and jury"). So, too the self is profoundly involved in love, even though the focus is the beloved, since on my analysis love is structured as a *sharing of selves,* so in that sense it is very much about the self, which is emphatically not to say that "all love is self-love." Self-love is not love.

Even if almost all emotions involve the self, it does not follow that all emotions are explicitly about the self. This is sometimes challenged, as we will see, by those who insist (in one sense or another) that all emotions are self-centered. But whether and in what sense the emotions *implicitly* involve the self is a more subtle matter. Thus in anger, the self is thoroughly involved but it is neither the object nor the focus of consciousness, and in moral indignation, the self might not be in evidence at all, only the violation and the violator. But the self, like a judge pointing a finger, is clearly present even if it is not the focus and seemingly not even in the scene. If I am proud of my brother, the emotion is quite explicitly about my brother, but as David Hume pointed out in his *Treatise of Human Nature*, my pride makes sense only insofar as I see my self in connection with my brother. So, too, in faith, awe, and admiration it may be the relative *insignificance* of one's self that is important to the emotion, but the self is thereby involved, no matter how intensely the focus may be on the object of the emotion (God, one's hero, or some exemplary individual). In fear there is the urgent question of what one should do as well as in what way one might be harmed, yet the focus of the fear is on the danger, not on one's self as such.

I mentioned above that there are theorists who have insisted (in some sense or other) that all emotions are self-centered. *Mea culpa.* Early in my work on emotions, I hazarded the very general empirical hypothesis that the ultimate strategy of all emotions was the maximization (or maintenance) of self-esteem. (In this, I sought to improve on Sartre's earlier suggestion that all emotions were a mode of "escape behavior," attempts to save face in confronting a difficult world.) I have backed away from this overly bold hypothesis, which I now see as rendering all emotions overly self-interested and perhaps even narcissistic. I have also come to loathe the notion of "self-esteem" because of its utter abuse by educators and pop-psych-gurus. But I still hold onto what I take to be a central insight: All adult human emotions, virtually by definition on my account, are more or less self-conscious. They are engagements of the self in the world, however primitive the self in question, even where the entire focus of the emotions seems to be aimed elsewhere, at another person's well-being, toward God, on the task in which one is busily engaged. In human beings, that is what makes emotions different from intellectual and other "cool" judgments. As strategies, they are concerned with, among other matters, the well-being of the self (its minimal condition being survival). In this, the dramatic strategy of anger is not so much the exception as the exemplary case.

I now call my former hypothesis into question primarily because I want to acknowledge that we are personally motivated in our emotions not only for the sake of ourselves but for the sake of others. Some of us, sometimes, can even be "selfless," so long as that means the total *submission* of the self and not its absence. This does not make emotions any less personal. But the self can itself be involved in many different ways. It can be submitted to a higher cause or, in love, can be expansive. It can embrace and encompass, even merge with other selves. We can get angry—and especially morally indignant—on the behalf of others as well as ourselves. We can avenge other people as well as seek revenge ourselves. And we feel sympathy and empathy for others when we ourselves have nothing at stake and nothing at risk. So while the self is involved in virtually every emotion, that does not mean that all emotions are self-centered or self-interested. But what also emerges from these considerations is the realization that the self in emotions is not a single substance, as Descartes suggested in his classic meditation on the self.

If the self is at least implicit in all emotions, it nevertheless appears in very different guises in our different emotions. Thus Hume, despite his denying the Cartesian self, argues that ideas about the self both cause pride and are what the pride is about, but these are *different* ideas. The cause, he says, is what we have done (some accomplishment or achievement), but the second idea is about the self more generally. Once we give up Descartes's overly abstract conception of the self as a "thinking thing" and look for the various roles that the self can play in the different emotions, we find that the self can be the agent of an ongoing action, the agent of a previous action, the victim of some calamity, the offended party, the beneficiary of an act or a situation, an innocent bystander, the agent or the victim (or both), the beneficiary or the offended (or both), and, of course, entangled with other people in all sorts of ways. Are these various selves *the same* self? Is the self we find in shame and embarrassment the same as the self we see in anger? Is the self that merges with another in love the same self that withdraws in sadness or for that matter in grief, even when grief follows love? When Nietzsche (1966) argued for the fragmentation of self ("a community of selves"), some of what he had in mind was the very different apprehensions of ourselves we have when in our various passions. So speaking simply of "the self" in emotion may turn out to be overly simplistic.

What we start to appreciate, as I think Hume and certainly Nietzsche appreciated, is that the self changes its shape and even its nature from one emotion to another. It is not as if there is one self, much less what earlier philosophers defended and attacked as a "soul-thing," that enters into our emotions. Animals may have a rudimentary sense of self, of themselves as threatened or encroached upon, but people, because they can be fully self-conscious, have a much broader range of emotions, even on the prereflective level. It is a matter of some debate whether animals can be ashamed or embarrassed or proud (although watching a German shepherd who has just misbehaved or accomplished a difficult task, it is hard for me not to think they can be), but the existence and importance of such emotions in human lives is not debatable. They are defined in terms of the self. If it makes sense to say that a German shepherd dog can be ashamed or embarrassed or proud then it must also make sense to say that it has some sense of self.

What is it to have a self (and a "sense of self")? I mentioned that Damasio writes boldly but speculatively about a core consciousness and a proto-self that exists even on the most rudimentary level of brain function and even in the most primitive organisms. Lewis Thomas (1974), years ago, argued that even the most primitive organisms, slime molds for instance, have a rudimentary sense of self, that is, some sense about what is *themselves* and what is *other*. But without being so speculative, we can say with confidence that animals (mammals and birds, in particular) who are afraid have some sense of vulnerability and those who are aggressive have some sense of defensiveness. (One should not jump to the unwarranted conclusion that animals who are afraid are afraid of death or that animals who are aggressive seek to kill their antagonist, for animals have no concept of *death*.) The interesting question here is what concepts, and in particular what concept of self, animals must have in order to have emotions. The overly skeptical reply that animals have no concepts and no concept of self just pushes the question back a step, so that it forces us to ask what *sense* of self an animal might have in order to have emotions (where we avoid the often overintellectualized concept of a "concept"). But it is evident that animals have some such sense of self if they have any emotions at all (and it is surely an unintelligible skepticism that still denies this.)

But having a sense of self is not the same as being self-conscious. It is highly debatable whether or to what extent animals have self-consciousness, that is, a sense of themselves *as* selves. Experiments with chimps and gorillas observing their behavior in front of a mirror with a paint smear on their forehead seem fatally flawed, if researchers assume that self-consciousness is *visual* self-consciousness. Many animals seem to depend much more or a sense of smell (notably less important in most human interactions, excepting perfumes and elevator and subway encounters). But without tackling this thorny issue, we can say with some clarity that animals may have emotions and therefore some sense of self, but they do not know that they have emotions and therefore are not self-conscious in anything like the sense that adult humans can be. Adult human beings, by contrast, can both recognize their emotions (even if they can also misidentify them) and be self-conscious about them. Even if biologists like Damasio and Thomas are willing to extend the notion of selfhood to virtually all living things so long as they display an in-mechanism of survival, the centrality of self in human emotion means much more than this.

Understanding the emotions as deeply involved with the self and interests helps us to understand another aspect of emotions that is often misinterpreted. Emotions, it is generally agreed, admit of degrees. One can be mildly angry, or one can be very, very angry. One can be just a little in love, or one can be "head over heels" in love. One can be a bit embarrassed, but one can also be very embarrassed, even humiliated or "mortified." But what is this *intensity* of an emotion? What does it mean to be a little bit emotional as opposed to very emotional? The intensity of an emotion is usually thought of as the "heat" of an emotion, as if a person who is a little bit angry will be a little bit agitated but a person who gets really angry or is in a rage will turn quite red and suffer from all sorts of physiological excesses (rapid pulse and heartbeat, heavy breathing, severe sweating, cramping, muscular tension, etc.), and this will all manifest itself in intense feelings, a particularly intense emotional experience. The anger is thus thought to be more or less intense on the basis of "how strongly one feels." But I have already suggested that the degree of physiological upset may sometimes be surprisingly independent of the intensity of the emotion and so too the sensations that accompany that upset. Autonomic nervous system–type sensations can be produced in various ways, by the onset of the flu, the ingestion of stimulants or vitamin supplements, but one soon realizes that these sensations are not in such instances symptoms of emotion. People get enraged over minor disappointments, but we do not thereby say that their anger is intense. Some people get very angry but may remain quite "cool" and controlled, perhaps because they already anticipate some devastating act of retaliation or revenge. We do not thereby dismiss their anger. But what, then, is the measure of the intensity of anger?

I would say that, for the most part, it is *the seriousness of the offense* that is the measure of the intensity of anger. But this cannot be an "objective" judgment. Otherwise, irrational anger and "overreacting" would be incomprehensible, for anger would always be proportional to the *actual* seriousness of the offense, however that would be determined. There will still be disputes over "objective" ethical standards, of course, whether the seriousness of the offense depends on the damage done, or, alternatively, the damage done to the agent's reputation, or rather, according to some moralists, the source, priority, and importance of the rule violated, etc. But the judgment in question is the *subject's* (or "subjective") judgment of the seriousness of the offense, *how personally the subject takes* the offense to be, or, indeed, whether there is any offense at all. So an insult that causes little damage to a person's reputation may nevertheless trigger rage, if he or she takes it sufficiently personally and personally considers it sufficiently insulting. "How strongly one feels," in other words, refers to the strength and certainty of the component judgments, not to one's bodily feelings. If an offense is taken very personally and as very serious, then the anger will be intense. By contrast, if an offense is not taken at all seriously, perhaps because the offender is a long-standing adversary from whom such comments are to be expected, or because he or she is a heckler or just a drunken stranger, then the anger will be less intense. In other words, the measure of the intensity of anger is one's sense of vulnerability and damage to the self. The measure of intensity, in other words, is an ethical judgment—how important the issue is in one's life—and not a physiological amplitude.

Naturally, the physiological symptoms of anger will usually be commensurate to the estimation of vulnerability and damage to self, but it is not these physiological symptoms that mark the intensity of the anger. The same is true regarding the intensity of other emotions. Fear and being afraid increases as one's sense of danger and vulnerability increases. (The intensity of vicarious fear, while watching a movie, for example, requires special treatment. One would have to bracket the estimation of danger and vulnerability within the scope of one's "willing suspension of disbelief.") In love, it is when the self feels most wrapped up and intimate with the self of another that love is most intense. The feelings (sensations) of love may be intense as well, but no one with any sense would want to measure the intensity of love just on the basis of intensity of feeling, much less the intensity of the physiological symptoms. Sprawled on the bed exhausted after having just *made* love, one's measurable feelings may be quite minimal, but the intensity of the emotion, in other words what we call *the feeling of love*, may be at its peak. The measure of an emotional experience has much to do with some sense of the extent to which the self is engaged, the degree to which one "takes it personally," and the importance of the issue.

"Taking it personally" refers not only to the evaluative judgments in the emotion but also to *reflective self-consciousness* or what many theorists would refer to as "second-order" consciousness, consciousness of consciousness (of the emotion). Thus in order to understand the central role(s) of the self in the structure of our emotions, it is necessary for us to open up the huge topic of consciousness. What does it mean for an emotion to be conscious?

There is a minimal sense in which all emotions are conscious, that is, they register on our sensibilities and they give rise to what can very generally be called "feelings," whether we notice them or not and whether we pay attention to them or not. Furthermore, we characterized emotions as engagements with the world, and so we can say that for any creature to have an emotion it must engage with the world, minimally by perceiving the world and having some stake and some role in what happens in the world. Thus minimalists like Jeremy Bentham have declared that even if animals do not think, they feel and thus have *interests*. (Stones, by contrast, have no interests.) Insofar as emotions involve or are anything like perceptions, we may call them minimally conscious if they involve seeing, hearing, smelling, tasting, or sensing (for example, someone's soft caress, or a dull pain in one's calf). If these are sufficiently weak, they may fall below the threshold of sensation and not be conscious, and therefore not count as feelings at all. But if they are above the threshold of sensation—and this is the essential point—they need not be noticed or attended to. So in one sense they may be conscious, but in another not.

A familiar example of this in psychology is subliminal perception, where an image appears so briefly that a subject does not seem to perceive it at all (and if asked will deny that he did), but, when asked certain relevant questions, quite evidently did "register" or see it. So, too, we sometimes see things without noticing them, but afterward we seem to remember them. It has been shown, for example by Robert Zajonc of the University of Michigan, that subliminal perceptions can affect our emotions. For instance, our preference for otherwise meaningless Chinese ideographs increases simply on the basis of repeated (subliminal) exposure and familiarity or in association with positive images (a happy face, for example) (1980). Zajonc's work has generated a good deal of controversy, especially due to a protracted debate with "appraisal theorist" Richard Lazarus. But what has emerged and is now generally agreed on is the idea that there are different levels of consciousness, some of which involve recognition (of one's own mental states), others that do not.

Consider Dan Dennett's example of what he calls "rolling consciousness," driving one's car over a familiar road while engrossed in an intense conversation (1991). But then one becomes abruptly aware of one's driving as something untoward happens that requires rapt attention (a car suddenly appears from a side road, or a tire blows out and the car swerves to the left). It is not as if the driver was paying no attention before—he did not run off the road or into another car—but he was driving on what we tellingly call "automatic pilot." But when he now attends to his driving it is not as if he is suddenly doing something else. Neither is he just doing what he was doing. So, too, when we have an emotion and become aware of it, it is not as if we are now feeling something else, but neither are we just feeling what we were feeling. One of the possible differences is that the self is now in focus, whereas before it was not. (This is why Jean-Paul Sartre says that the self only appears in reflective consciousness but that the emotions themselves are not reflective.)

Without yet invoking any theory of consciousness, we can say that in the first sense, simply registering on the senses, any feeling, must (by definition) be conscious (sometimes called "first-order consciousness"), but in further senses, noticing or attending to or knowing that one has a certain mental state, not all feelings and not all emotions need be conscious (all lumped together as "second-order consciousness"). In what we have said so far, it is clear that something like a sense of self must be possible on a fairly primitive level of consciousness (whether or not in slime molds). But self-consciousness is a clumsy way of referring to a variety of types of emotional awareness that may or may not be possible in a few non-language-using animals (although it would be relatively rare) but are pervasive in adult human emotion. Indeed, self-conscious emotions may not only require the use of language but the mastery of a fairly sophisticated language that includes (minimally) a vocabulary of emotions and self and a way of "locating" the emotions in our psychology and in our lives.

Jean-Paul Sartre made a distinction between "prereflective" and "reflective" consciousness, to mark off these two kinds of awareness, of the world, first of all, and of ourselves, secondly. ("First- and second-order" is used in more recent work by psychologists Marcel and Lambie; another way of making the distinction is "phenomenal" versus "access" consciousness by cognitive scientist Ned Block.) But Sartre immediately realizes that his distinction between prereflective consciousness and reflective self-consciousness is far too simple, so he muddies the picture considerably as he insists that although the "I," the self, appears only on the reflective level of consciousness, some version of the Cartesian *cogito* ("I think") must appear even on the prereflective level. He describes a typical episode of prereflective consciousness as the experience of "streetcar to be overtaken," noticeably without an "I" (as opposed to the reflective "I must catch that streetcar"). But it is clear enough that the "I" is implied in the former even if not thought or perceived as such. Thus we might further distinguish between "self-consciousness" and "reflection," and among different kinds or "levels" of self-consciousness. I introduce this not to confuse an issue that may have looked straightforward but in order to appreciate how complicated our emotional lives are with regard to the self and consciousness, and this is even before we get to the labyrinth postulated by Sigmund Freud. I want to suggest that the two-level distinction is far too crude, especially when we are talking about phenomena as intriguing as the connection between emotions and the self. Self-consciousness and reflection cover a wide range of distinctly human capacities. Perhaps most dramatically, this affects not only our knowledge of emotions but the very nature of the emotions themselves.

In chapter 10, I mentioned that Sartre's colleague Maurice Merleau-Ponty wondered at length whether we could even comprehend what our experience would be like (and what it once was like, in our infancy) without language. Or what nonlinguistic animal experience is like. This is, I said, a profound question, because it is not as if we can simply "peel off" the additions of language to our experience in order to then have access to "raw" or linguistically undigested experience. Our language (or more accurately the concepts we have because we use language) permeates all of our experience, even the most inchoate and inarticulate. (The limit experience would be something like pure pain, or pure sensation, but even then we have to ask whether the experience would be the same if we didn't recognize it as pain or as the kind of sensation that it was.) So can we appreciate what anger is for a dog, or a bird, or a monkey? In one sense, obviously yes.

But in another, deeper sense, probably not. And the same question reiterates with regard to people from other cultures, or (just to invite trouble) persons of the other gender. This is a question that has dogged us since the beginning of this book: whether our emotions are to some extent shaped as well as defined by the language (and the metaphors) through which we identify and describe them. The answer is "yes, to some extent." Our language or perspective shapes and defines "to some extent" both our particular emotions but also the overall shape of our emotional lives.

What this means is that our emotions are already saturated with reflection and self-consciousness and they cannot be understood in any "prereflective" form. Here, I think, we can see why Sartre was so troubled by his own claim that there is a prereflective consciousness quite apart from reflective consciousness, and why his early essay on the emotions in which he presumed this distinction (and insisted that all emotions were prereflective) was ultimately unsatisfactory. There is, as Merleau-Ponty insisted, no clear separation, even in theory, of prereflective and reflective consciousness. Our emotions are already infected by reflection and self-consciousness. It is only a question of how crude or articulate are the concepts that make up our emotional judgments and with which we identify and describe them. Just after waking up or with a bit too much to drink, those concepts may indeed be crude and barely articulate, and self-consciousness and reflection may be minimal. The emotions will be crude and minimally self-conscious as well.

But in an aesthetic context, or in the poetry of love, or in deep vengefulness and resentment, the concepts constitutive of our emotional responses may be thoroughly thought out, deeply reflective, and wholly self-conscious. And this reflection and self-consciousness will be definitive of those emotions. Our sense of romantic love is a thoroughly reflective emotion. People are in love and they celebrate the concept of love and they are very self-aware when they are in love. (It is well-known that men and women sometimes "discover" that they are in love, but the critical point is that their love is fully realized only once they recognize that they are in love.) The notion of a purely prereflective love would yield little more than animal attraction and some sense of affectionate attachment. Important, yes, perhaps even "basic," but hardly the stuff of romance, poetry, and song.

All of this raises serious challenges to the overly simply distinction between two kinds or "levels" of consciousness. First of all, the distinction is inapplicable as such to adult human emotions, insofar as all emotions are to a certain extent reflective. But second, I think that the very idea of two levels of consciousness is impoverished. Within the realm of reflective and self-conscious emotions there are many different discriminations that can and need to be made. In general, we distinguish between a person who is conscious—that is, just going about his or her business, and someone who becomes self-conscious, that is, who is keenly aware of how his or her behavior (or looks, or demeanor) may appear to someone else. Or, he or she may scrutinize his or her feelings, for instance, to question whether they are warranted in the situation or not. ("Do I really have reason to be jealous, just because she is talking to him?") It is easy enough to imagine someone, perhaps yourself, blushing and acting nervously and being embarrassed *without noticing it*. When a friend points this out, you get really embarrassed, as your emotion becomes fully self-conscious. (Notice the difference between these two senses of "self-conscious.")

It might be worth noting that in American English, at least, to say that someone has become "self-conscious" is to say that he or she has become at least slightly embarrassed, so that when we become self-conscious about our embarrassment we tend therefore to be *doubly* embarrassed. (In German, by contrast, *selbst-bewusstsein* suggests something more like pride or self-confidence.) So it is one thing to say that an emotion is self-conscious in that the self is its object and another to say that it is self-conscious in the sense that one is reflectively aware that one has that emotion. So in the latter sense even the explicitly self-conscious emotions, for example, shame, embarrassment, and pride, can be either self-conscious or not. In other words, we are talking about a complex system of discriminations here, not just a single one.

With almost any emotion or perception, we can make a number of distinctions among merely having, registering, noticing, attending to, and understanding the emotion. We can add to this the different levels and kinds of understanding, from (emotionally) understanding that "something bad seems to be happening" to (emotionally) understanding exactly what it is, how it happened, how it came about, its implications and consequences, and its larger significance. Here is a quick (not necessarily emotional) analog: Glancing sleepily at my digital clock by the bed at four in the morning, I might not even notice what time it is—although I clearly saw it. (It was right in front of my open eyes.) Or, I might notice the time, think nothing of it, and then immediately forget (or did I never really pay attention?). Or, I might notice the time, think nothing of it, but nevertheless be able to tell you—were you to ask—what time it is. (This might be considered a variation on subliminal perception—noticing but not really paying attention. But here, too, I think there are several distinctions and not just one.) Or as I look I might casually think that I have to get up in three and a half hours. Or I might go into a panic about not getting enough sleep. Or I might start asking myself how I can keep my job when I go to the office so tired all the time. Or I might start cursing the fact that I have to work at all. Or I might start thinking about the curious way that time seems to slow down at night. Or I might reflect (as a philosopher) on what Saint Augustine or the neo-Hegelian John McTaggart had to say about time. At every stage of this progression, I might have reason to say that "I was conscious of the time," but this would have very different meanings and implications.

So, too, we can be conscious of our emotions (or, our emotions may be conscious) in a number of different ways or on a number of different "levels." (I hesitate to call them "levels" insofar as it suggests they are hierarchically ordered, one "on top" of another.) In a tense situation, I suddenly realize (that is, recognize) that I am upset. I am agitated, sweating, edgy. But I was so before I noticed that I was so, and it is evident that my emotional disturbance did not begin just when I noticed it. Now that I notice my upset, however, I am not sure what I am upset about. Then I remember a brief confrontation I had with a colleague on the way out of the office and the way I slammed the door, and I realize that I must be angry. But at what? I may or may not be able to pin this down, given the brevity and the seeming banality of that particular meeting. But then I remember earlier confrontations, a few of which were downright offensive. So now I understand my present anger not so much in terms of this one brief meeting but in terms of a whole history with this fellow. And I notice, as I have before, that this person's demeanor more than superficially resembles the behavior of my older brother: dismissive, disdainful, superior. So now I have to wonder just what it is—and who it is—that I am angry about. And then I start wondering, am I really angry, or maybe I'm just getting defensive. I'm now trying to understand, really understand, my emotion. Perhaps I begin to suspect that there is some deeper explanation of my getting upset, and I try to remember what my psychoanalyst taught me years ago. But then, as I replay today's encounter in my mind, I start to appreciate the innuendo and the irony of what my colleague just said, and I get angrier. I drop my attempt to understand in a "deeper" way and just focus in more closely on the details of the meeting. As I start to think about possible (but missed) rejoinders, I get angrier still, until I realize (reflectively) how foolish this is. I am angry at a pompous ass, and I know that it's bad for my health not to mention my peace of mind. So I get angry at myself for getting angry, and then I laugh (a little) at the absurdity of this self-convoluted turn. I start to reflect on what an angry person I am and how hard it is for me to just relax and I resolve to do something about that. (At this point, I sit myself down and start to meditate, or, at least, I count to ten.) I finally become fully aware of my anger, but only now that it is passing.

These different levels of reflection or different kinds of awareness also suggest very different roles for the self in reflection. People with a high level

of intellectual intelligence may understand their emotions in one sense but
not in others. People with good social intelligence may understand quite
well what the effects on other people and one's relationships might be but
not understand in a theoretical sense what is at stake. People with a keen
strategic intelligence, who may seem rather stupid when it comes to either
other people's feelings or any theoretical concerns, may nevertheless
understand very well what they need to do, which emotions are strategic,
what steps they have to take, what expressions they need to make, and what
actions to perform in order to get what they want. Thus one angry person
may understand his anger in a deeply theoretical way. (Perhaps he or she is
a psychoanalyst, or a neurologist, or an emotion-theorist.) Another might
be aware mainly of the repercussions of her anger on her friends and
family, and on her own sense of congeniality. Still another might plot an
exquisite revenge, seeing quite clearly what needs to be done but thinking
only tangentially about the mechanisms involved in all this.

Thus we can see how intricately reflection on emotion reshapes, blends,
and mixes in with the emotions. But I certainly do not want to ignore the
fact that we are also capable of reflection in a more detached way, and this
is what explains both our freedom and responsibility regarding our emotions and the misleading impression that reason (reflection) is systematically opposed to our emotions. It is true that we are (sometimes) rational
beings who can counter and sometimes control our passions. We are rational beings insofar as we are capable of thinking, reflecting, and using language to characterize as well as recognize our emotions, and this means
that we can more or less "dispassionately" (or at any case, at one step
removed) consider our own emotional behavior. This is especially the case
in reflecting on past emotions, in retrospect, and during the course of
long-term ongoing emotions. Thinking back, we can see that what we
should have felt or *should have* done and resolve to handle such matters
differently in the future. And in the throes of anger, guilt, or love we can
ask, "Why am I so angry?" "Why should I feel so guilty?" "Why do I love
her so?" and take steps to examine, explore, and perhaps adjust our emotion. So reflection does serve an important function that (whether or not
we include it as part of our emotional experience) allows it to question
and challenge our emotions and suggest alternative emotional paths. It is
in this sense that we can, sometimes, distinguish our emotions from
reflection and recognize a freedom that is unimaginable in nonlinguistic
animals and infants, or, for that matter, in relatively unreflective folks who,
it may be quite accurately said, are "not in touch with their feelings."

Once we have learned to reflect on our emotions and made a practice of
self-monitoring we gain a profound sense of "free will." This does not
mean, as we discussed in chapter 17, that we can now feel whatever we

would like to feel. But it does mean that we can make resolutions, resist our surging feelings, and fight our obsessions, even if this in practice amounts to no more than dragging our feet and screaming "no! no! no!" all the way. But reason (reflection) is never really dispassionate and it is never free from the concerns and perspectives of the self. And so it is never simply at odds with the passions but always, and by necessity, in league with at least some of them. Thus Nietzsche suggests that what we call reason is just another passion, and it is sometimes the strongest of them. But with a more modest and modified conception of reason and reflection that sees them not as separate "faculties" nor as wholly dispassionate, but as essential to the *somewhat* detached ability to distance oneself and characterize and question our emotions in language, we can understand one of the things that makes us most human, the fact that we can become self-conscious, reflect on and describe our feelings, make resolutions, and profoundly change our emotional behavior. This is the source of our freedom and our responsibility for our emotions. And that is why, whatever else we might understand about the neural mechanisms of emotions, we need to take responsibility for our emotions and appreciate the central role they play in our ethics and the extent to which they determine a good part of who we are.

20

Emotional Experience ("Feelings")

In chapter 11, I discussed the idea that emotions are feelings. I allowed that (in accordance with common usage) emotions are feelings, but only so long as we expand this notion far beyond the limited notion that feelings are essentially sensations. Some of the feelings involved in emotions are straightforward bodily sensations (for instance, feeling flushed), as William James pointed out, but many more involve the body in more interesting ways, reflecting tendencies to act, for example, or a sense of vulnerability or aggressiveness. But among the feelings involved in emotions are also feelings about the world, thus involving intentionality. So I experience my beloved as lovely, my enemy as hateful, my self as shameful. But at this point we realized that we had already stretched thin the notion of feelings. I want to further expand it to include the feelings that are consequent but also constitutive of self-consciousness and reflection, including, especially, those "emotions about our emotions" that are so often a part of our emotional life. At this point, the simplistic notion of *feeling* is no longer appropriate, so instead, I want to broaden the topic to *emotional experience*, where emotional experiences may involve feelings, or at least, they embody dispositions to have feelings but are by no means limited to those.

Many years ago, with William James on my mind, I denied that emotions were feelings at all because I thought that the feelings that James pointed to—the bodily sensations that accompanied the physiological symptoms of emotional excitement, including rapid pulse, heavy breathing, sweating, and such—were not nearly so essential to emotion as judgments about the world. It is through such judgments, I argued, that emotions were relevant to ethics. (Sweating and heavy breathing are of no moral significance at all.) Having made that point, however, I later pulled back from the insistence that emotions are not feelings and I came to acknowledge that perhaps emotions even necessarily involved feelings. But I now want to seriously explore what *kinds* of feelings are involved in emotion. I do not deny that bodily feelings of the sort James points to are incorporated into emotion, but I think that there is much more going on by way of feeling than just these. Early on, I pointed out that the word "feelings" covers a wide range of phenomena, from Jamesian sensations to very sophisticated intuitions and emotions in all of their complexity and intelligence. It also includes a wide variety of emotional experiences, many of which would not ordinarily count as feelings. The problem with the Jamesian analysis, I now see, is that it has an impoverished account of feeling. Or rather, it reduces all of the richness of emotional experience to the singular sensations of the most primitive bodily feelings.

Since James, the very idea of emotional experience has had an incredibly hard time of it in the recent history of both philosophy and psychology, not to mention in animal behavior studies. For almost half a century, as I noted earlier, behaviorism ridiculed any reference to experience of any kind as "unscientific," "merely subjective," and "ineffable," on those few occasions when it allowed that there might be some such thing as emotional experience. But even when the fact that we have emotional experience is accepted without question, one can describe with some ease what the experience is of, while it is no easy matter to describe the experience itself. That is, describing the tree that one perceives is rather straightforward. ("It is more than twenty feet tall, it has a straight singular trunk with brown bark, it has leaves that are rather needle-like, etc.") But describing the perception of the tree is a very different matter, for then we have to take explicit account of our perspective, of the way we see it, of the way it seems to us, and this may be extremely difficult. Granted that we all describe the world from our own perspective in any case, but we rarely describe or make explicit what our perspective is. This makes perfectly good sense. If all emotions have intentionality, as I have insisted, then the description of an emotional experience will mainly be a description of what the emotion is *about*, namely, the world, to which our language is most suited. (Very few people ever learn to describe their experiences as such, as opposed to what their experiences are about. Poets specialize in this rare skill.) Thus the temptation of science-minded behaviorists to describe the situation in the world (for example, the experimental apparatus) in terms of the objective facts of "stimulus" and "response," as neither of these (supposedly) has anything essentially to do with experience.

But, as I also insisted, what the emotion is about must also be understood as subjectively perceived, from a first-person point of view. Thus the absurdity of behaviorism. I follow some of my philosophical colleagues in taking subjectivity and the description of emotional experience as a description of "what it is like" to have a specific emotion, where the description of *what it's like* necessarily includes a description of the world *as experienced* —as threatening, as offensive, as lovely, or as depressing. Thus having an emotion is not just an experience like "seeing green," which may well be ineffable in the sense that it cannot be described to someone who has not had that experience (for instance, to someone who has been blind from birth). But neither is it just another "objective" description of the objects or situations in the world. Emotional experience is best described in terms of the way the world seems to, and is grappled by, the person having the emotion.

But in order to analyze the many dimensions of emotional experience, let me begin with William James, who did rightly identify physical sensations as one ingredient of emotional experience. And because he firmly tied these sensations to physiology, we can exactly specify the sensations in question. (Thus blushing—when the capillaries in one's face dilate—is accompanied by the feeling of "being flushed," feeling hot, etc.) James's examples tend to focus on the autonomic nervous system, that is, on such matters as hormone secretion, increased pulse and heartbeat, sweating, etc. Today's proponents of "basic emotions" also tend to stress the importance of these basic physiological processes, so emotional feelings for them are also pretty much restricted to simple sensations. The feelings caused by the autonomic nervous system are certainly familiar feelings in emotion, but they are not at all the only or the primary feelings in emotion, much less the essential ingredients in emotional experience.

In chapter 11, I briefly suggested that the bodily sensations involved in emotional experience are by no means all the product of the autonomic nervous system. I noted that James mixes together a number of very different sorts of feelings. But notice that even though he highlights the experiences that are caused by the activation of the autonomic nervous system, the truth is that (since our focus is usually riveted on the object of the emotion) we usually do not even notice any of these sensations at the time. It is only *after* the emotion has been going on for a while—or after the emotion is over—that we become keenly aware of such sensations. Immediately following the close call on the highway we pull off to the side of the road and *then* we notice our fast breathing, the fact that our heart is pounding, the sweat on our palms, and the dampness that drenches our shirt. It is usually only in a brief lag in anger, on in a quick moment of reflection, that we notice how tense we are, how our fists are clenched, how aroused we are, and (if we are near a mirror) the contortions in our face. In the leisure of love one might well come to notice the warm feelings that one enjoys in the presence of the beloved, but even so, our focus will be entirely on the beloved and not on our feelings. So even where autonomic nervous system sensations are involved, they may play only a marginal role in emotional experience.

But experiences produced by the autonomic nervous system are only a very small if dramatic and obvious part of the picture (much exaggerated in importance in psychological theory). In the preceding examples one can distinguish, if not sharply, the involuntary responses of the autonomic nervous system and the tensing of our voluntary muscles. This is not to say that the tensing of our muscles in emotions is always willful or intentional. Indeed, the charm of facial expression in contemporary psychological theory (as well as in real life) is that these responses are for the most part involuntary, even if they involve the voluntary musculature. In fact, most of us cannot accurately produce them even if we try to do so (for instance, in an acting class or when feigning an emotion). James plays suggestively with the observation that we can voluntarily (to some extent) control our facial expressions—for instance, we can smile—and this in turn will alter our emotional experience. I think James has struck a rich vein of insight here, but the dimension of emotional experience that is caused by such voluntary behavior should not be conflated with those experiences that arise from the autonomic nervous system, or with those experiences that are caused by the "involuntary" or seemingly automatic tensing of the voluntarily musculature. The feeling one gets when one's face is in a grimace or a frown is not the same kind of feeling one gets when one's pulse beats faster or one's face flushes red. But these are all feelings that may be constitutive of our overall emotional experience.

We are only occasionally aware of our facial expressions, and our facial expressions are much more in evidence when we are engaged with other people. (Indeed, people who exhibit elaborate or dramatic facial expressions when we spy them alone strike us as extremely odd or eccentric.) But while we are engaged with other people, we are usually attentive to what is being said or done, to the other people and their facial expressions and what they signify, not our own. Because we often don't notice them, we don't usually think of our facial expressions as manifesting themselves in feeling, that is, as contributing to our experience. We think of facial expressions as strictly "external" and public, feeling as internal and private. But every emotional facial expression has its own distinct "feel," whether or not we notice or pay attention to it. A frown feels very different from a smile, as James suggested, and a phony smile feels quite different from a real, spontaneous smile. Crying because one is sad feels quite different from weeping because one is peeling onions. Making a face in disgust feels very different from making a face out of annoyance. All of this is very subtle, but it all goes into what we vaguely refer to as the "feeling" we have when we have a certain emotion, an emotional experience.

With all of the fascinating recent work on the face and facial expression, it is easy to lose sight of the rest of the body. It is not just the facial muscles that tense in characteristic ways; so do the muscles of the body. So in anger one clenches one's fists, and in love one reaches out to caress or embrace one's beloved. In shame one hides one's face, and in sadness one withdraws. Again, we are often not aware of what we are doing with our body, but it is an essential ingredient in our emotional experience. When we are told as children to "stand up straight," this is not just a matter of how we present ourselves to the world, our "posture." It has a direct effect on how we feel, and how we feel about ourselves. "Hold your head up high" is a bit of good Jamesian advice. It will indeed make you feel a little bit better about your place in the world. But if we are usually not aware of our own bodily comportment, think of how quickly (and often accurately) we "size up" someone else on the basis of their way of holding themselves. A man who is stoop-shouldered already gives us something of a psychological portrait, an unintended confession of sorts. A woman who is ashamed of her body and uncomfortable about her sexuality holds herself in certain ways (and, of course, dresses in certain ways). How she moves may tell us much more about her than what she says, and her feelings about herself may in fact be much more evident in the bodily feelings she does not notice than it is in the feelings that she rather abstractly reports to us.

The relevant expressions and the feelings that are caused by them have to do not only with how we "hold ourselves" but with how we move. Thus the kinesthetics of one's shifting and moving body, the dynamics of movement, one's gait, the rhythm of one's walk, are all revealing and contribute to the overall fabric of our emotional experience. In joy we skip alone merrily. A brisk walk is a mark of someone "in a good mood," and taking a brisk walk may indeed make one feel good, not just because it is good exercise (or because one feels righteous about doing exercise) but because it is productive of energetic, vital feelings. By contrast, a slow, aimless shuffle is a critical dimension of the experience of sadness or depression. This is not to say, of course, that a slow, aimless shuffle is always a sign of sadness or depression. It may be just an expression of relaxation or lethargy. But this is just to say the obvious, that there is rarely a one-to-one correlation between any complex bit of behavior—including facial expressions—and emotions. Affect programs, those neurological-hormonal-musculature syndromes I described back in chapter 1, might be an exception to this, but, even so, those define a very limited set of behaviors—and with them a very limited set of experiences. Most peoples' postures and rhythms betray a good deal about them, not just how they feel at the moment but how they feel about themselves in general. However varied the behavioral expressions, our movements and the dynamics of our movements provide a major ingredient in our experience, and they are not at all like the particular sensations (the feeling of your heart pounding, a sinking feeling in your chest) that James and the Stoics were talking about.

At this juncture I would like to raise a serious question about the fact that we embellish our physiological vocabulary with such metaphors as "feeling as if my heart is about to burst" and even "I have a sinking feeling in my chest." The question is whether our metaphorical descriptions are based on an insightful observation concerning the details of our experience (which then becomes something of a thoughtless cliché for describing such experiences) or rather (or to what extent) our emotional experience is in fact shaped and partially determined by these metaphorical descriptions. The hydraulic model, for instance, was based on some readily identifiable sensations, at least in a few select emotions (such as anger and excitement). But such metaphors as "blowing up" or "ready to burst" are not just descriptions. They shape and suggest a way of experiencing (and not just talking about) our emotional life. Thus everything we have described so far in this chapter, from the sensations produced by the autonomic nervous system to the experiences that are part of the dramatic roles and behaviors that we choose for ourselves is processed through the quasi-poetic language we use to discuss and describe our emotional life. What we experience in our emotions, in other words, is not just the product of our senses but of our intelligence as well. The fact that this intelligence quickly becomes frozen into thoughtless inanities does not change this in any way. What we experience is what our language allows us to experience.

Most expression consists not of immediate muscle contractions but of mediated action, action that has a point and a purpose and proceeds over time (even if only a few moments). Accordingly, our emotional experience consists not just of feelings (filtered through language) but of the ongoing experience of voluntary and often willful action. We experience ourselves as *agents*, as doing something, as "expressing" ourselves. There may be a distinction between the expression of emotion that follows the emotion immediately and more or less automatically and the protracted and deliberate courses of action that emerge "out of" the emotion. (Peter Goldie [2000], for instance, pursues this distinction at some length.) I do not think that this distinction is clear or alters much the notion of emotional experience. Thus anger immediately followed by lashing out (verbally or physically) is, to be sure, one kind of experience, while vengeance, which may follow the incident which sparked anger by months or even years is another. But the difference, I suggest, is that the person experiencing the latter is consumed by thoughts and plans, fully conscious of the anger, while someone experiencing the former may have a fairly minimal experience of "just having to do this right now." But I would argue that the experience of seeking vengeance and the eventual feeling of satisfaction are an important part of the experience of protracted anger just as much as the "action tendency" in immediate anger is an important aspect of that experience. But perhaps what both cases show us is that an essential part of getting angry is the experience of *wanting to do something*, so the emotional experience of anger is in part the experience of agency, whether this is realizable in the circumstances or not, and consequently an experience of desire, the often overwhelming felt need to *do something*.

The point I am now making is that the experience one has in having an emotion is not just, as I used to think, a value-drenched perception of the world. It also essentially involves desire and action, and thus the body, but the body in its various dimensions. The primitive mechanisms identified by the basic emotions theorists are part of the experience, but the voluntary and more sophisticated expressions of emotion in behavior are also correlated with various experiences of place and posture, of poise and imbalance, of movement and of hurry and repose, of intentions and aspirations, of desires and perceived outcomes. But our more directly action-oriented and even deliberate behavior also provides a critical ingredient in our emotional experience, a further reason for not thinking of our emotions as essentially passive. The felt desire to do something is a part of almost every emotion (the possible exceptions are some of the aesthetic emotions that James talks about, but even there, I am doubtful. It is hard to listen to a moving piece of music without feeling the need to sway or tap one's foot, for example).

I am here invoking the experiential manifestation of what Dutch psychologist Nico Frijda has famously called "action tendencies," which he takes to be definitive of emotion. An action tendency is not just a muscle movement or muscular tension. It is itself directed toward an action. It would be saying too much to say "directed toward a goal," but one might think of such a movement as a truncated version of goal-directed behavior. Thus when one clenches one's fist in anger it is the first step in getting ready to punch someone. In embarrassment the various gestures of shrinking away and withdrawing, even if never quite coming to actual withdrawal, are obviously getting ready to do so. Thus the intention to do something, like intentionality, is a part of emotional experience.

But the role of goals in intentional behavior is by no means straightforward. A lover need not intend to make love when he caresses his beloved any more than a man intends to hit someone when he clenches his fist, but nevertheless the gesture *means* something, and this meaning is captured in the direction of the action. It is important that we do not take the intention here to be goal-defined as such. There are intentions that are only steps on the way. This raises interesting questions about the status is of such goals that give direction to behavior without being a goal as such. A quick non-problematic example is playing a sport just for the fun of it. One shoots a couple of racks of pool or goes bowling with a friend without trying to win, but there is a sense in which just "playing around" nevertheless demands that the end in sight is playing as well as one can. Otherwise, one can hardly be said to be playing pool or bowling. The action tendencies in emotion are like this too. They express intentions without necessarily being aimed at achieving any particular action, and the experience of the emotion reflects these complex intentions. So I would insist that the experience of having an emotion includes the experience of such truncated bodily preparations for action and even such "playing around" as well as the more protracted and deliberate goal-oriented expressions of emotion.

When we talk about emotional experience, however, what we mainly talk about is the whole dimension of intentionality. We may or may not notice the various sensations and modes of awareness that we have discussed so far, but we are almost always aware, to some degree, of what our emotions are about. (This is even true when we don't know what they are about, when the object of the emotion is obscure or eerily unrecognizable.) The core of emotional experience—and the language with which we describe our emotional experience—is defined by the judgments that constitute the emotion. One might argue that judgments as such are not experienced at all, but this, I think, is a quibble. We experience the world via our judgments, which is why I say that that our emotions are shaped or structured by judgments. Thus an essential part of the experience of anger is the experience of being wronged or of having one's intentions frustrated. An essential part of the experience of love is the experience of finding another person attractive and desirable, being drawn to her or him, and later finding this person to be more or less indispensable to one's life. An essential part of the experience of grief is having suffered a terrible loss because one was (and is) bound to another person, who is now lost. Again, each of these descriptions is not just a description of "items in our public world," although, to be sure, it refers to those too. But the person who angers us, the person whom we love or for whom we grieve is not just a person in the world but the person *as experienced* from the peculiar perspective of the emotion and the person who has the emotion.

Grief points to another odd feature of our emotional experience, briefly mentioned in chapter 7. In a great many emotions, part of the experience is not of what is there in the world, but what is *not there*. Thus Plato has Socrates describe love as a "lack," and grief, of course, is precisely that, the terrible absence of someone who once was so close. That is yet another reason for not confusing the objects of emotion with the objects that are actually there in the world (which is not to deny the obvious, that—certain ontological quandaries aside—absences are real in the world). But let me generalize this. Every desire, every aspiration, is defined by an absence, namely the absence of what is desired or aspired to. (This was the argument that Plato—via Socrates—made in the *Symposium*.) In my earliest work on philosophical psychology, I coined the clumsy phrase "requiredness" to refer to such experiences, not knowing at the time that the Gestalt psychologists had beaten me to it by a decade or two. But the fact that our emotional experience can be about absences as well as presences once again greatly expands the scope of what we mean by "experience" far beyond what is usually intended by either "sensations" or "feelings."

Similarly, an emotional experience is not just an experience of the present. Even if we think of an emotion as a process over time, there is a seductive temptation to think of each moment of the experience as being about a present state of the world. But this, too, gives us a limited and impoverished sense of phenomenology. Just as an emotion can be about absences as well as presences, so, too, every emotion also has what various authors (some of them following Heidegger) have called the *background*, aspects of the emotion that are not in focus or conscious but nevertheless must be understood as a necessary ingredient for the intelligibility of the emotion. (We find this notion in John Searle's analytic philosophy [1983] as well as in Hubert Dreyfus's Heideggerian philosophy [1990].) Much of the background is, as the word suggests, historical. It has to do with the history of the situation, of the people involved, of the relationship, of the emotion. Thus it makes no sense to speak of grief in the absence of a love that has been lost, and it makes no sense to talk about anger in a situation in which no one has any interest or investment. One gets angry, as we have been saying, because his intentions have been thwarted or frustrated or he has been offended, and those intentions or one's sense of self provide the background against which the emotion is intelligible. This, too, is part of our emotional experience even though by its very nature it is rarely focused upon as such.

It is possible, of course, to have an emotional reaction (and thus an emotional experience) in the absence of any background of emotional investments and such: Artificially stimulating affect programs would no doubt give rise to such an experience, real enough, but utterly meaningless. Indeed, that is why we would not even call it an emotion. The Schachter-Singer experiments of 1962 provide an illustration of such meaningless experiences (1962). In that experiment, subjects were injected with a stimulant (and told it was just vitamins), and asked to interpret their resultant feelings. It turned out, not surprisingly, that people understood their experiences on the basis of the circumstances in which they found themselves. A control group, however, reported discomfort but no emotion. I have no doubt that they had an experience (agitation and arousal), but it was not an emotional experience. It had no meaning.

All emotions are meaningful, and almost any emotion of any significance will involve a background of other emotions. An extreme but telling set of examples involve *trauma*. After a serious trauma, a wartime experience, rape, or having lived through sexual abuse or a terrible accident, one may not remember the actual experience at all, or, alternatively, one may have vivid repeating and confusing flashbacks, but few emotions of a once traumatized person can be adequately understood without taking into account his or her traumatic background. Or to put it another way, more generally, no emotion can be said to have any depth without reference to a rich background of emotional experiences.

This is what we mean, I think, when we say that someone has "soul," that their emotions are deep and rich in background. (Of course there is no presumption of pleasantness here. "Soul" usually indicates a tragic or challenging background, not a happy one.) Again, overly strict theorists may object that the background, however important it may be for interpreting or understanding an emotion, is not itself an object of experience. But again, I do not want to quibble about this. It is very difficult to say what is *in the experience* once we start talking about those aspects of emotional experience that are not the focus of consciousness or fully reflective. How much of the background of one's life in love must be conscious in order to grieve? How many of the fragile tendrils of one's self-esteem must be in evidence in order to understand one's anger? It is probably enough to say that emotional experience is unintelligible without understanding the background of an emotion. This is enough to conclude that the background is part of one's emotional experience.

In addition to the background we can also discern another dimension of emotional experience, what I've called with some desperation *frame experiences* (I've tried to do better, but none of the theorists in the field seems to have any term that is more informative). A good example of an unembellished frame experience is what we now call the experience of *déjà vu*. The term is relatively new, but the experience is quite common (though it is often conflated with any experience of familiarity). Nathaniel Hawthorne complained that there was no term for an experience he described in 1863: "I was haunted and perplexed by an idea that I had . . . seen this strange spectacle [a vast kitchen in an English manor house] before." It is an experience—no matter of what—that seems to be an echo or a repetition of another, which, however, never seems to have been. Dreams are often like this: One dreams of a strange but seemingly familiar house, or one meets a complete stranger who seems to be an old friend. Alan Brown, a professor in Dallas, has traced the history of theories of *déjà vu*, from the idea that it is caused by fatigue when perception and emotion are out of sync, to the opposite theory, that being too relaxed allows the imagination to play these tricks on us (2004). The idea that *déjà vu* experiences remind us of forgotten dreams is an obvious candidate and, after Freud, the idea of the emergence of repressed memories became another.

Today, of course, the favored explanations have to do with small brain malfunctions (mini-seizures) or they involve "dual processing." It is suggested that the brain has distinct modules for memory and familiarity, and though these are usually correlative, on occasion they are not. But whatever the neurological explanation the phenomenology is fascinating. And what it points to is a distinction between the content of our experience—*what* is being experienced—and the *frame* of that experience—the overall sense of how it fits into our experience. Other familiar frame experiences would include feeling uncomfortable and feeling threatened. To be sure, when we feel uncomfortable or feel threatened we usually recognize the appropriate object, something discomforting or something threatening, but on rare occasions we find ourselves feeling uncomfortable or feeling threatened by utterly inappropriate objects, or even by nothing at all. And most students (and their teachers) have had the following experience: Sure that they have a great idea they shoot up their hand and eagerly wait to be called upon. But when they have their chance to speak, they realize to their considerable embarrassment that they have nothing to say. It is not that they forgot what they wanted to say (although this will probably be their excuse) but rather as though they had the keen sense of having something to say they in fact did not. Thus I want to suggest that there is one more dimension of emotional experience that is usually melded in with the emotion's object but nevertheless deserves independent recognition. Indeed, in my wilder moments (and in the final chapter) I would hazard a guess that a good deal of what we call spirituality is just this, a frame experience with no object in particular. More down to earth, it is what is going on in a good many moods, especially those that Heidegger designates of particular ontological significance.

Following the last chapter, however (and Heidegger too), we have seen that an emotional experience is never just about the world. It always involves, in one way or another, the self engaged in the world, the self with interests and concerns in the world. Our explicit ethical judgments both reflect and express our always-evaluating experience of the world, our interests, and our concerns. In the last chapter, I argued that the emotions are tied up with the self and its concerns in many different roles and different guises. Accordingly, other dimensions of emotional experience have to do with these different roles and different guises. In some emotional experiences (for example, of anger) we feel active and if not in control then at least aggressive. In other emotional experiences (for example, of sadness) we feel passive and victimized. Thus our feelings include our sense of engagement, of activity or passivity. Anger energizes us, readies us for action. Sadness feels in part like enervation, and we watch with some helplessness as the world goes by us. Some sense of control is also part of our emotional experience. "Falling" in love, as the expression indicates, is partly an experience of loss of control. Hatred, by contrast, often involves a sense of power (thus distinguishing it from resentment, which does not.)

Sometimes, this sense of control is experienced as something of a countercurrent in emotional experience. When we get angry, if we have been well brought up, one part of the emotional experience will be the experience of trying to restrain oneself. When you get sad or depressed, an important part of your experience may well be a kind of desperate cheerleading activity, trying to get yourself up and involved in the world. And, finally, all of this involves all sorts of feelings about the self, not only self-esteem and the lack of it, but self-love and self-loathing, confidence and lack of confidence (often geared to the particular situation), awkwardness and gracefulness, generosity and courage as opposed to miserliness and cowardice, and so on. These often form the core of our emotional feelings and experiences, and the bodily feelings that go along with them are more like the soundtrack to a movie than they are, as too many emotions theorists would make them out to be, a concert unto themselves.

Finally, I think that we should reject the distinction between reason, reflection, and thought, on the one hand, and feelings, emotions, and emotional experience on the other, a residue of the tired old "reason versus the passions" dichotomy. To say what I think should be obvious, we experience thoughts. And many if not most human emotions involve thoughts. Thus I would insist that we include *thoughts* as essential ingredients in human emotional experience. Angry thoughts, tender thoughts, humiliating thoughts, are often the most palpable manifestations of anger, love, and shame, respectively. But among the thoughts that constitute our emotional experiences are those thoughts that are about the emotions we experience. Thus I get embarrassed, which provokes the thought "this is so embarrassing," and this provokes a further emotion, as I get embarrassed about being so visibly embarrassed, and this in turn provokes the thought "Oh, no, now I am *really* embarrassed." It would be difficult to separate the thoughts from the emotions here and, for that matter, to separate the thoughts from one another as well. But all of this is to insist that reflection is not, for the most part, something that stands apart from or "above" the emotions. Thus reflection is *part* of our emotional experience. This is not to insist that all emotions are reflective or self-conscious, nor is it to suggest that only creatures who can have thoughts can have emotions. Nor is it to deny that there is a more or less "dispassionate" sort of reflection that is quite distinct from the experience we have of a particular emotion or mood that puts us in the position of being able to make resolutions and such without being stuck in the emotion itself. (We will come back to this in the last chapter.) But it is to say that our emotional experience is rich and complex and often involves the sophistication and intelligence that can only come with language and self-knowledge, even if mistaken or self-deceived.

So what is emotional experience? I think it is what James and others were groping for when they insisted, with some reason, that an emotion is essentially a *feeling*. But I hope it is evident by now that I consider emotional experience to be much more than that. It is a complex of many experiences; sensations; various ways of being aware of the world, our own bodies, and intentions; and also thoughts and reflections on our emotions, all melded together in what is typically encountered as a single more or less unified experience.

21

The Universality of Emotions:
Evolution and the Human Condition

Ever since Aristotle (at least), the search for an ethics has turned to the question of human nature, on the reasonable assumption that the good life for humans should be something geared to actual human beings, how they live, what they desire and aspire to, and what moves them. Even those who would speak of "absolute ethics" commanded by God are well aware of the necessity that his commandments must be those that are appropriate to creatures like ourselves, whatever more that they may assume about us above and beyond our merely worldly selves. So the question becomes, What is it to be human? And what moves us, not just as Christians, or as Americans, or as middle-class Europeans, or as peasant Chinese, but as human beings? One way of defending absolute values may be to imagine commandments imposed by a God who rules over all of us—even if we sharply disagree which or what being that might be. But another is to find those emotions and motivations that all people have in common, and this quest for human nature goes on quite apart from any theological predilections. Theology and nature come together, however, in what is often called "natural law theory," most famously formulated by Saint Thomas Aquinas.

So it is not surprising that it is often said, by way of both profundity and platitude, that people are, "deep down"—that is, in terms of their "basic emotions"—all alike. We all tend to think this when we express such platitudes as "people everywhere are essentially the same." We watch a well-made film from Iran or Sri Lanka or Los Angeles or the jungles of South America and no matter how different people may be, they all seem to express similar anxieties and suffer from the same losses. Children everywhere laugh and play in that unmistakable human child manner. Invasions and violations are greeted with anger, dangers with fear, the disgusting with disgust, the surprising with surprise.

The psychologist Gardiner Lindzey summed up what many people think in 1954 when he wrote, "emotions, as biological events, are the same the world over." Today, contemporary psychologists like Paul Ekman (1984) and Carroll Izard (1977) make this claim on the basis of extensive cross-cultural comparisons of facial expressions of emotion and their recognition. Neurologists such as Paul MacLean (1980) and Jaak Panskepp (1982) have made such claims on the basis of the common structure and functions of the brain, especially its more "primitive" subsystems. Philosophers have long made similar claims just on the basis of common sense and the everyday observation of what has traditionally and not without theoretical bias been called "human nature." Customs, laws, governments, marriage and mating rituals, table manners, and religious beliefs may vary from culture to culture, but emotions, at least certain "basic" emotions, are assumed to be the same from Mount Abu and Baghdad to downtown Cleveland, with variations appropriate to culture and circumstances, perhaps, but with some basic core nevertheless. This would seem to hold out the promise of a universal basis for ethics as well as defense of the "basic emotions" thesis.

It is an appealing thesis, that emotionally we are all the same. But what does this mean? An easy but obviously inadequate interpretation is that everyone has emotions, that is, some emotions or other, although these may be very different and expressed very differently as well. But this cannot be what is intended, for the very antithesis of the universality claim is the idea that different people and different cultures have such different emotions that they cannot comprehend each other. The problem is not Mr. Spock, who does not have emotions, but Edgar Rice Burroughs's Martians, who have such different emotions and different expressions that we Earthlings cannot understand them. But it is not Martians we are talking about, but fellow humans. So it is suggested, for instance, that Japanese culture is so different from American and European culture that the Japanese have some emotions that we do not, and vice versa. But even this does not deny the universality thesis.

The question is not whether some people or cultures have some emotions that others do not (although even this is contested) but whether there are some emotions that everyone has, regardless of culture or upbringing. But even here, we have to distinguish between whether everyone has the emotions in question or whether they have the capacity or potential to have them. The latter is a much weaker claim and, again, of not much interest. It is rather like saying that everyone could speak Chinese if they had been brought up in China with Chinese parents. Well, yes, but the analogous question would be whether everyone does in fact speak Chinese, and the answer is obviously "no." So the universality thesis is not nearly as clear as it might at first seem.

The most arguable and interesting claim is that there are some emotions that everyone actually has. We need to make allowances, of course, for people who are in one way or another emotionally defective. But it would not be just those with brain injuries or Vulcan heritage who might be deemed emotionally defective. If the universality thesis is true, then there might well be whole cultures that are either emotionally defective or emotionally deceptive. Because it would seem, at least on the surface, that some cultures lack one or another basic emotion. (We will see some examples in the next chapter.) Here, I would like to explore the plausibility of the idea that that there are at least some emotions, if only crude, unrefined emotions, that everyone has.

One (but not the only) basis for such a claim is that emotions are "biological events," as Lindzey suggests. Of course, he made this claim in the heyday of behaviorism, so the idea that emotions might be anything other than biological events would have been difficult to defend. And yet insofar as emotions are biological events they may be the same across the entire species (and in higher animals with similar brains as well), but they also might not be. Different breeds of dogs, for example, have very different temperaments as a result of breeding, that is, genetics. Their emotions are biologically based, but they are not the same even within the species. Among humans, we know that the races differ in their genetic constitution, for example in their tolerance for alcohol and lactic acid. So, too, we know that cultures, families, and individuals differ in their emotional temperament, and although many of these differences are a matter of culture, experience, and upbringing, we cannot simply conclude, as some would as a matter of ideology, that none of these differences are a matter of biology. This remains a difficult and obviously controversial matter, especially when it comes to questions about race and gender (see Stephanie Shields, *Speaking from the Heart*). I will avoid even the "obvious" questions, such as whether women are more sensitive and nurturing than men, and whether some races have a more "natural" talent for mathematics or sports. But race and gender force us to modify our query. Insofar as emotions are biologically based, are they therefore universal? And, conversely, if emotions are universal, does that show that they are biologically based?

I would argue, if basic emotions are biologically based this does not entail that they are universal, and they might well be universal without being biologically based. An emotion might be universal because of the common conditions and circumstances of human life, for instance, the fact that we all need food and water, have needs and desires, the fact that we get hurt, get sick, and die, the fact that we are born only after a man and a woman have had sex and conceived and at least one of them has stayed around long enough to assist our survival, and the fact that we live in social groups. This is somewhat dramatically called, by the existentialists, especially, *the human condition*, and it alone would explain why we have many emotions in common, especially fear, anger, sadness, disgust, and some form of affection or at least a feeling of dependency. The circumstances of life are such that we all face dangers, feel frustrated or offended by our fellows, feel disappointed and suffer loss, encounter things that are disgusting, feel closer to some people than to others. We do not need a notion like "affect programs" to understand the universality of these emotions.

But given that the circumstances that constitute the human condition (and to some extent, the mammalian condition) have been true for a very long time, it is not unreasonable to suppose that some of our responses (and a great many of our mammalian cousins' responses) have evolved along with other inherited features. In animals, what evolved were bigger brains and more complex behaviors, group affiliations and intragroup rivalries, more varied forms of competition, flight, and aggression. In humans, we evolved our still-bigger brains, our upright postures, our ability to speak and understand languages, and our more complex societies. But "evolved along with" is a tricky expression. It does not follow that our responses, especially our emotional responses, were "selected for" by virtue of their adaptiveness. In fact, it does not follow that any of our current features were "selected for," as opposed to being the residuum of natural selection that eliminated those creatures or early humans with other features that did not foster survival, for instance the Neanderthals, who supposedly lacked the brain power of their rival Cro-Magnons. But surviving with a feature does not mean surviving because of a feature, and universality and a biological basis prove much less than some evolution enthusiasts would maintain.

Our disposition to anger, for instance, might in fact be a by-product of a more general sense of aggressiveness in response to violations of territory. Aggressiveness is inherited and the capacity for anger comes along with it. Erotic love might be a culturally refined variation of a natural sense of attachment to those closest to us combined with a biological desire to mate and reproduce. (I take it that it is undeniable that there is a biological desire to mate or to attempt the activities that will result in mating, but it is not at all clear that there is any natural desire to reproduce. Watching two dogs go at it, for example, it is pretty evident that despite the intensity of their attempts to do what they are doing there is considerable confusion on their part why they are doing it. So, too, while people sometimes have sex with the explicit intention to reproduce, there is scarce evidence of any such supposedly unconscious intention in cases of "casual" sex.) So the fact that we might have a certain in-born propensity to have certain emotions does not mean that those emotions as such have been "selected for" by evolution. They may well be co-evolved or coincidental, what the late great paleontologist Stephen Jay Gould of Harvard University illustrated with his comparison to "spandrels" in architecture. These are forms that were not designed as such but naturally occurred with the design of arches in gothic buildings. So, too, there may be features of human temperament and personality that were not selected for but nevertheless emerged through evolution.

In any case we do not inherit emotions as such in the way that we inherit brown or blue eyes, for instance, or opposable thumbs. We are not born angry, or shameful, or happy. As I said before, what we inherit is the *capacity* to have an emotion. The comparison again is that we inherit the capacity to speak a language (although this, too, has been said to be coincidental with other inherited traits). But we do not inherit any particular language capacity. What language we learn depends on what language we are taught and surrounded by. This is not to deny that there is some in-born capacity to speak language, as Noam Chomsky and more recently Stephen Pinker have argued. But the idea that we inherit the *capacity* to speak a language leaves lots of room for debate, in the absence of much more detailed knowledge of the brain, about what it is that is actually inherited and how much is learned. So, too, the idea that what we inherit is the *capacity* to have an emotion leaves lots of room for debate.

What are these emotional capacities? Perhaps we inherit the capacity to be aggressive but learn to get angry when we learn what it is to be offended. Perhaps we learn to love when we learn to sublimate and transform our desire for sexual companionship. And learning these emotions is, like the capacity for speaking a language, very much dependent on growing up in a suitable environment and being exposed to one emotional environment rather than another. (This seems pretty evident in couples who reiterate their parents' relationship.) To be sure, we inherit *some* capacity, and it goes without saying that if people have an emotion they have the capacity to have that emotion. But whether we inherit the capacity to have any particular emotion by no means follows from this.

Nevertheless, it is a plausible hypothesis that some of our species-wide emotional responses, if there are such, may have been the result of natural selection processes that eliminated those who did not display such responses. Fearless creatures may well have been devoured by predators or killed by stronger rivals, so only creatures who felt fear (and acted accordingly) survived. Overly timid creatures may well have been taken advantage of and been blocked from mating such that the population consisted increasingly of more aggressive creatures (or, at least, more aggressive males). And, in line with the famous study by Robert Axelrod that we discussed in an earlier chapter, humans and other creatures who were wholly selfish and lived in groups tended to be shunned and consequently perished, while those who allowed others to take advantage of them also perished, leaving mostly those who cooperated with others and were willing to punish those who refused to cooperate. This explained not only the evolution of cooperation but also the evolution of punishment, in other words, both the evolution of sympathy and affiliation and the evolution of righteous indignation. These twin emotional responses are to be found in most human beings and most human cultures (and some animal cultures as well). The exceptions are, accordingly, startling, for instance, the infamous Ik of Africa, reported by Colin Turnbull, and the now extinct peace-loving Morioris of New Zealand, reputedly wiped out by the more warlike Maoris.

These are terrific and plausible stories. The hard question is whether they are anything more than stories, "just-so stories," according to Stephen Jay Gould. (The phrase "just-so stories" comes from Rudyard Kipling's animal stories for children, "How the Leopard Got Its Spots," "How the Rhino Got His Thick Skin," and the like.) Given any feature of contemporary creatures or humans, so long as it is not evidently maladaptive or dysfunctional (and sometimes even despite that!), a clever storyteller can weave a tale explaining how or under what circumstances that feature might have been adaptive, or at least once was so. Thus the best and most famous evolutionary storyteller of all, Charles Darwin, explained many behavioral traits, including some emotional responses, as "once serviceable," signifying that they once served a significant (that is, adaptive) function but do so no longer. But even if we can supply a plausible story for some basic emotions, that is not sufficient reason to conclude that these emotions were specifically "selected for" as part of the biological human personality.

For example, David Buss has attempted to create such a story for jealousy, and this has aroused considerable excitement and opposition regarding both his particular hypotheses and the general field of "evolutionary psychology" to which he has contributed. And while I do not want to enter into that debate (Buss having once been my student and now my friend and colleague) I will simply express some skepticism with the *specificity* of such efforts. I do not doubt that our psychological make-up in general is the result of evolution (as is everything about us), namely, it has survived the obstacles and threats that have faced us in the past. But whether a particular emotion such as jealousy evolved as such is a question about which I am willing to be agnostic. Yes, we are creatures who have evolved, but not everything about us is a "product" of evolution. A great deal of our emotional repertoire we learned collectively in the context of particular circumstances, only some of which have the universality of the human condition.

Does this mean that we are stuck with what Peter Goldie and Paul Griffiths have both criticized as an "avocado-pear" model of basic emotions, a hard core of "hard-wired" neural circuits and a squishy fruit covering provided by culture? I think not, and I would join them in rejecting this. Our neurology is nothing if not plastic and our emotions depend both on developmental neurology and the environment, including culture. With this in mind, let me consider a very different way of understanding a basic emotion. An emotion is basic, we might suggest, if it is central and perhaps essential to a certain way of life. It may or may not be based on a distinctive neurological syndrome, and it may or may not be central and essential to human life as such, part of the human condition. Consider the emotions of fear and anger. There are, clearly, neurological syndromes associated with these emotions. But what makes one afraid or angry and how this is expressed will surely differ from culture to culture and situation to situation, not to mention the many refinements that daredevils and manipulative managers have created.

Nevertheless, something like fear and anger seem "basic" to human existence, even if they cannot be explained in all specifics by reference to discrete neural syndromes. But on this conception of basic emotions, it is clear that an emotion (that is, an emotion-family or "system") might yet be more basic to some cultures than to others. So anger is a basic emotion in New York City but not (until recently) in Tahiti. That is, an emotion is basic depending on its importance in a social context, not just its neurological origins. If any emotion is universal, it is because of the human condition, not evolution or genetics or neurology. I do not doubt that culture and biology are the *yin* and *yang* of our emotional inheritance. But in our enthusiasm for the *yang*, let's not ignore or neglect the very rich *yin* we have to work with. Dr. Stephanie Brown is a social psychologist at the University of Michigan who has raised a storm with a study summarized recently by John Schwartz in the *New York Times*: "Men would rather marry their secretaries than their bosses, and evolution may be to blame." The idea is that evolution "programs" men to prefer mates with inferior and less-threatening status. Needless to say, there was a howl of public protest. At the end of the piece, however, Dr. Brown confessed that, "I don't think it's ever possible to really separate out what proportion of a behavior is shaped by evolutionary history and which parts are shaped by our environment or culture." I believe we can leave the issue there.

22

Emotions Across Cultures

Whether or not some emotions are universal, it is fairly obvious that, at least in the details, emotions and emotional life differ from society to society. Just take a trip from Scandinavia to the Mediterranean, or take a drive from downtown Boston to rural Nova Scotia, or from Miami to Tallahassee. Think of the stereotypical personalities of Denmark in contrast with those of Sicily, of Minnesota in contrast with those of Los Angeles, of Western Australia in contrast with those of rural Japan. The differences fall along several different dimensions. First of all, there are evident differences in the overall intensity of the emotions, or at least in the overt expression of the emotions. This may be due, as we saw before, to differences in the estimation of the importance of various issues, for instance issues having to do with "honor." It may also be due to very different display rules, what sorts of emotions and emotional displays are deemed appropriate. Second, the repertoire of emotions differs, at least in emphasis and frequency, but perhaps also in the appearance of novel emotions or what we think of as normal (even basic) emotions that are notably absent. Third, the nuances of emotions (within emotion "families") will differ considerably. Fourth, what *causes* a particular emotion might well differ from culture to culture. Fifth, the modes of expression and the contexts in which these expressions are appropriate differ according to cultural mores and display rules. Sixth, emotions typically lead to action, and the appropriate courses of action are also, in part, culturally determined. Seventh, there are various verbal expressions of emotion, and this greatly complicates both the nature of expression and the nature of the emotion.

In particular, there is the language that one uses to report and describe emotions, and it cannot be simply presumed that the various words we translate from one language to another refer to precisely the same emotion, even if it is very likely they will refer to emotions that might be recognized as being from the same family.

Let me begin, however, by saying something about the most obvious and usually overemphasized source of differences between cultures, namely differences in what *causes* emotions. In fact, this is the least interesting of all cultural differences. It is, nevertheless, intriguing and often amusing. Psychologist Carol Tavris (1982) tells a story:

> A young wife leaves her house one afternoon to draw water from the local well. She saunters down the main street, chatting amiably with her neighbors, as her husband watches from their porch. On her return from the well, a stranger stops her and asks for a cup of water. She obliges, and in fact invites the man home for dinner. He accepts. The husband, wife, and guest spend a pleasant evening together, and eventually the husband puts the lamp out and retires to bed. He wife also retires to bed—with the guest. In the morning, the husband leaves early to bring back some breakfast for the household. Upon his return, he finds his wife again making love with the visitor.

Tavris asks, "at what point in this sequence of events will the husband become angry or jealous?" That depends, she says, on what tribe and culture he belongs to:

> A Pawnee Indian husband, a century ago, would in fury bewitch any man who dared to request a cup of water from his wife.
>
> An Ammassalik Inuit husband who wants to be a proper host invites his guest to have sex with his wife; he signals his invitation by putting the lamp out. (The guest might feel angry if this invitation is not extended.) An Ammassalik husband would be angry, however, if he found his wife having sex with a man in circumstances other than the lamp game, such as that morning encore, or without mutual agreement.
>
> A middle class husband in America would get angry with any guest who, however courteously, tried to seduce his wife, and with the wife, who, however hospitably, slept with their guest.
>
> A husband who belonged to the polyandrous Toda tribe of southern India would find the whole sequence perfectly normal, nothing to raise a fuss about. But a Toda husband and wife would be angry with any man who tried to start an affair by sneaking around the husband's back.

The differences in repertoires of emotions can be understood, if with some caution, in terms of stereotypical personalities. The point to be made

immediately here, to hold off charges of political incorrectness, is that
political and cultural stereotypes are not just caricatures imposed by
unsympathetic and even hostile outsiders. People *live* their stereotypes.
The stereotype of the Texan, to start with my home territory, with a
temperament of calm and courteous reserve punctuated by excessive
expressions of noisy enthusiasm and backed up by an unmistakable pen-
chant for violence, is not just one that has been imposed by New Yorkers
and Hollywood. Indeed, even without outsider stereotyping, according to
Molly Ivins, the typical Texan response is to play into the stereotype, exag-
gerate it, even reduce it to absurdity. (Austin and Dallas columnist Ivins
is great on this, telling in her extremely amusing way how when she first
started going to New York she cranked up her Texas twang and dress.) But,
to make the obligatory point, a stereotype is only a stereotype. It is not an
ideal type. It is not an average or a generalization. There are many Texans
(I am one of them) who don't fit the stereotype at all, but this by itself is
not an argument against it. Indeed, I still play the role of the amused but
alienated outsider, with a temperament very much at odds with the stereotype. But there is something of a cultural paradigm at work here, nevertheless, by way of role models and literature and shared activities and even
the folk psychology, which, I must say, tends to be a bit more folksy in
Texas than elsewhere. To describe the emotional stereotype is not to paint
an ideal picture nor to portray a typical citizen but to capture a certain
constellation of emotional tendencies that are striking mainly in contrast
to other cultures and against the background of some usually provincial
conception of "human nature."

Let's look again at anger. Anger is not the same from group to group
even in our culture. In more morality-minded subcultures (and a subculture can be as small as a family or a local ethnic community, as large as a
worldwide religious community) anger tends to be expressed as moral
indignation. The difference between anger and moral indignation, as I discussed in an earlier chapter, has to do with the essential moral component
of the emotion. By contrast, in more individualistic groups in which
autonomy and self-interest rule and blaming other people is considered a
weakness, anger will more likely be frustration, with a minimum of blame
and a certain amount of humiliation. In other individualistic groups it may
be expressed as annoyance, which may be devoid of moral consideration
but may, nevertheless, include an element of blame. In other words, the
differences in anger-like emotion will have much to do with the nature
of the mode of engagement with the world that one or another group or
culture embraces. In groups that have strong moral convictions and a
tendency to blame, indignation will seem "natural." In groups that have
strong sense of autonomy and self-interest, frustration will be common but

indignation rare. In groups that have strong sense of "leaving each other alone" annoyance will be more common. So, on the one hand, it would make good sense to say that all three groups get angry, but the nature of the anger is quite different in each.

Let's look at two actual examples, with certain subgroups in America as our contrast. The contrast I have in mind is the American subculture of commuters and rush hour interstate drivers, among whom anger is very common. The mode of anger will vary, of course. Some feel indignation, others feel frustration, still others mere annoyance. But whatever the mode of anger, it is easily provoked, even by minor inconveniences and offenses. The two examples are far-flung, first the Polynesians of Tahiti, second the Utkuhikhalingmiut ("Utku") Inuit or Eskimos of the Canadian Arctic. The claim has been made, of both groups, that "they don't get angry," or, at least, that anger is rare and not easily provoked. (The lack of traffic is just a partial explanation.)

This claim was made about the Tahitians as far back as they have been known to Europeans. An officer with Captain James Cook, during his exploration of the "Friendship Islands" in 1770, noted in his log that the people of Tahiti were "slow to anger and soon appeased." Robert Levy, an anthropologist with psychoanalytic training, studied them two centuries later and came up with similar conclusions. It is not that Tahitians never get angry, but when they do they experience the anger as unwelcome and alien, and they do not get angry nearly so often or so easily as we do. Anger is not, in other words, a prevalent emotion in their society. (This is not the case, I should point out to potential tourists, in a city like Papeete, where the European influence has been so pervasive that the bars are as dangerous as in Marseilles.)

Why is this? Without even hinting at possible racial differences—what the Europeans believed for several centuries—we can much more convincingly point to their cultures. Tahitians live (or lived) in a land of plenty. They had little reason to squabble about who took what from whom. They were an island. They had no serious wars or invasions and few visitors. (Captain James Cook was killed in Hawaii, a larger island that had a much more violent people and became a candidate for U.S. statehood.)

The Utku were studied by female Canadian anthropologist Jean Briggs, and she tellingly entitled her book on them *Never in Anger*. Among the Utku, anger is a genuine rarity. Briggs suggests that even in circumstances that we would find intolerably frustrating or offensive, the Utka do not get angry. Where most of us would be resentful or furious, the Utku are merely resigned. Anger is not only unreasonable, it is all but unintelligible. According to Briggs, there is not even a proper word for it. The Utku word used to refer to anger—for example, in the behavior of female Canadian anthropologists—translates as "childishness." She does describe in considerable detail one of her hosts, an older man of some distinction, who was known for what was locally considered his bad temper, but his more than usual provoked anger was nevertheless much less frequent, less ferocious, and more reservedly expressed than what we might expect. Perhaps "never in anger" is a bit of a stretch, but it is again clear that anger plays much less of a role in Utku society than it does in our own.

Such differences in emotional repertoires have to do with not only the differences in cultural "choices" of emotions—the fact that one culture finds a great deal to be angry about while another finds relatively little—but also with the way that emotions are viewed in the culture, notably, whether they are viewed with approval or disapproval. Obviously the two are related and feed one another. Anger is so demonized in Tahitian society that people are terrified to get angry. If a culture thinks that anger is dangerous and demonizes it, as people do in Tahiti, it naturally follows that children are strongly discouraged from getting angry, are reprimanded or punished when they do, that incidents inciting anger are avoided when possible, and that anger when it does arise is not easily or energetically expressed. By contrast, in much of current America—and let's focus this mainly on the subculture of commuters and interstate drivers—anger is expected and even much celebrated, not withstanding its dangers in a society where handguns are legal. What is interesting, however, is that rarity of anger and disapprobation do not strictly go hand in hand. The Tahitians, as I just mentioned, demonize anger. They talk about it all the time. In Levy's observations, they "hypercognize" anger. They are virtually obsessed with it. And this talk, in turn, has a dampening effect on anger. It against this background that we should appreciate the trauma of the occasional outburst of murderous anger when a young man "runs amok." Among the Utku, by contrast, we might note that anger is hypocognized, it is rarely talked about and the Utku do not even have a vocabulary for talking about it.

But why, then, is anger so rare among the Utku? It has been suggested that Briggs is wrong about them, that they do not lack anger but, to give it the Freudian twist, they repress it. Or, without the psychoanalytic apparatus, it is suggested that the seeming absence of anger is in fact the result of a set of display rules that forbid its expression. This might be a plausible suggestion with regard to the Japanese, where the expression of anger is clearly regulated by considerations of social status and propriety. But there is little evidence for this among the Utku. What does explain the lack of anger goes to the very heart of our "cognitive" theory of the emotions, emotions defined in terms of their engagement with the world and anger defined, at least in part, by the concepts of blame and offense. Briggs describes the situation, the language, and the worldview of the Utku in admirable detail. Their situation is severe. They live in a harsh climate where a blizzard can catch them at any time. The only thing to do, when caught in a blizzard, is to sit down and wait for it to pass. Any active effort is more likely to be fatal. What is striking is the fact that the Utku do not, in general, blame each other for their harsh circumstances. The absence of blame means the absence of anger, at least, most forms of anger. We might interpret the bad temper of Briggs's host as annoyance or frustration and so argue for a much weaker thesis, that anger as such is rare among the Utku though some forms of annoyance or frustration may occasionally be seen. In any case, all I want to argue for here are the significant differences between cultures in terms of their emotion repertoires, not the absolute difference that might be indicated by the literal thesis "never in anger." The Utku share with us the capacity for anger. What is striking is how little that capacity gets realized or encouraged in their culture.

The insight that, philosophically, the Utku are taught resignation and patience rather than indignation and anger is, once again, a confirmation of the sophistication and intelligence of emotions. Their emotions are a way of understanding and coping with their difficult world. But now, let's go back to those commuting Americans. Most of them have fairly expensive late-model cars, capable of ninety-plus miles an hour (although few drivers have actually tested that, at least more than once out of curiosity). They have watched television commercials in which the same cars are shown speeding down some beautiful country or seaside road (driven, we are reminded, by professional drivers), utterly devoid of traffic. Many of the cars now stalled or creeping along in the commuting traffic jam are "sport utility vehicles," designed, in theory at least, for off-the-road performance. Modern drivers are in a hurry, frustrated, impatient, bored, tired from waking up too early or after a long day's work, feeling entitled to a quick, exciting, unimpeded ride, just like those promised in the TV commercial. That sense of entitlement, in confrontation with the rudeness of the real world, tells us all that we really need to know about the cultural background of anger. I would not generalize this disposition to anger beyond the automobile subculture (and perhaps some kindred subcultures, for instance, the subculture of beleaguered airline passengers). But wherever we find a strong sense of entitlement we are likely to find a strong disposition to anger. I leave it to you to contemplate how far this reaches in American society.

The repertoire of emotions in a culture (or a subculture) depends not only on the cultural background and the environment but on the way people talk and think about their emotions. In our society, conversations often tend to focus on outrage, envy, resentment, and, in a very different

mood, romantic love. We talk very little about grief, very little about gratitude, although these two emotions form the foundation of a great many
extended conversations and so are "basic" emotions in other cultures.
Among the Kaluli of Papua, New Guinea, for example, grief and gratitude
form two of the central themes of the entire culture, while American males,
to be very specific, seem to feel very uncomfortable with both of them.
Some years ago Boston psychologist Shula Sommers (1984) did an extensive analysis of attitudes toward gratitude, in American and a few other
societies. What she found was that American men, in particular, found
gratitude a humiliating emotion and talked about it infrequently. They
might often be heard, after winning a sports or political contest, thanking
God or their mom, but thanking a colleague or an underling is quite dis-
comfiting, suggesting that one did not do it alone. Gratitude presupposes
so many judgments about debt and dependency that it is easy to see why
supposedly self-reliant American males would feel queasy about even talking about it. In Papua, New Guinea, by contrast, interdependence and
mutual dependency is taken for granted so expressions of gratitude are
highly ritualized. So, too, as we saw in an earlier chapter, Americans feel
very uncomfortable with grief and limit its expression as much as possible
to the confines of a funeral service. In Mediterranean and Maori societies,
by contrast, mourning is highly ritualized and grief is a constant theme in
their societies. I do not want to judge, here, and say that the one is necessarily better than the other. But the differences are revealing, and they say
a great deal about who a culture is. (For instance, *schadenfreude* is an
example of an emotion that most people both have and recognize, but we
never bothered to invent a word for it, since we do not think that we
should approve of it, so we had to import a label from German. Similarly,
there is no English word for "sadness at the success of others" but nonetheless it is a very familiar emotion—Gore Vidal says somewhere that
whenever one of his writer colleagues enjoys a success, some little part of
him dies.)

But the cultural differences in emotions include more than differences of
frequency and intensity of emotions (or emotion families) that are familiar
to us. There are also emotions that are unknown to us, both in the senses
that that we do not know of or about them and that we do not experience
them. Two much-discussed emotions that are unknown to Americans
and Europeans are the Japanese emotion *amae* and the Ifaluk emotion of
fago. *Amae* is an emotion of "indulgent interdependence," according to
sociologists Herman Smith and Takaka Nomi, and it is, according to a
distinguished Japanese scholar, Takeo Doi and now by broad agreement
"distinctive to the production and reproduction of Japanese culture." It is
what makes Japanese child-rearing distinctively different from American

child-rearing. Japanese babies are taught from the start the importance of dependency and the emotional rewards of clinging and security. The Japanese mother, by common cultural consensus, does not let her baby out of her sight, and only rarely out of her arms, for the first two years. The "spoiled child," according to the Japanese, is an American (mis)conception. According to Doi, *amae* is the Japanese basic emotion, "more universal than Freud's two instincts, sex and aggression." According to E. F. Vogel, another Japan scholar, "Amae is experienced by the child as a 'feeling of dependency or a desire to be loved,' while the mother vicariously experiences satisfaction and fulfillment through overindulgence and over-protectiveness of her child's immaturity." What should also be noted is that *amae* is not so much an emotion had by either the child or by the mother so much as it is the emotion that defines the mother-child bond itself. This fits with the general portrait of the emotion, which is one of interdependency.

The distinction between independence and interdependence gives rise to an important organizing principle in doing crosscultural comparisons of emotion, according to Hazel Markus and Shinobu Kitayama. American and European societies, for the most part, tend to prize independence and self-sufficiency, and their emotions reflect this. Asian societies, by contrast, tend to insist on interpersonal interdependence, and their emotions reflect this in turn. This is, to be sure, a gross oversimplification, but it does capture an important dimension of cultural difference, even if most societies occupy something more like a middle ground on the spectrum. Traditional American culture, for instance, is a complex of individual self-reliance and community sensibilities. It is hard to imagine American history without both of those, no matter how much we fantasize, celebrate, and over-emphasize the "lone wolf" image of the cowboy or spy. So, too, Japanese society is, to be sure, defined by ferocious loyalties, whether of samurai to their lords or salarymen to their companies, but individual excellence is nevertheless prized—so long as it is positioned within the community and not an excuse for self-aggrandizement. But understanding Japanese *amae* obviously does require an appreciation for the potent value of bonding in that society, just as understanding American anger requires an appreciation for the robust value of entitlement.

Fago is translated by anthropologist Catherine Lutz (1988) as "compassion/love/sorrow," who deals with it at length in her important book, *Unnatural Emotions.* The subjects of the book are the people of the island of Ifaluk in the South Pacific (in the Caroline Islands) and *fago,* she claims, is the definitive and in that sense basic emotion in that society. The overall thesis of the book is worth relating. Lutz is part of that generation of anthropologists that rebelled against the universality of emotions thesis and insisted instead that both the emotions and emotional language are shaped by culture and "socially constructed." She rejected the Jamesian question, "what is an emotion?" and replaced it with a more open-ended question about the variable roles and functions of emotions in particular societies. She therefore rejects the idea of "natural' emotions and insists that the emotions are unnatural, which is not to deny that they are somehow based in biology but rather to insist that they are fundamentally cultural products. This is a view introduced in the early sixties—to howls of indignation—by the great American anthropologist Clifford Geertz: "not only ideas but emotions are cultural artifacts." The social constructionist view as an oppositional view in psychology was developed by James Averill and Rom Harré. But in anthropology the social constructionist perspective became the coin of the realm, as evident and beyond question as the universalist thesis had become among the basic emotions theorists.

Fago is the recognition of suffering in the lives of the Ifaluk and their insistence on interpersonal kindness in the face of that suffering. Maturity, according to the Ifaluk, consists above all in the ability to nurture others. If the focus of American anger is the offensiveness of the world and the extent to which others are to blame for one's misfortune or frustration, the focus of *fago* is the fragility of life and the preciousness of connections to others. Relationships can be severed, abruptly. Love cannot be understood apart from loss. *Fago* is the recognition and the attempt to cope with this fragility and vulnerability. It is, according to Lutz, a vigorous optimism in the face of suffering, bolstered by the sense that human caring can control the cruel ravages of fate.

The combination of compassion, love, and sorrow sounds to us (as it first sounded to Lutz) like a contradiction. Love, she writes, is a positive, activating emotion, while sadness is negative and enervating. I have already argued that this "positive-negative" notion of "valence" is too simpleminded to capture the complexity of most emotions, and of love and suffering in particular. But what was required for Lutz to understand the Ifaluk was to come to understand this combination that makes little sense to us. If we think of love as unqualified enthusiasm we will not understand *fago*. It is only when we come to appreciate love, even in our society, as a complex of attachment and vulnerability, both of these present in the emotion itself, that we start to make some headway. But *fago*, if Lutz is right (and she did struggle for quite some time to understand it), is not readily translatable into English and the emotion is not easily understood by foreigners.

There is considerable controversy surrounding what all of this means, whether *amae* and *fago* really are different emotions or whether it is Japanese and Ifaluk *languages* that pick out different combinations of emotions that are in fact universal and familiar to us. "Social construction" theorists tend to argue the former while basic emotions theorists tend to argue the latter. Strong universalists will even insist that there are no untranslatable emotion terms, and the widely read accounts of *amae* and *fago* are proof of this. They may not be translatable in a one-to-one word fashion, like English "anger" to French "*colére*" and Polynesian "*riri*." But they are translatable, as "indulgent interdependence" and "compassion/love/sorrow," respectively. A weaker claim is that they may not be exactly translatable (in fact, no word in any language can be translated without loss into any other language), but we can nevertheless "hone in" on the meaning of foreign emotion words, and this in turn allows us to empathize, at least to some degree, with the people who have that emotion. But on the other side, social construction theorists would argue that any coincidence of emotions and emotion terms, would be just that, a coincidence. Each culture "constructs" its own emotion repertoire, and while we might well expect that (due to the human condition as well as human physiology) many emotions would turn out to be similar, this would have nothing to do with the universality of emotions. A weaker conception, which I myself have suggested, is that biology and culture are the *yin* and *yang* of emotional life. The idea that emotions are either *just* biological or *just* cultural is, I think, unsustainable.

But this does not answer the challenge above, whether exotic emotions like *amae* and *fago* are really different emotions or whether it is the languages that differ and pick out different combinations of emotions. I think that there is good reason to think that there are any number of processes, involving any number of combinations and successions of emotions, not all of these have names. In fact, it may well be that most of them do not have names. The names of emotions, it has been suggested, are mainly used in retrospect, to rationalize or understand what in fact was an extremely complex and confused stream of responses and experiences. Thus we sum up the incredibly convoluted sequence of emotions involved in even the most routine case of "falling in love" and establishing a life-long relationship by calling it all "love," when in fact this is a process that may include the entire social repertoire of emotions, from anger to zeal. So, too, we summarize the dynamic interplay of fear, resentment, and anger by simply calling it "anger," but we should not pretend that this is a label for a single, distinctive "state of mind."

There is no reason, I have argued all along, to think of the emotions as discrete psychic entities. To puncture the image of boundless emotions I suggested toward the end of chapter 18, let me insist that there is no psychic universe in which millions of emotions are floating around, most of them unconscious and unrecognized. That image may be entertaining, but it is absurd. What is true, and where the social construction theorists are right, is that every culture creates a language and a vocabulary for talking about emotion according to its needs and contingencies, and it is this language and vocabulary that carves out what might seem (within that language community) like discrete psychological entities but are in fact complex, contextually defined processes. But it is not as if every culture creates its own emotions. If there is good reason for being skeptical about the basic emotions thesis, there is also good reason to be skeptical of the strong social constructionist claims. Whether or not there are physiological universals, it is the role and function of particular emotions in the particular circumstances of a culture's (and an individual's) existence, as well as biology, that determines the nature of our emotional lives.

23

Happiness, Spirituality, and Emotional Integrity

"Be here now!" was one of the dubious pearls of wisdom in the 1960s, but with regard to happiness, at least, it was it was always a nonstarter. Happiness, as we discussed in chapter 6, is never momentary but necessarily spreads out over time. But our emotions more generally are rarely momentary. Emotions are processes, and even brief emotions take time, refer to the immediate past and anticipate the immediate future. Most emotions, however, are very much involved in time. They involve memory and anticipation. Hope and fear are about the future, possibly even the rest of one's life. Anger engages the past, and often, the rather extended past, going back to childhood. True love may not be "forever," but it usually aspires and imagines itself to be enduring and open-ended. Emotions are not just momentary mental states. They are also the means by which we transcend the momentary, even the means by which we transcend ourselves.

On the other hand, the "Be here now!" formulation suggests something of great importance that I have been defending throughout this book. It is what my friend Sonoma guru Sam Keen has called "*the passionate life.*" It is a conception of the good life that many people admire but few philosophers preach. Many philosophers, including Aristotle and many eastern philosophers, too, have sermonized about happiness and the virtues, but all too often, the conception of happiness that emerges is rather tame and has mainly to do with being a good citizen, a congenial person, and enjoying peace of mind (*ataraxia*) and even a lack of passionate turbulence (*apatheia*). In contrast, the passionate life is defined by its sometimes vehement emotions, by its impassioned engagement, by its ardent quests, grand but futile ambitions, and embracing affections.

The passionate life is sometimes characterized (for example, by Goethe in *Faust* and by Kierkegaard and Nietzsche) in terms of frenzy, vaulting ambition, essentially insatiable goals, and impossible affections. It is what Nietzsche in particular referred to as a "Dionysian" temper, a life captured in dynamic rather than static metaphors, notions of "energy," "enthusiasm," "charisma," even mania. The passionate life embraces the values of Romanticism and the image of the suffering but sometimes manic artist. It may well be occasionally weighted down with despair and *weltschmertz*, but it will probably be buoyed by joy and exuberance as well. I want to make room for such "perverse" conceptions of the good life in contrast to both ordinary morality and "being a good person" and to the life of mere contentment and satisfaction. That, too, I suggest, is a version of happiness, but it is radically different from what we talked about in discussing Aristotle's otherwise persuasive notion of *eudaimonia* (doing well).

The passionate life may be exemplified by the romantic image of the suffering artist, but it is not at all unfamiliar in contemporary life. Youthful people around the world understandably prefer driving rhythms in their music and in their daily lives seek out the excitement of risk-taking and thrill seeking. Later in life, too, we appreciate enthusiasm and passion. We demand (perhaps foolishly) *charisma* in our politicians and excitement in our lives. We admire and aspire to the passionate life and treat peace of mind and the absence of passion as merely "relaxing," time off from an otherwise driven life. One could, of course, hold a hard line and insist that no such life could possibly be happy, and I certainly know and read many social critics and psychiatrists who maintain this. But I think that a more generous and realistic view is that the demands of a creative and spirited life—or any life that is defined by difficult and continuing challenges—makes it evident that we need to broaden or even reconsider the notion of happiness. Happiness is not, contra Aristotle and many of his predecessors and successors, necessarily a life of moderation and peace of mind. I think, like Nietzsche, that one can make a good case either that happiness is not incompatible with turmoil, suffering, and unhappiness but even depends upon it, or that happiness as we have been taught to think of it is not the most important thing in life (see Bellotti, 2004). Indeed, even Aristotle allowed that happiness might well include some pain, suffering, and failure. It is just that these could not be the definitive qualities of a happy life. But all of this should open up for us the question, What it is that counts as happiness?

For Aristotle, we noted, happiness refers to the more or less "objective" features of virtue and success, such as being healthy, well-off, respected by one's peers and being successful in one's profession. (For Aristotle, this would be pretty much restricted to being a statesman or a philosopher, but we can certainly expand this list to include all of the many careers, professions, and livelihoods in which contemporary citizens are engaged.) For many people today, by contrast, happiness is too often conflated with the mere feeling of happiness, or with just *feeling happy*, a momentary experience that need have nothing to do with one's accomplishments, virtues, well-being, status in society, or prospects for a good life. The most wicked, pathetic failure might have happy feelings, at least occasionally, and, of course, such feelings can be artificially induced by any number of drugs, pharmaceuticals, operations, and exercises. (The feeling of ecstasy is, not surprisingly, produced by a drug with that name.) But in between more-or-less objective success and merely feeling happy there is a rich spectrum of options, which may or may not include success and may or may not include happy feelings. Notably, there is what Ed Deiner and others call "subjective well-being," which presumably takes account of one's fortunes in the world and one's over-all well-being and presumes a fair amount of happy feeling, but does not wholly depend on either of these. But also, there is a "second level" of happiness, beyond doing well, feeling happy, and having subjective well-being, and that lies in the refection that one is happy. Reflection, I want to argue, is essential to happiness.

To put it very simply, to be happy is not just being well engaged and feeling good. It also requires the reflective recognition that one is happy. I have argued that one cannot begin to understand adult human emotion without taking into account the powerful ability to reflect on our emotions. But as I have been urging for quite some time, and especially in chapters 19 and 20, such reflection is not a process entirely separate from the emotions reflected on. When we reflect on our own ongoing emotions the reflection becomes part of the emotion. It is only in this ongoing emotive-reflective process that an emotion becomes fully conscious. In my discussion of love in chapter 4, for instance, I argued that being in love ultimately involves the recognition *that* one is in love and one might say that it is the reflective recognition that *completes* the emotion. In anger too, the realization "I am so angry!" is not a commentary or report on anger but an important part of the anger. So, too, with happiness. One might have a flourishing but unthinking life and have a sense of subjective well being, but adult human happiness requires something more, the knowledge that one is indeed happy.

With these considerations, I suggest that we should modify our statement in chapter 6 that happiness is not, properly speaking, an emotion. We might say that happiness is a kind of "meta-emotion," an ongoing summary evaluative judgment about our being in the world. It is a kind of all-embracing emotion, one that is not just about any particular aspect of our lives but about our lives as a whole. Thus happiness, as I want to consider it here, is neither a feeling nor just a matter of "subjective well-being" nor an objective achievement but an emotion that is about the sum of all of our other emotions, the way they add up in our lives and the life they add up to. And this creates just the space we need to include and account for the passionate life and those romantic notions of happiness. The question is not whether we enjoy our lives, or even whether we have a sense of subjective well-being. It is rather a question of how we evaluate the course of our lives, given our aspirations and our values, what we really want to do or accomplish in our lives. It is very much like the Stoic "affirmation" that we give not just to our particular emotions but to our emotional lives as a whole.

An artist or a writer or a social worker or an entrepreneur may enjoy only a few brief moments of contentment and satisfaction (and perhaps not even that). But if he or she is living the life that he or she wants and needs to live and understands that frustration is an essential and perhaps incurable aspect of that life, I do not see why we cannot call such a person happy. He or she may be like Albert Camus's Sisyphus, living a life of assured frustration (rolling the rock up the mountain with great difficulty, only have it crash back to where he began). But Camus assures us that we must consider Sisyphus happy insofar as he enthusiastically accepts and throws himself into his futile task. Camus further compares Sisyphus to all of us, and so do I. A passionate life may be always vulnerable to despair but it is not a life of despair. It all depends on how we *think* of things.

This is not to say that a person can live a life of complete misery and failure and still be happy. Aristotle's "quasi-objective" insistence remains. But what counts as a life of misery and failure is by no means so easily recognizable as Aristotle presumed. I think that Nietzsche's criticism of the classic Greeks is just right on this issue, that even Aristotle, when you get right down to it, had an overly staid view of the passions and no appreciation at all of the passionate life, however essential he may have made out the passions, in general, to be. There are many ways to be happy, and being an aristocratic Greek philosopher is but one of them.

Happiness depends on those moments (which may be plentiful or sparse) in which one gets a glimpse of our lives as a whole or, at least, of some substantial portion of our lives from the necessarily limited perspective of our current life experience. (This is what Heidegger suggests in his somewhat morbid emphasis on *angst* and "Being-unto-Death.") It is such reflection on our lives as a whole that completes our happiness. Not that thinking that one is happy alone makes one happy, to be sure. (This, perhaps more than any other emotional judgment, is liable to self-deception.) All of the ingredients, including some of Aristotle's "quasi-objective" virtues and accomplishments, must already be there. But happiness is a compound experience not just composed of the many aspects and activities of one's life but made up of an intricate interweave of all-embracing meta-emotions and holistic reflection.

It is by way of this conception of happiness as something of a super-emotion involving both emotions and reflection that we can finally understand the concept of *emotional integrity* that I have been dragging along for most of this book. As the word would suggest, integrity has to do with "wholeness," so emotional integrity has to do with the unity of our emotional life. Now one might think that emotional integrity is no more than emotional consistency, but this would be a serious misunderstanding of the concept. One can be wholly consistent in his or her emotional life if he or she is sufficiently obsessed or fanatic. That is the very opposite of what I have in mind here. Obsessing on a single emotion, blindly and without critical reflection, seems to me to be the virtual opposite of emotional integrity. Emotional integrity is not just consistency in one's emotional life (where the easiest consistency or unity, to be sure, is an exclusive focal point, a single set of beliefs, and a single emotion). Integrity implies richness and profundity rather than simplicity. The religious fanatic, for instance, is someone who utterly lacks emotional integrity.

A slightly less erroneous version of the same misunderstanding is the idea that emotional integrity is no more than emotional coherence, which allows for a much broader mix of emotions but is still much too limited and need not include reflection. Leading a simple, conflict-free life (what the Stoics called *ataraxia*) would be like this, but it, too, dramatically fails to count as what most of us would call a full and happy life. But the Stoics were absolutely right about this: Emotional integrity (or what they considered the virtuous life) necessarily involves second-order reflection as well as first-order feeling, and in line with the romantic conception of the passionate life I briefly defended above, I would want to allow for a mixed, even conflicted, repertoire of feelings, emotions and reflections, including dissatisfaction, self-criticism, lack of contentment, and real ethical dilemmas, that is, impossible choices and engagements. Again I would want to say that a life without any such sense of conflict is a limited life indeed. Just to be affluent in a world that contains so much poverty, for instance, should be enough to guarantee some such a sense of dissatisfaction and conflict. Those who deny or rationalize away this ugly fact do not thereby have more integrity but less.

In fact, some of the people I would highlight as exemplary in emotional intelligence are those unusual physicians, executives, and politicians who have cultivated the remarkable ability to "compartmentalize," separating off the incredible pressure of a high-responsibility position (fighting a war as prime minister, treating horrible casualties after some cataclysmic disaster, standing up against withering opposition for a noble principle) from the rest of their lives. How one does this, I do not know, but it means that the emotional integrity of some people who live the most fulfilling lives is by its very nature segmented and divided in a dramatic way, and their integrity depends on

—it is not in spite of—this radical separation. A happy life with emotional integrity is not a life without conflict but a life in which one wisely manages emotional conflicts in conjunction with one's most heartfelt values.

It will be evident to some readers that this concept of emotional integrity is a version of the existentialist concept of *authenticity*. What this means (in Heidegger and Sartre, for instance) is none too clear, but it certainly has a lot to do with the agreement of our prereflective engagements in life and our larger reflective outlook. But this distinction is, as I have also been indicating, too simplistic, and so, too, authenticity cannot be a simple match between what we feel (our engagements with the world) and what we think of ourselves and our being in the world. Sartre, in particular, gives the character he calls "the Champion of Sincerity" (in *Being and Nothingness*) a hard time, because (as becomes evident in his novels and journalism as well as his philosophy) he had dim view of what passes for sincerity in his fellow citizens, which was more often a cloak for hypocrisy and bad faith than a virtue. If we think of sincerity as a simple "match," there is ample reason for suspicion. Thus authenticity is much better conceived of as a dynamic complex of thoughts, emotions, and social interactions (Sartre's "Being-for-Others"), and better yet as emotional integrity, which does not have the individualistic implications of authenticity and has built into it the idea of social virtue as well as existential individuality. Emotional integrity is essential to the good life, fully embracing our being with others as well as our need to live in accordance with our (and others') values. Emotional integrity is, contrary to the bent of some existentialists, anything but narcissistic and internally directed. To the contrary, I would suggest that it suggests an ideal of transcending ourselves by allowing us to become the person we most want to be.

With this in mind, let me finish up by noting another meta-emotion that involves an even more radical form of transcendence, and that is *spirituality*. Spirituality is a meta-emotion that transcends the merely personal by taking into account our larger (or more modest) place in the universe. It thus incorporates many of those emotions that constitute happiness, but in an importance sense it transcends the self, or, more accurately, it expands the self to suprahuman if not cosmic proportions.

Love and compassion, although they are assuredly ingredients in spirituality, are limited by their specificity. (Adam Smith argued against love as a virtue for just this reason.) *Agapé* or the "love of humanity" is much more all-embracing, and the love of all of nature even more so. Such love, not so much for a particular person, and compassion, though again not just for a particular person or any particular group of people, is what we mean by spirituality. Whatever else it may be, spirituality involves such passions, and against those spiritual traditions in philosophy and religious thought that downplay the passions, I would insist that the spiritual life is also a passionate life. But it is not therefore "mindless." To the contrary, it too, as a meta-emotion, requires thought and knowledge. It is not, accordingly, at odds with science and reason but in league with science and reason. For most of Western history and virtually all of Eastern philosophy, religion, philosophy, spirituality, and wisdom are deeply interconnected and inseparable. Again, spirituality is not at odds with thought and reflection but dependent upon it. All too often, the prototype of a spiritual experience is taken to be the blissful oblivion of a "mystical experience." But without suggesting anything about such an experience here, I want to counter that by saying that most spiritual experience is inseparable from thought. Indeed, in one of my books, I define spirituality as "the thoughtful love of life."

One thought in particular is essential to spirituality, and, not surprising, it is a thought that is also an emotion. It is the emotion of *gratitude*. In ordinary life, being "ungrateful" is considered a serious vice, whether in a single instance or as a long-term defect of character. In all of those instances where gratitude is appropriate or even mandatory (from getting good service from a waiter to having one's life saved by a total stranger), being ungrateful is a sign or symptom of a lack of character, not just an absence of generosity but a damnable failure to appreciate what is done for you by others. Ingratitude reflects the inability to appreciate other people and, worse, a grudging resentment of one's own vulnerability and the refusal to admit one's debt to others (see Sommers, 1984). Barbara Fredericks (2003) rightly argues that gratitude "broadens and builds." It is not just a "positive" view of life. It is a way of putting one's life in perspective.

Thus it is all the more important to feel gratitude for what is most valuable to most of us, namely, our lives. Late in his short life, Nietzsche (1992) exclaimed in one of his most heartfelt exclamations: "How could I fail to be grateful to my whole life?" This despite the many sufferings and pains of his life, not to mention his disappointments in his career and the utter indifference (and occasional hostility) in his public reception. But one of the questions that has always intrigued me about such cosmic gratitude, and it certainly bothered Nietzsche as well, is *to whom* one should feel this gratitude. As an emotion, gratitude is defined, at least in part, by its "object," namely the reception of a gift of some kind. But the object (in this case one's whole life) seems to be incomplete. If a good friend gives me a book, I am not just grateful for the book. I am grateful *to him* for giving me the book. This acknowledgement of the other's agency seems essential to the emotion. But if spirituality need not include a belief in a personal God, then how can one be grateful for one's life and all of its blessings? Nietzsche talks rather obscurely about "affirming one's life," but this seems to rather beg the question. *To whom* should one be grateful for one's life? The Christian philosopher Robert C. Roberts has no problem with this question, nor do most Christians, Jews, Hindus, and Muslims. But I do, as do many Buddhists. To whom indeed?

Being grateful "to the universe" is a limp way out of this quandary. But personifying the universe solves the God problem only by displacing it. Thus Camus, an atheist, populates his hero Sisyphus's world with gods and goddesses who are maliciously enjoying his fate (at whom he can rail in "scorn and defiance"). But this literary ploy is part and parcel of Camus's own recognition that the universe cannot be, as he so often claims, merely "indifferent." (Indeed, he gives the game away when he has his antihero Meursault "open his heart to the *benign* indifference of the universe" at the end of *The Stranger*.) But does it make sense to be grateful *to the universe*? I can imagine Dr. Roberts saying, Isn't this really being grateful to God without admitting it?

Perhaps one could avoid God by claiming to be thankful "to chance," or perhaps "to luck," as one might be thankful in roulette or the state lottery (one is surely not thankful to the casino or the state). But, again, the effort seems limp. The *to whom* question gets begged again. Manufacturing an evasive impersonal agent to whom to be grateful does not seem convincing. But, then, are we stuck with being ungrateful about the single gift that matters most?

Rather, I think the "to whom?" question is misplaced here. We should reject the easy move from gratitude as an interpersonal social emotion to cosmic gratitude for one's whole life. This may make good sense for a theist, for whom there is something akin to an interpersonal relationship with God (but even Kierkegaard, the most powerful author on this, expresses deep anxiety about the peculiar one-sidedness of this particular relationship). And one can, of course, personify the universe as Camus does, but I think that there is another solution, more radical in that it severs gratitude for one's life altogether from the interpersonal emotions. It is, I think, still gratitude, but it shines a light on what even interpersonal gratitude is all about, which is not merely being thankful *to someone* but being properly humble about one's own modest place in the world.

Gratitude, in other words, is a philosophical emotion. It is, in a phrase, appreciating the bigger picture and having a chance to play a role in it, no matter how small. In relationships, gratitude is seeing a particular act or transaction as part of a larger ongoing relationship. So viewed, "opening one's heart to the universe" is not so much personifying the universe as reflecting on as well as feeling and expressing a cosmic gratitude, that is, expanding one's perspective, as the Stoics insisted, so that one comes to appreciate the beauty of the whole as well as be absorbed in our own limited projects and passions. That is spirituality. It is, perhaps, the ultimate happiness, and it is an ideal expression of emotional integrity.

Annotated Bibliography

Let me first recommend two of my own books for a collection of some of the classic texts in the history and theory of emotions and for background readings in existentialism:

Solomon, Robert C., ed. *What is an Emotion?* New York: Oxford University Press, 2004. Includes selections from Aristotle, Seneca, Descartes, Spinoza, Hume, Darwin, James, Freud, Ekman, Lazarus, Frijda, Schachter and Singer, Sartre, Lutz, Nussbaum, De Sousa, Griffiths, and many others.

———, ed. *Existentialism.* New York: Oxford University Press, 2004. Includes selections from Kierkegaard, Dostoevsky, Nietzsche, Heidegger, Sartre, Camus, and others in the existentialist tradition.

Aristotle. *Nicomachean Ethics.* Translated by W. D. Ross. Oxford: Oxford University Press, 1948. The classic ethics text by one of the great philosophers.

———. *Rhetoric.* Translated by Jon Solomon. In *What Is an Emotion?* Edited by Robert C. Solomon. New York: Oxford University Press, 2004. Selections from three of Aristotle's works specifically on the nature of emotion.

Arnold, Magda. *Emotion and Personality.* New York: Columbia University Press, 1960.

Austen, Jane. *Pride and Prejudice.* New York: Penguin Classics, 2002.

Averill, James R. *Anger and Aggression: An Essay on Emotion.* New York: Springer-Verlag, 1982. An excellent study by one of the best "social construction" theorists of emotion.

Axelrod, Robert. *The Evolution of Cooperation.* New York: Basic Books, 1985.

Ayer, A. J. *Language, Truth, and Logic.* New York: Dover, 1952.

Beck, Aaron T. *Anxiety Disorders and Phobias: A Cognitive Perspective.* New York: Basic Books, 1990. A good study of the many ways that fear can go wrong.

Becker, Gavin de. *The Gift of Fear*. New York: Dell, 2000. A book by a well-known security expert in Hollywood arguing that we need to learn to trust our feelings of fear, as they may impel us to take action that will saves our lives.

Bedford, Errol. "Emotions." In *Essays in Philosophical Psychology*. Edited by D. Gustafson. New York: Doubleday-Anchor, 1963. One of the important early essays on emotions in the Anglo-American "analytic" tradition.

Bellotti, Ray. *Happiness Is Over-rated*. Lanham, MD: Rowman and Littlefield, 2004. A challenging study that argues that happiness is *not* the most important thing in life.

Bentham, Jeremy. *An Introduction to the Principles of Morals and Legislation*. New York: Hafner, 1948. The classic introduction to "utilitarianism" and the reduction of ethics to considerations of pleasure and pain.

Ben-Zeev, Aaron. *The Subtlety of Emotions*. Cambridge, MA: Massachusetts Institute of Technology Press, 2000. A rich and subtle book by one of Israel's foremost psychologists of emotion.

Bharatamuni. *Natyashastra*. Translated by M. Ghosh. Calcutta: Granthalaya, 1967. Bharata lived and worked somewhere between 200 B.C. and A.D. 200. He was the most original Indian writer on the arts and the original authority on the *rasa* system.

Blum, Lawrence. *Friendship, Altruism and Morality*. London: Routledge and Kegan-Paul, 1980. An early work in the Anglo-American "analytic" tradition on the importance of feeling in ethics.

Briggs, Jean L. *Never in Anger*. Cambridge, MA: Harvard University Press, 1975.

Brown, Alan S. *The Déjà Vu Experience: Essays in Cognitive Psychology*. New York: Psychology Press, 2004. Summarized in "The Tease of Memory." *Chronicle of Higher Education* (July 23, 2004).

Buss, David. *The Dangerous Passion*. New York: Free Press, 2000.

Camus, Albert. *The Stranger*. New York: Alfred A. Knopf, 1988.

Carroll, Noel. *The Philosophy of Horror*. London: Routledge, 1990. A wonderful study of horror books and movies and an analysis of what it is that people enjoy about them.

Charland, Louis. "The Natural Kind Status of Emotion." *British Journal for the Philosophy of Science* (2002).

Csikszentmihalyi, Mihaly. *Flow: The Psychology of Optimal Experience*. New York: Harper, 1991.

———. "Reconciling Cognitive and Perceptual Theories of Emotion: A Representational Proposal." *Philosophy of Science* 64 (December 1997).

Damasio, Antonio. *Descartes' Error*. New York: Putnam, 1994. A pioneering work in neuropsychiatry that argues against the "Cartesian" split between reason and emotion.

———. *The Feeling of What Happens: Body and Emotion in the Making of Consciousness*. New York: Harcourt, 1999. A bold work that attempts to develop a theory of self and consciousness starting from the context of the neurosciences.

Darwin, Charles. *The Expression of Emotions in Animals and Men*. Edited and introduced by Paul Ekman. 1862. Reprint, New York: Oxford University Press, 1998.

Davidson, Richard, H. H. Goldsmith, and Klaus Scherer, eds. *Handbook of the Affective Sciences.* New York: Oxford University Press, 2002. A very substantial collection of essays on the emotions, especially the neurophysiology and medical ramifications of emotion.

Dawkins, Marian. *On Animal Suffering.* Oxford: Oxford University Press, 1980.

Dennett, Daniel C. *Consciousness Explained.* Boston: Little Brown, 1991. An ingenious and unusually entertaining account of the nature of consciousness in cognitive science.

Descartes, René. *The Passions of the Soul.* Translated by S. H. Voss. Indianapolis: Hackett Publishing Co., 1989. One of the classic essays on the emotions by the great French philosopher.

Diener, Edward. *Culture and Subjective Well-Being.* Cambridge: Massachusetts Institute of Technology Press, 2003.

Dixon, Thomas. *Emotions: The Invention of a Psychological Category.* Cambridge: Cambridge University Press, 2004. A bold new study of the origins of the concept of "emotion" and the substitution of this psychological category for traditional ethical and theological conceptions of "the affects and the passions."

Doris, John. *Lack of Character.* New York: Cambridge University Press, 2002.

Dreyfus, Hubert. *Being-in-the-World: A Commentary on Heidegger's Being in Time, Division I.* Cambridge: Massachusetts Institute of Technology Press, 1990.

Eisenberg, Nancy. "Empathy and Sympathy." In *Handbook of Emotions.* 2d ed. Edited by Michael Lewis and Jeannette M. Haviland-Jones. New York: Guilford Press, 2002, 677–91.

Ekman, Paul. *Emotions Revealed.* A book that brings together the thoughts and theories of one of the seminal and most important figures in the twentieth century psychology of emotions, emphasizing the expression of emotion.

———. "Expression and the Nature of Emotion." In *Approaches to Emotion.* Edited by K. R. Scherer and Paul Ekman. Hillsdale, NJ: Erlbaum, 1984.

Ekman, Paul, and Richard Davidson, eds. *The Nature of Emotion.* New York: Oxford University Press, 1994. An imaginative collection of questions and comments by many leading contemporary social scientists.

Elster, Jon. *Alchemies of the Mind.* Cambridge: Cambridge University Press, 2000. An excellent study of emotions and rationality with some good historical studies and a detailed study of strategies of rationality, the author's specialty and the subject of his many other books.

Faccio, Peter. *Shakespeare* (audio tapes). Chantilly, VA: The Teaching Company, 1999.

Frank, Robert H. *Passion Within Reason.* New York: Norton, 1988. One of the few books on emotion by an excellent economist, arguing that the emotions are an unappreciated dimension of economic studies.

Fredericks, Barbara. "Gratitude, Like Other Positive Emotions, Broadens and Builds." In *The Psychology of Gratitude.* Edited by Robert Emmon and Michael E. McCullough. New York: Oxford University Press, 2003.

French, Peter A. *The Virtues of Vengeance.* Albany: SUNY Press, 1983. The author not only defends vengeance and demonstrate its prevalence throughout our history and our literature but also praises its virtues as essential for morality and justice.

Freud, Sigmund. *Introductory Lectures to Psychoanalysis.* New York: Norton, 1966. The classic introduction to psychoanalysis by the man who invented it all.

Frijda, Nico. *The Emotions.* Cambridge: Cambridge University Press, 1986. A wide-ranging and deeply insightful study of emotions by one of the great social psychologists of our times.

———. *The Laws of Emotion.* Mahwah, N.J.: Lawrence Erlbaum Associates, Inc. [LEA, Inc.], 2006. The most recent wide-ranging and deeply insightful study of emotions by one of the most distinguished social psychologists.

Gerstein, R. S. "Capital Punishment: A Retributivist Response." *Ethics* 85 (1985).

Gladwell, Malcolm. *Blink: The Power of Thinking Without Thinking.* New York: Little, Brown and Co., 2005. A best-seller arguing that intuition is sometimes better than drawn-out ratiocination.

Goldie, Peter. *The Emotions.* Oxford: Oxford University Press, 2000. An excellent study by a contemporary British philosopher and literary theorist who discusses the role of narrative in emotions.

Goleman, Daniel. *Emotional Intelligence.* New York: Bantam, 1995. The book that made the phrase "emotional intelligence" part of our everyday conversation. A best-seller when it appeared, sparking a wide interest in what was going on in emotions research.

Gordon, Robert. *The Structure of Emotions.* New York: Cambridge University Press, 1987. A cognitive science study of emotions in the Anglo-American "analytic" tradition.

Greenspan, Patricia. *Emotions and Reasons.* New York: Routledge, 1988. An important early book on emotions and rationality, raising difficult questions about cognitive theories of emotion.

Griffiths, Paul E. *What Emotions Really Are.* Chicago: University of Chicago Press, 1997. A bold and challenging book written from an evolutionary biological perspective and largely dismissive of philosophical and cognitive accounts of emotion.

Guignon, Charles. *Heidegger and the Problem of Knowledge.* Indianapolis: Hackett Publishers, 1983.

Halpern, Jodi. *From Detached Concern to Empathy.* New York: Oxford University Press, 2001. An important and sensitive book by a philosopher in the health professions trying to break the model of medical detachment in favor of more empathetic treatment of patients.

Harré, Rom. *The Social Construction Theory of Emotions.* Oxford, UK: Blackwell, 1986. An introduction to "social construction" theories of emotion by one of its main originators.

Hegel, Georg Wilhelm Friedrich. *Phenomenology of Mind.* Translated by J. B. Baillie. New York: Cosimo, 2006.

Heidegger, Martin. *Being and Time.* Revised edition, New York: Harper San Francisco, 1962.

Hochschild, Arlie. *The Managed Heart.* Berkeley: University of California Press, 1983. A ground-breaking study in sociology of the pressures, tensions, and coping behavior of people (e.g., airline stewardesses) who have to carefully "manage" their emotions in their work.

Hume, David. *A Treatise of Human Nature.* Edited by L. A. Selbe-Bigge. Oxford: Clarendon Press, 1973. One of the classic studies of human nature by one of the great English-speaking philosophers. Book II includes an ingenious study of the passions, and book III argues that morals depend on sentiment rather than reason.

Ivins, Molly. *You Got to Dance with Them What Brung You.* New York: Vintage, 1999.

Izard, Carroll. *Human Emotions.* New York: Plenum Press, 1977.

———. "Emotion." In the *Encyclopaedia Britannica,* XIIIth edition, 1982.

Jacoby, Susan. *Wild Justice.* New York: Harper and Row, 1983.

James, William. *Principles of Psychology.* New York: Dover, 1890. One of the great works in American psychology and the textbook for generations of psychologists at the beginning of the last century. It includes an important chapter on emotion, which is a slightly revised version of the famous essay below.

———. "Does Consciousness Exist?" In *Writings.* New York: Library of America, 1988.

———. "What Is an Emotion?" In *What Is an Emotion?* Edited by Robert C. Solomon. New York: Oxford University Press, 2004. This essay on emotion set the stage for much of the research on emotion throughout the twentieth century.

Keen, Sam. *The Passionate Life.* New York: Harper, 1976. The author was, in his words, "overeducated at Harvard and Princeton" and was a professor of philosophy and religion at "various legitimate institutions," a contributing editor of *Psychology Today* for twenty years and then a freelance thinker, lecturer, seminar leader, and consultant.

———. *Hymns to an Unknown God.* New York: Bantam 1995.

Kenny, Anthony. *Action, Emotion, and Will.* London: Routledge and Kegan-Paul, 1963.

Kotchemidova, Christina. "A Brief History of Cheerfulness: From Good Cheer to 'Drive-by Smiling.' " *Journal of Social History* (2005). An interesting study of the American obsession with "cheerfulness" and its recent origins and functions.

Kübler-Ross, Elisabeth. *On Death and Dying.* New York: Harper and Row, 1975. A classic study of death and dying by the author who brought such concerns out of the hidden cellar of philosophy and medicine into the light.

Landsman, Janet. *Regret.* New York: Oxford University Press, 2003. A thorough study of the nature of regret as a dynamic process of comparing reality and possibility.

Lane, Richard. *The Cognitive Neuroscience of Emotion.* New York: Oxford University Press, 1999. A good introduction to the fascinating work going on in the contemporary neurosciences on emotion.

Lazarus, Richard S. *Emotion and Adaptation.* New York: Oxford University Press, 1994. A book that brings together the thoughts and theories of one of the most important figures in the twentieth-century psychology of emotions, emphasizing the role of appraisal and coping in emotional processing.

Leary, M., J. Landel, and K. Patton. "Motivated Expression of Embarrassment." *The Journal of Personality* 64, no. 3 (1996).

Le Doux, Joseph. *The Emotional Brain: The Mysterious Underpinnings of Emotional Life.* New York: Simon and Schuster, 1996. A bold and original study of fear and the details of neurological processing.

Levi, Robert. *The Tahitians.* Chicago: University of Chicago Press, 1975.

Lewis, Michael, and Jeanette Havilland-Jones, eds. *A Handbook of Emotions.* 2d ed. New York: Guilford Press, 2000. An excellent topical collection of essays on various emotion topics, aspects, and particular emotions.

Lutz, Catherine. *Unnatural Emotions.* Chicago: University of Chicago Press, 1988. An important anthropological study of the cross-cultural concerns in the study of emotions, which the author explains as largely cultural (rather than biological or "natural").

Lyons, William. *Modern Philosophy of Mind.* London: Penguin, 1996. An important philosophical study of emotions as feelings in terms of a causal-evaluative account.

MacLean, Paul D. "Sensory and Perceptive Factors in Emotional Functions of the Triune Brain." In *Explaining Emotions.* Edited by Amelie Rorty. Los Angeles, University of California Press, 1980.

Manstead, Anthony S. R., Nico Frijda, and A. Fischer. *Feelings and Emotions.* Cambridge: Cambridge University Press, 2004. An excellent collection of essays from an important conference in Amsterdam a few years ago.

Mencius. *Mencius.* Translated by D. C. Lau. New York: Penguin Books, 1970.

Merleau-Ponty, Maurice. *The Phenomenology of Perception.* New York: Routledge Classics, 2003.

Mill, John Stuart. *Utilitarianism.* Indianapolis: Hackett Publishers, 1979. A classic and popular introduction to utilitarianism by one of the most important English philosophers of the nineteenth century.

Miller, William I. *Anatomy of Disgust.* Cambridge, MA: Harvard University Press, 1997. A delightfully written study of disgust in literature and psychology.

Moran, Richard. *Authority and Estrangement.* Princeton: Princeton University Press, 2000.

Morreall, John. *Taking Laughter Seriously.* Albany: SUNY Press, 1983. One of the most serious recent texts in the philosophy of humor.

Murphy, Jeffrey G., and Jean Hampton. *Mercy and Forgiveness.* New York: Cambridge University Press, 1988. An excellent study by way of a debate between two leading political philosophers about the justification of vengeance versus the virtue of forgiveness.

Neu, Jerome. *A Tear Is an Intellectual Thing.* New York: Oxford University Press, 2004. A wide-ranging collection of studies of topics and individual emotions, including jealousy, boredom, and pride.

Nietzsche, Friedrich. *Beyond Good and Evil.* Translated by W. Kaufmann. New York: Random House, 1966.

———. *On the Genealogy of Morals.* Translated by W. Kaufmann. New York: Random House, 1967. One of the seminal books by one of the most outrageous modern philosophers, in which he diagnoses much of morality as an expression of resentment.

——. *The Gay Science.* Translated by W. Kaufmann. New York: Random House, 1968. Another seminal book by one of the most outrageous modern philosophers, full of great insights.

——. "Why I Am So Clever." In *Ecco Homo.* Translated R. J. Hollingdale. New York: Penguin Books, 1992.

Noddings, Nell. *Caring.* Berkeley: University of California Press, 1984. An important feminist study in the tradition of challenging (male) principle-based impersonal conceptions of morality with conscientiously more "feminine" concerns.

Noé, Alva. *Action in Perception.* Cambridge: Massachusetts Institute of Technology Press, 2005.

Nussbaum, Martha. *The Therapy of Desire.* Princeton: Princeton University Press, 1996. An excellent study of the Stoic philosophers and their theories of emotion.

——. *Upheavals of Thought.* Cambridge: Cambridge University Press, 2001. This is the author's own neo-Stoic theory of emotion, which includes a substantial study of compassion and analyses of emotion in great literary and musical works.

——. *Hiding from Humanity.* Princeton, Princeton University Press, 2004.

Oatley, Keith. *Best Laid Schemes: The Psychology of Emotions.* Cambridge: Cambridge University Press, 1992. A difficult but original study of emotions from a cognitive science point of view.

Ortony, Andrew, Gerald Clore, and Allan Turner. *The Cognitive Structure of Emotions.* New York: Cambridge University Press, 1988. An important contribution to the cognitive analysis of emotion.

Panskepp, Jaak. "Toward a General Psychobiological Theory of Emotion." *Behavioral and Brain Sciences* 5 (1982), 407–67

Parrott, W. Gerald. *Emotions in Social Psychology.* New York: Taylor and Francis, 2000. A good collection of classic writings by leading social scientists.

Pennebaker, J. W., M. R. Mehl, and K. Niederhoffer. "Psychological Aspects of Natural Language Use: Our Words, Our Selves." *Annual Review of Psychology* 54 (2003), 547–77.

Plato. *The Symposium.* Translated by P. Woodruff and A. Nehamas. Indianapolis: Hackett Publishers, 1988. One of Plato's great texts, a series of speeches on love (eros), some serious and profound, some not so much so.

Prinz, Jesse. *Gut Reactions.* New York: Oxford University Press, 2004. An excellent book and a challenging resurrection of the Jamesian view of emotions as physical feelings brought about by primitive physiological reactions.

Robinson, Jenefer. *Deeper Than Reason.* New York: Oxford University Press, 2005. An excellent new book challenging the cognitive view of emotions in favor of more primitive physiological feelings together with an analyses of our emotional responses to great literary and musical works.

Rorty, Amelie, ed. *Explaining Emotions.* Berkeley: University of California Press, 1980. An excellent interdisciplinary collection by an important philosopher.

Russell, James. "Basic Emotions." *Psychological Review* (1993). An important challenge to current work on cross-cultural comparisons of emotional expressions.

Salovey, Peter, Marc Brackett, and John Mayer. *Emotional Intelligence: Key Readings.* Port Chester, NY: Dude Publishing, 2004.

Sartre, Jean-Paul. *The Emotions*. New York: Citadel/Lyle Stuart, 1948. An early phenomenological study of emotions and a direct attack on the theories of both Freud and William James.

——. *Being and Nothingness*. Translated by H. Barnes. New York: Philosophical Library, 1956. One of the great books in phenomenology and the central text of French existentialism.

——. *Nausea*. Translated by Lloyd Alexander. New York: New Directions, 1964. A good critique of Sartre's grim view of "true reality" is Colin Wilson's *Anti-Existentialism*, excerpted in Robert C. Solomon, ed. *Existentialism*. New York: Oxford University Press, 2004.

Schachter, Stanley, and Jerome E. Singer. "Cognitive, Social, and Psychological Determinants of Emotional State." *Psychological Review* 69 (1962). Also in *What Is an Emotion?* Edited by R. Solomon. New York: Oxford University Press, 2004. One of the classic experiments on emotion that challenges the Jamesian theory and insists on a cognitive dimension to emotion recognition.

Scherer, Klaus, A. Schorr, and T. Johnston. *Appraisal Processes in Emotion*. New York: Oxford University Press, 2001. Provides an outline of the fundamental ideas and history of the appraisal notion, and reviews basic assumptions, theoretical orientations, and controversies.

Schweder, Richard, and A. Levine, eds. *Culture Theory*. Cambridge: Cambridge University Press, 1984. An excellent anthropological collection on the cross-cultural study of emotions, including essays by Jerome Bruner, Richard Schweder, and Clifford Geertz.

Searle, John R. *Intentionality*. Cambridge: Cambridge University Press, 1983.

Shields, Stephanie. *Speaking from the Heart: Gender and the Social Meaning of Emotion*. Cambridge: Cambridge University Press, 2002. An excellent study of gender-specific aspects of emotions and emotion research.

Singer, Irving. *The Nature of Love*. 3 volumes. Chicago: University of Chicago Press, 1973. A classic study of the history and origins of contemporary "romantic" love.

Smith, Adam. *A Theory of the Moral Sentiments*. 1759. Reprint New York: Oxford University Press, 1976. An early study by the great economist in which he argues that human ethics is based on sympathy, a natural moral sentiment.

Solomon, Robert C. *About Love*. Lanham, MD: Rowman and Littlefield, 1993, 2001. An elaboration of the theory of love briefly suggested here.

——. *The Passions*. Indianapolis: Hackett Publishing Co., 1993. Originally published in 1976, my original book on emotions, a strong statement of the cognitive ("emotions are judgments") view.

——. *Not Passion's Slave*. New York: Oxford University Press, 2002. The first volume of a trilogy on the nature of emotions.

——. *The Joy of Philosophy*. New York: Oxford University Press, 2002. A book on the central role of the passions (including joy) in philosophy.

——. *Spirituality for the Skeptic*. New York: Oxford University Press, 2003. A study of spirituality, from a naturalistic and sometimes skeptical point of view.

——. *In Defense of Sentimentality*. New York: Oxford University Press, 2004. The second volume of a trilogy on the nature of emotions.

———. *Thinking about Feeling*. New York: Oxford University Press, 2005.

Sommers, Shula. "Adults Evaluating Their Emotions." *Emotion in Adult Development*. Edited by Malatesta and Isard. New York: Sage, 1984.

de Sousa, Ronald. *The Rationality of Emotion*. Cambridge: Massachusetts Institute of Technology Press, 1987. A very original and lively book on the relationship between emotions and rationality, including a wonderful chapter on laughter and humor.

Spelman, Elizabeth. "Anger and Insubordination." In *Women, Knowledge, and Reality*. 1st ed. Edited by A. Garry and M. Pearsall. Winchester, MA: Unwin Hyman, 1989, 263–73.

Spinoza, Baruch. *Ethics*. Malibu, CA: J. Simon, 1981. Also in *What Is an Emotion?* Edited by Robert C. Solomon. New York: Oxford University Press, 2004. One of the early great books in modern philosophy by a brilliant and much-persecuted Dutch thinker.

Stearns, Peter N. *Jealousy: The Evolution of an Emotion in American History*. New York: New York University Press, 1989. Another excellent study of the changes in a dangerous emotion in American history.

Stearns, Peter N., and Carol Stearns. *Anger: The Struggle for Emotional Control in America's History*. Chicago: University of Chicago Press, 1986. An excellent study of the changes in the rules of regulation of a dangerous emotion in American history.

Stevenson, Charles L. *Ethics and Language*. New Haven: Yale University Press, 1960.

Stocker, Michael. *Valuing Emotions*. New York: Cambridge University Press, 1996. An excellent study of emotions and their relation to values.

Tavris, Carol. *Anger: The Misunderstood Emotion*. New York: Simon and Schuster, 1982. An excellent study of anger, emphasizing both the cultural differences and the strategic importance of anger, especially in the women's liberation movement.

Thomas, Lewis. *Lives of a Cell*. New York: Viking, 1974.

Thurman, Robert. *Anger*. New York: Oxford University Press, 2004. A study of anger by one of the leading Buddhist scholars in America.

Twain, Mark (Samuel L. Clemens). *Following the Equator*. New York: Harper and Brothers, 1912.

Walton, Kendell. *Mimesis and Make-Believe*. Reprint, Cambridge, MA: Harvard University Press, 2005. An ingenious book to account for the fact that we have emotions with regard to fictional objects.

Williams, Bernard. *Shame and Necessity*. Berkeley: University of California Press, 1993. A challenging attempt to understand shame and honor in ancient society and the modern differences between shame and guilt.

Wollheim, Richard. *On the Emotions*. New Haven, CT: Yale University Press, 1999. An important study of emotions by an important twentieth century philosopher and master aesthetician.

Zajonc, Robert. "Feeling and Thinking: Preferences Need No Inferences." *American Psychologist* 35 (1980), 151–75.

Index

Printed in Great Britain
by Amazon.co.uk, Ltd.,
Marston Gate.